MG
X POWER SV

MG XPOWER SV

DAVID KNOWLES

THE CROWOOD PRESS

First published in 2005 by
The Crowood Press Ltd
Ramsbury, Marlborough
Wiltshire SN8 2HR

www.crowood.com

Dedication
To Babe and Arthur – they put my hat on.

British Library Cataloguing-in-Publication Data
A catalogue record for this book is available from
the British Library.

ISBN 1 86126 678 2

Design and typeset by Focus Publishing,
11a St Botolph's Road, Sevenoaks, Kent TN13 3AJ

Printed and bound in Singapore by Craft Print
International

Acknowledgements
As you will very soon see, this story has been shaped with the input of people at the heart of the project. At the head of the list are the three men who have been – and remain – so central to the project: designer Peter Stevens, chief engineer Giordano Casarini, and production manager Ian Moreton. These three have been the powerful trinity who have kept the project going, often through difficult periods as dramas have played out in the background. It goes without saying that without the generous help that Peter, Giordano and Ian have given me, this book simply could not have been written – just as without them, the MG XPower SV could not have been built.

I must also single out for special mention Nick Stephenson, deputy managing director of Phoenix Venture Holdings, and the man with the vision to see the potential of what would become the MG XPower SV. It was Nick Stephenson who, only a few years earlier, had seen the potential of the sports car studies that led to the MGF – and not only is Nick a good businessman, he is a genuine car enthusiast and a fun person to be with, a combination that one doesn't always find in a single package.

I would also like to give special mention to Steve Hudson, for Steve played an important part in the early part of a project that later changed direction. So often historical records unfairly 'airbrush out' people whose contributions to a story stopped part-way through, and I am pleased to have the opportunity to acknowledge the part one person made to this story, even though he moved on to other things before it came to fruition.

Julian Mackie is the talented professional photographer who took the superb, specially commissioned shots for this book, with whom I spent a highly enjoyable day dodging the combined forces of half the United Nations (or so it seemed) while he photographed Nick Stephenson's Trophy Blue MG XPower SV on Salisbury Plain.

It almost goes without saying that also I owe an enormous debt of gratitude to my publisher – in particular Crowood's commissioning editor, Nick Wright – and my family – wife Shirley and daughters Katie and Emily – for their gracious mixture of encouragement and forbearance.

Finally, I will do my best to acknowledge here as many of the other key people who have helped bring this story to life. So many have contributed that it will be hard to mention them all, and so for any omissions, I sincerely apologise. From MG Rover itself, in addition to the people already referred to above, I must thank: Greg Allport, Antonio Ara, Peter Beale, Paolo Corradini, Vittorio Filippini, Stefano Garuti, Alistair Herschell, Alun Isaac, Kevin Jones, Tim King, Andy Kitson, John Linforth, Paul Linnell, Biagio Maltese, Wayne Nation, Rob Oldaker, David Sharples, Ramin Tolouie, John Towers CBE, Keith Twigg, John Wallbank, David Watson.

And from the various outside partners and others who have generously provided their assistance there is Rob Aherne (editor, *Autocar* magazine), Dave Anderson (Anderson & Ryan), Craig Anderson (Anderson & Ryan), Roy Axe, Phiroze Bilimorio (Project X), Dr Aaron Colombo (Belco Avia), Alistair Cusick (photographer), Pete Edwards (Anderson & Ryan), Giancarlo Grinza (OPAC), Nick Gwinnutt, Clive Hawkins (ARIA), Ted Higgins (David Price Racing), Frank Hook (QCR Motors), Richard Hopkins (Emap), David Humphreys, Sean Hyland (Sean Hyland Motorsport), Colin Jones (Dove), Paul Kneeshaw (Project X), Terry Lee (photographer, Mark Longmore (DANA Automotive), Mark Longmore (DANA), Frank Mandarano, Harris Mann, Janet Mills (BBC *Top Gear* magazine), Peter McKenzie (DPS Composites). Nik Moore, Rod Morris-Kirby (HP Chemie Pelzer), Dan Poulson (Omitec Telematics), David Price (DPS Composites), Bruce Qvale (BMCD), Steve Randle (Randle Engineering), Kate Rowland (SP Group), Angelo Sacco (OPAC), Enrique Scalabroni, Dominic Simpson (Randle Engineering), Filippo Spalla (Belco Avia), Richard Springall (CARAN Design), Tim Springett (DPS Composites), Martin Starkey (SP Group), Pete Trafford (BBC *Top Gear* magazine), Mike Whitestone (photographer), Dave Woods (XK Engineering).

Contents

Foreword

It is very rare for an automotive designer to be given almost total responsibility for a design project as exciting as the MG XPower SV. I was fortunate enough to have been given that opportunity by the Phoenix Board members, who took on the enormous task of restructuring and reviving the MG and Rover brands after the departure of previous owners BMW. This foreword gives me a chance to thank John Towers, Nick Stephenson, Peter Beale and John Edwardes for their unwavering support of, and enthusiasm for, this project: without these four it simply would not have happened. It is also a fact that our most enthusiastic development driver, Kevin Howe, is also the chief executive of MG Rover, and his input and feedback was invaluable.

In the early days of the SV project I had the chance to hand pick a very small team of skilled, loyal, and highly motivated 'mates' to make the absurdly challenging timetable achievable: this book gives the reader the chance to learn more about this great team. I must also give my personal thanks to Ian Moreton, without whom we could not have made a single car; and to Giordano Casarini, without whom it would not have been so spectacularly well engineered. During the course of the project, we were extremely well 'shadowed' by author David Knowles. His probing questions often caused our team to re-examine our aims and objectives, and David was a great sounding-board for gaining an outside view of the progress of the SV's development. I hope that both readers and SV customers will not only be entertained by this book, but will also gain an insight into the singular passion that all the team had for the project. We all like to think that the cars exude the essence of that passion.

Peter Stevens

The MG XPower SV has been very much a team effort, led by Peter Stevens (at right) and his colleagues Ian Moreton (left) and Giordano Casarini (centre). (MG Rover)

Introduction

This book comes just as MG enters yet another turbulent period of its eighty-year history: lesser car marques would have disappeared before now, but MG has something special that makes it a true survivor. Many people mistakenly assume that the depth of the MG marque goes no further than the MGB, the ubiquitous 'affordable sports car' with which MG's evolving parent company – from British Motor Corporation to British Leyland – earned millions of dollars of US currency. However, the genuine importance of the MGB in MG history can blind us to the fact that occasionally in the past, MG strove to be much more than the commonplace; sometimes an MG was a giant killer, pitching beyond its weight and upsetting the accepted status quo. There have been a handful of MG cars for which this maxim holds true – and each one has been striking in its audacity, often taking a surprising leap into the heart of Motorsport territory and scattering the opposition. The new MG XPower SV offers the potential of a similar promise, but arguably the gestation of this new MG supercar is more complex and fascinating than most, and involves an intriguing tangle of interlinked people and their

The MG XPower SV in production form – the most powerful MG production car by a long way, and undoubtedly the most exotic road car ever to wear the famous octagon. (Julian Mackie)

stories which together contribute to an unusual and exotic pedigree.

What has been particularly rewarding for me in the writing of this story has been the opportunity to watch that story unfurl, to see its evolutionary progress through new stages and blind turnings, and to share in the excitements and frustrations along the way. I have been most fortunate to be able to follow the story in such a way, for most histories are written long after the events have had a chance to settle and be edited for posterity: here the facts are still fresh and have been given added life through the generous co-operation of the talented group of people involved. And that group of people is surprisingly wide-ranging, for not only is this a story of a project that has been vital to the struggles of a company striving to grow under an often hostile spotlight, but it is also an uplifting tale of partnership and co-operation between businesses from around the world that collectively feed into a 1,000-mile production line.

The initials 'MG' derive originally from those of the 'Morris Garages' of Oxford, where the first custom-built cars were built; nowadays, the main home of MG may – for the time being at least – be Longbridge, but in the case of the SV, the spirit of this mighty beast really lies in Modena, Italy, where each SV begins to take shape. For this new supercar, at least, then, MG surely now stands for 'Modena Garages'.

chapter one

MG Beginnings

The first architect of MG was Cecil Kimber, hired by William Morris in 1921 as sales manager for Morris's garage business in Oxford. In March of the following year, Kimber stepped up to the position of general manager, and within a matter of months he began 'customizing' the Morris Oxfords, cars that originated at his patron's main business down the road in Cowley. By the beginning of March 1923, Kimber had already overseen the creation of the distinctive octagonal MG logo, and fourteen months after that, the badge formed part of a Morris Garages trademark application (Trademark 490090) that assigned the badge for use on 'motor cars and motor chassis – The Morris Garages Limited'.

Kimber's special MG race car of 1925 was 'Old Number One' (left), but within eight years the MG sports car pedigree had evolved as far as the virtually bespoke MG K3 Magnette (right). (MG Rover)

Kimber may have made a lucrative business out of 'hotting up' Morris Oxfords and Cowleys, but his ambitions were much grander than that: he could see a future for MG in more specialized, purpose-built machines – and in his eyes, the more special the better. When Morris Motors Ltd brought out their own Morris Occasional Four, Kimber was alarmed to find that it undercut the price of his own Morris Garages Chummy, and he was spurred on to look for other, more exclusive opportunities – to run where Cowley would not follow. The most successful of his early experiments was a sporting four-seater tourer, based on the Morris 14/28 chassis. This car had a rakish body of highly polished aluminium and drew many admiring glances: there was no other Morris product quite like it.

No story of MG worth its salt can easily eschew mention of 'Old Number One', even if only to show respect to what Kimber personally regarded as his first 'real MG sports car'. What started as a humble Morris

Kimber's first MG supercar was the 18/100 'Tigress', a car whose grand style promised a great deal but sadly failed to make a significant inroad into the 'thoroughbred' market. (MG Rover)

Cowley chassis was modified by Frank Stevens, a Morris Garages employee based at the garage's Longwall premises, and fitted with a modified Hotchkiss engine built by Stevens's colleague Charlie Martin. Fitted with one-off bodywork by Carbodies, the end result was ready in time for Kimber to compete in the Land's End Trial of Easter 1925, which involved a run from Slough to Land's End in Cornwall. Eventually, partnered by his friend Wilfrid Mathews, Kimber made it to journey's end and won a gold medal.

In the years to come, the car acquired an almost heroic status, which some – including one or two contemporary MG employees – would argue was out of all proportion to its real significance in the scheme of

things. It was not until two years later that Kimber and his men began serious work on their first 'real' MG in production terms – but 'Old Number One' has maintained a romantic association as the first 'proper' MG sports car, and therefore the 'origin of the species'.

Just before Christmas 1927, Kimber and his men began work on their first production 'MG' road car that could be regarded a true MG in its own right, rather than a modified Morris, marrying a Morris Light Six engine to a chassis of MG's own design. The spring of 1928 saw the MG Car Company (proprietors: Morris Garages Ltd) come into being, taking over responsibility for MG manufacture in readiness for the August launch of the new MG 18/80 Six. The new car was announced in The Autocar of 17 August 1928, and made its debut at the Olympia Motor Show alongside the MG Midget, also new at the show. By this stage, MG production was increasing, and by 1929 a new home was needed: MG moved out of Oxford and down the road to Abingdon-on-Thames, where the marque would stay for the next fifty years.

SUPERCAR ROOTS

By 1930, the genteel MG 18/80 had evolved considerably, and the lessons learned were applied by Kimber and his increasingly versatile team in the

The K3 Magnette is for many enthusiasts of classic MG sports cars the 'ultimate' MG. (MG Rover)

The 1933 Mille Miglia

It is just after half past two on a Sunday morning on a mild, still spring night in Brescia, in the heart of northern Italy; but nobody is asleep – even the children are out playing in the street. The excited chatter and hubbub of the crowd – held back by ropes and planking between flag poles on either side of the road – echoes off the ancient walls of the buildings that surround the square. Dazzlingly bright arc lamps mounted overhead light up the faces of small boys perched in the chestnut trees as well as the large, chequered-edged banner stretched high across the archway that marks the exit from the square, framing the backdrop of the black night sky and the ribbon of road that fades out of view into the outskirts of the town and to the countryside beyond in the direction of Verona. While the carabinieri maintain a watchful eye on the crowd, elegant ladies parade up and down the press stand, and a small noisy group of men clamber on to the town bandstand, bottles raised in celebration of the party spirit, their guffaws almost drowned by the gramophone music straining from the tannoy system.

There has already been one false alarm when, to cries of 'macchina!', a Lancia Astura appeared – and turned out to be nothing more than an early retiree from the race who was simply on his way home. Suddenly, though, there is an exclamation as someone sees more headlights weaving through the gloom, and there is the sound of a bugle accompanied by the growing roar of a racing engine at full pelt. Race officials – until now in idle conversation – move into position by the improvised timekeeper's post to greet the car rushing headlong into Brescia, its headlamps freshly illuminating the scene as it bursts into the square and heads towards the chequered flag. Brakes squeal as the car shudders to a halt, and the

The 1933 MG K3 Magnette, in similar trim to the form in which the three cars raced at the Mille Miglia. (MG Rover)

enthusiastic crowd – shouting 'magnifico! Gli Inglesi!' surge around the British Racing Green machine and its two occupants.

Behind the wheel is the substantial bespectacled figure of the Englishman Captain G.E.T. Eyston, with local hero Count Giovanni 'Johnny' Lurani hunched wearily alongside. In eighteen hours they have just covered 1,024 hard-fought miles, and have been the first car to finish the 1933 Mille Miglia. Within minutes, another car – this time a red Fiat Ballila, driven by Ricci – races into the square to more partisan acclaim; but then suddenly a third car – like the first, an MG K3 Magnette – roars up, and in so doing ensures that together the MGs wrest the Mille Miglia team prize – the 'Gran Premio Brescia' – the first time that it has been won by a non-Italian team. It is 42 minutes before another car in the MG Magnette's class crosses the finishing line, while overall race victory goes to the legendary Tazio Nuvolari in a fire-breathing 2.3 litre straight-eight 'Scuderia Ferrari' Alfa Romeo. The four finishing MG drivers – Eyston, Lurani, Earl Howe and H.C. 'Hammy' Hamilton – are surrounded by excited spectators as seasoned racer Howe is heard to remark that this has been the greatest race in which he ever competed. MG has made its mark in Italy, and the story of the 'vetture inglesi' will be talked about for a long time to come.

Results of the Mille Miglia Saturday/Sunday 8–9 April 1933 The three MG K3 Magnettes entered by Earl Howe and managed by Hugh McConnell finished as follows: George Eyston/Count Giovanni ('Johnny') Lurani (car number 39, registered JB 1475, chassis K3003; 1st in class); Earl Howe/Hugh Hamilton (car number 42, registered JB 1472; chassis K3001; 2nd in class); Sir Henry 'Tim' Birkin and Bernard Rubin (car number 41, registered JB 1474, chassis K3002; did not finish, but set new record for Brescia road section of the course).

building of the first true MG factory race car: the 18/100 B-type 'Tiger' or 'Tigress'. Preliminary details of this new car appeared in *The Motor* in February 1930, and soon it emerged that the actual debut was to be at the two-day Brooklands 'Double Twelve' of Friday and Saturday 9 and 10 May 1930, at the hands of Leslie Callingham of Shell Petroleum. Sadly, the engine ran its bearings barely two hours into the race. This proved to be the last serious competitive outing for the Tiger, and before long the model faded from the scene as Kimber reluctantly abandoned the project. But in that same race, the hoards of MG Midgets entered had been rather more successful, the highest finishing third in its class and fourteenth overall.

In the wake of this triumph, Kimber announced a limited series of replicas of the MG Midget race cars, claiming them to be identical in every respect to those that raced at Brooklands; but even while he turned his attention to exploiting the smaller sports car market, he still harboured grander ambitions.

As the original Morris Minor-based MG 'M' Type Midget proved successful, Kimber and his engineering team developed the Midget philosophy of low-cost, accessible sports car motoring – but they did so by developing their own chassis and specially adapted running gear. The 'M' Type Midget was swiftly overtaken by a family of 'J' Type Midgets, which also helped give rise to a related family of mid-sized cars with small, high-revving six-cylinder engines: the MG Magna and Magnette ranges. By this time – arguably the heyday of pre-war MG development – the range was becoming almost bewilderingly complicated for such a small company; but at the top of the family tree emerged what was unquestionably MG's first real 'supercar'.

The MG K3 Magnette evolved in the Abingdon workshops in December 1932, two prototypes being built in readiness for the 1933 season. One of the prototypes was despatched to Monte Carlo, where it made a promising if unexpected debut (James Wright breaking the class record for the Monte des Mules hillclimb); whilst the second car – fitted with a prototype sloping nose – was shipped under the watchful eye of ace mechanic Reg 'Jacko' Jackson to Italy in the first week of January for five weeks testing and reconnoitre in preparation for the 1,000-mile Mille Miglia road race of 8 and 9 April, where a team was to be entered by Earl Howe and managed by Hugh McConnell, chief scrutineer at Brooklands.

Howe, the archetypal English aristocrat, had entered the 1931 Mille Miglia in his substantial ex-Caracciola Mercedes tourer, and this car was employed on the reconnoitre as a glorified support truck. The convoy of prototype K3 and the Mercedes made their way down into Italy, meeting local small-car racing hero Count Lurani at Milan. At Modena, the équipe called on Scuderia Ferrari, where Enzo Ferrari and the great Italian racing driver, Tazio Nuvolari greeted them; and at Molsheim they called on Bugatti, where Monsieur Bugatti studied the car, voicing his opinion that the front axle was not strong enough. Reg Jackson soon telephoned back to Abingdon, and as a result the design was modified in time for the race. Such was the interest in the MG entry (only five of the 98 cars entered in the race were non-Italian) that they were greeted in Rome by the British Ambassador, the King of Italy and Mussolini – although undoubtedly part of the reason for this hospitality was the fluid situation in European politics; after all, in 1933, Adolf Hitler had become Chancellor of Germany.

Late March saw Earl Howe's team of three K3 Magnettes sailing out of the Cornish village of Fowey aboard the SS Florentine, bound for Genoa, and then on by road to Brescia for the start of the 1933 Mille Miglia. The drivers were Count Lurani (partnered by Captain George Eyston), Sir Henry 'Tim' Birkin (accompanied by his friend and Bentley team-mate Bernard Rubin) and Earl Howe (accompanied by University Motors salesman Hugh 'Hammy' Hamilton). At the start of the race, Earl Howe solemnly shook hands with his colleagues and – as Eyston would recall later the same year in his autobiography *Flat Out* – said: 'You are racing for England and MG. Do your very best.' The local band played 'Soldiers of the King' and then the race began, first off being some small Fiats and then the MG Magnettes.

Lurani and Eyston's car was the first MG off, but it was followed three minutes later by Birkin, and then Rubin. Birkin drove like a man possessed to draw the Maseratis into challenge; as Eyston later wrote:

> It was 'Tim' Birkin who laid the foundations of what was to be a great and glorious victory – and for Tim the selfless, a sacrifice. He knew his mission, and he achieved it as only he could have done. His was the task of breaking up the opposition, the very fast Maserati driven by Tuffanelli, the Italian crack. Not for him the plaudits of the multitude. He was the wrecker. How greatly he achieved is proved by the fact that he opened the race with a series of smashed records. For at Bologna, 129 miles away, he had averaged over 87 miles an hour. Here were daring and courage. On towards Rome, imperial Rome, and Sir Henry still led, and the Maseratis had been left behind. Tim had done his duty.

Eventually the engine of Birkin's car suffered from its extreme punishment and he was forced to retire. Much of the opposition, however – especially the crucial Maserati opposition – had also suffered; the gearbox of Tuffanelli's Maserati 4CTR was shattered on the Futa pass, while the only other four-cylinder 1,088cc

Maserati was about an hour behind, and the coast was therefore clear for Birkin's team-mates. It was nevertheless not an easy race for them – over a thousand miles on public roads in a giant figure-of-eight throughout northern Italy – but the two surviving MG Magnettes eventually won through to finish first and third in their class, and snatch the team trophy.

After the 1933 Mille Miglia, much effort at Abingdon went into the racing version of the MG Midget – the famous 'J4' – using a mélange of (J2) Midget and Magnette parts selected expressly for their racing merit. The J4 was only produced in a handful of numbers, but went on to inspire many replicas, and contributed to later racing Midgets. Meanwhile, the

The R-Type Midget, brainchild of MG chief designer H.N. Charles, was a technological tour-de-force that was sadly short-lived. (MG Rover)

success at Mille Miglia had fired the imagination of both the public and the motor-racing fraternity, and there was great excitement when it was learned that Tazio Nuvolari himself (overall victor of the 1933 Mille Miglia) would be competing in a K3 Magnette at the Ulster TT race in September of the same year. Nuvolari had driven into Brescia at the end of the Mille Miglia less than three minutes after the Eyston/Lurani Magnette. At Ulster, and with MG's Alec Hounslow along for the ride as race mechanic, Nuvolari simply climbed in the car, grasped the peculiarities and principles of the pre-selector gearbox with the aid of little more than gesture and hand-waving, and went on to win the race outright, famously wearing out eight sets of tyres in the process.

It is easy for us to look back nostalgically at cars like the K3 Magnette, but Peter Stevens – nowadays responsible for the way MGs are designed – is keen to

point out that while cars like the K3 were constrained by contemporary technology, even so they demonstrated clever solutions to problems. 'When you look at MG's competitors in those days, when other people put petrol tanks way out at the back they either broke the back of the chassis or the bodywork – the Riley Brooklands and some Bugattis were prime examples of that' he observes. 'It was a very neat solution for MG to make a slim slab tank as they did, which had other benefits such as altering the weight distribution by the minimum amount between a full and an empty tank. So at the time it was kind of modern and practicable, and it is only nowadays that we tend to see it as a "retro" feature…'

MG R-TYPE

By the spring of 1935, Kimber was pushing the frontiers of MG racing development to the limit – and, as it happened, chancing his arm when it came to financing such ventures. There is a school of thought that by 1935, Kimber was in danger of becoming rather as Enzo Ferrari did in later years: too much fascination in the racing shop, at the expense of the production shop. Chief designer at MG was H.N. Charles, and it was he who was responsible for the remarkable racing Midget known as the R-type. This car was impressive for several reasons, in particular because it married a supercharged 113bhp 746cc engine (pretty remarkable in itself) with a unique 'wishbone' chassis equipped with all-independent suspension. The latter was an idea still fairly much in its infancy, and the early R-types handled in a slightly peculiar manner, even though their ability on the circuit significantly outclassed the similarly engined but traditional-chassis Q-type. Charles had resorted to a box-section wish-bone chassis, the prototype of which was fabricated by Frank Stevens – the same person responsible for modifying the chassis of Kimber's 'Old

Number One' ten years beforehand. As a consequence of the lightweight chassis and minimal bodywork, the R-type was a featherweight 1,421lb.

On 6 May 1935 was the racing debut of the R-type at the Junior Car Club International Trophy Race at Brooklands, where Bill Everitt and Malcolm Campbell managed to bring home chassis 'RA0260' to a well-deserved class win, with Doreen Evans immediately behind in 'RA0255'. More race entries took place, but what promised to be a rewarding career for a factory MG racer was cut short in the summer of 1935 when Sir William Morris suddenly sold his MG interests into his Nuffield Motors concern, and new manager Leonard Lord moved swiftly to close down the MG racing shop, killing further work at Abingdon on the promising but expensive R-type.

IN CONCLUSION

Looking back from the perspective of nearly seventy years, Peter Stevens sees the R-type as a seminal MG supercar:

> The engineering in that car was marvellous. I was fascinated quite early on when I started reading up on MG history to find how modern that car was for 1935. One thing I believe is that if you look for pointers in history, you don't look at things like the shape of a door handle or details round a tail-light; you should instead look at the philosophy of the car, and the R-type came at a point when MG's philosophy was more advanced than anybody's. It had that 'Y'-shaped back-bone chassis which is remarkably like that of the first Lotus Elan, and it had big perforations with flanged holes to make it stiff but extremely light, and of course it had novel all-independent suspension. Funnily enough they didn't know quite where to seat the driver in all that – but you just know that the next one, if there had been a next one, would have been phenomenal…

chapter two

MG Evolution

FROM TA TO MGB

The process of evolution after 1935 took a considerably different course to that which preceded the great purge; the TA Midget was the first of a new generation of Morris-engineered cars with simpler engines and engineering that outraged MG purists (and there have been MG puritans at all stages of the marque's history). With new eyes on the financial bottom line, there was little room for the 'excesses' of the higher echelons of Motorsport, and while MGs would prove very effective in many levels of competition, they rarely competed at the same levels as they once had.

War intervened in the development of MG sports cars, as it did in so many other fields; but after the conflict was over, something strange happened: MG was 'discovered' by the Americans. The apocryphal story is that former UK-posted American 'GIs' took large numbers of MG sports cars back with them after the war, because the T-type Midgets were so different to the large barge-like family sedans they had been used to back home – but in truth the reality was

The MG TC Midget exemplifies the seminal 'classic' MG Midget. (MG Rover)

The MGC GT'S' was Abingdon's last home-grown attempt at a dedicated race car. (Bill Price)

somewhat more prosaic: yes, the T-type Midget was 'discovered' by US servicemen, but rocketing sales in the USA were more down to the combined concerted efforts of Nuffield Exports at Cowley and canny salesmen such as Kjell Qvale, coupled with the growth of the Sports Car Club of America, which made racing European sports cars both fashionable and attainable.

The first post-war MG was the TC Midget, introduced in October 1945, and since regarded by many as a paragon of simple beauty; but real volume sales did not come until the following generations: the MG TD of 1950, the TF of 1953, and then the enormous leaps to the MGA of 1955 and, of course, the MGB of 1962. Each of these models rightly holds a place in the motoring hall of fame, but even their most ardent supporters would hardly categorize them as 'supercars'; this was because MG had moved firmly into the volume sector, satisfying the substantial demand for affordable sports cars.

ABINGDON'S LAST SUPERCAR?

In the middle of the 1960s, MG's parent BMC seemed almost invincible, with a wide product range and numerous factories churning out large volumes, including Britain's best-selling car, the Austin-Morris

'ADO16' 1100 range. In motorsports too, BMC was sweeping all before it, the main weapon in this assault being the giant-killing Mini Cooper. MG's home plant of Abingdon played a fundamentally important role in this Motorsport pre-eminence, and yet there was some small disappointment in certain parts of the MG camp that most of the effort within Abingdon's 'Comps' department was concentrated on other marques.

A possibility to redress the balance appeared to present itself in 1966 when BMC sanctioned the building of a small number of alloy-bodied competition versions of the new GT version of the MGB/MGC range. 'Comps' had long fostered friendly relationships with Motorsport-minded friends at Pressed Steel, the organization principally responsible for the MGB bodies, and they were persuaded to allow special, very limited runs of alloy panels using the tooling intended for the normal steel pressings. Although clever 'dodges' were adopted, the actual pressings that resulted from these endeavours were not of a particularly high quality in their raw state, but after the ministrations of a skilled aluminium welder, they did result in sets of light alloy panels for the MGB.

When it came to the GT version, BMC agreed to develop a more muscular-looking style with flared wings, and the first such car was built during 1967 as an 'MG GTS', using the still secret MGC floorpan, but racing at the Targa Florio in Sicily during April as an 'MGB', complete with B-series four-cylinder engine. This car was later joined by a second – by which time the 'proper' MGC six-cylinder 3ltr engines were in place – and both had limited racing exposure at Sebring and the Nürburgring.

There were tentative thoughts both of taking the MGC GTS rallying, and of building a very small number of high-priced road-going replicas – harking back to the pre-war concept of an exotic MG sold to help the factory racing efforts. Sadly this was not to be, however, as BMC's merger with Leyland in the spring of 1968 had far-reaching effects; one of these was a dramatic review of the company's motorsports agenda, and the MGC GTS was one of the victims of this process, along with the MGC itself, killed off in the summer of 1969 after 8,999 examples had been built.

Arguably there was little else 'exotic' about the MGB family after that, with the honourable exception of the MGB GT V8 – a promising marriage of the MGB GT body and the all-alloy ex-Buick 3.5ltr Rover V8 engine, launched in August 1973. The MGB GT V8 offered good performance for its day – *Motor* tested one and achieved a 0–60mph (0–80km/h) time of 7.7sec – but unfortunately it eventually fell victim to corporate finances and politics, not to mention the Arab-Israeli conflict of October 1973, which damaged sales of all 'big-engined' cars. The MGB GT V8 lasted just three years, and sold only 2,591 examples – even less successful than the MGC. Within another three years, the MGB itself fell victim to a combination of circumstances, and the Abingdon factory eventually shut its doors in 1980.

THE MG EX-E: THE AUSTIN-ROVER SUPERCAR

By 1985, after the major pruning imposed on the former British Leyland, the principal automotive business still in government ownership was 'Austin Rover'; they were responsible for producing a range of volume cars including the classic Mini, the five-year-old Austin Metro (and its MG derivatives), the larger Austin/MG

This original Austin Rover Design studio artwork shows the aircraft influences that helped shape the most futuristic MG concept seen at the time of its debut in 1985. (MG Rover)

Photographed by the author in 2004 at the Heritage Motor Museum, where it now resides, the MG EX-E still looks stunning. (Author)

The MG EX-E concept was intended to marry Austin Rover's brand new bespoke V6 engine and four-wheel-drive transmission from the Metro 6R4 programme. (MG Rover)

Mighty Metro: The MG Metro 6R4

The importance of the Mini Metro of 1980 to British Leyland cannot be overstated, but by itself it could not rebuild a company that so often had been on its knees. However, the Metro (as it soon became known) captured the public imagination, and it was clear that the role of the new car as a 'giant killer' had great public appeal – much as had been the case with the original Mini. By the end of 1981, what would become BL's rallying contender for the 'Group B' class began to take shape behind closed doors, much of the initial work being carried out by Patrick Head of Williams Engineering at Didcot. To be successful in the fiercely competitive rallying arena, it was agreed that the new car would need a bespoke chassis and all-new mid-mounted engine, four-wheel-drive and a centrally mounted differential. For marketing purposes the appearance of the car would resemble the production MG Metro as closely as possible.

Before long the first prototype was running, and Austin Rover asked their old friend Tony Pond to help with the development testing. The public announcement of the MG Metro 6R4 – standing for six cylinders, rally, four-wheel drive – took place on Friday 24 February 1984, where it was also announced that the car would be making its competition debut in April. In the launch briefing, Austin Rover's commercial director Mark Snowdon announced that 'although we will not make a final commitment to international rallying until the prototype Metros have proved themselves in competition, we would not announce the car at this stage if we were not

confident of its ability.' Pitching high, Snowdon went on to say that 'it is our ambition to win the world championship with this exciting car.'

After a toe-in-the-water entry with the prototype (fitted with a cut-down V6 version of the Rover V8 engine) on 31 March 1984 at the York Rally, development of both the 6R4 and its bespoke engine continued throughout 1984. Five days before Christmas, a 'ride-and-drive' was conducted at Austin Rover's Gaydon test facility, with senior management in the form of Ray Horrocks and Harold Musgrove driving prototypes 002 and 003 around the test track. Musgrove finished his drive full of enthusiasm, and gave the go-ahead for the programme. By February 1985, the low-volume facility at Longbridge was building the first of the planned production run of 200 cars, while the unique V64V engine and transmission assemblies were built at Austin Rover's Radford branch in Capt Martin Road.

But unfortunately for the Metro 6R4, events in the world of rallying developed fast, and in the wrong direction for Austin Rover's Wunderkind: the Group 'B' rally class was suddenly given notice of cancellation by the end of 1986 after a series of horrific accidents, culminating in one where Henri Toivenen (brother of Metro 6R4 driver Harri Toivenen) was killed, along with his colleague Sergio Cresto, when their Group 'B' Lancia crashed and burst into flames in Corsica on 2 May 1986. As a

The MG Metro 6R4 was about as far away from the basic Austin Metro as one could hope to get. (MG Rover)

Mighty Metro: The MG Metro 6R4

The MG Metro 6R4 in early 'Computervision' guise, before the car evolved to the ultimate version, shown opposite. (MG Rover)

result, the 6R4's promising international career was cut short, the best result being a third place on the November 1985 Lombard RAC Rally for Tony Pond.

In May 1987, the Austin Rover Motorsport division closed down, and Austin Rover stopped work on the 6R4. For the cars themselves, however, a competitive future remained: Metro 6R4 registrar David Sims of Derby believes that 233 6R4 bodies were built, and of those at least 200 must have been built into complete cars in order to comply with homologation requirements. Even now, twenty years later, 6R4s can be seen actively competing in motorsports.

Maestro and Montego ranges, and the Honda-derived Rover 213/ 216 range. At the top of the range was the Rover 'SD1' family, which at ten years of age was nearing the end of its life. Waiting in the wings was a new large car, codenamed 'XX', its design the result of a close working partnership between Austin Rover and Honda.

Unlike British Leyland, which had arguably suffered from a lack of coherent design and engineering, and had been further hampered by a lack of investment in design itself, Austin Rover chairman Harold Musgrove had hired Roy Axe as his director of design in 1981, and had funded a major investment both in a new design studio and the recruitment of good quality staff. Axe came from Chrysler, and when Chrysler subsequently closed its substantial design centre at Whitley, near Coventry, it meant that Axe was able to cherry-pick

many of the staff he needed. Among these was Gerry McGovern, who later became the principal designer of the MGF sports car.

Roy Axe brought a new perspective to the importance of good design, and equally importantly the benefits of good public relations and effective corporate self-publicity, and he was keen to champion the cause of 'image cars' that, while not necessarily major profit earners in themselves, would help generate interest in, and public awareness of, the new company as well as generating showroom traffic for the dealers. An obvious candidate for an 'image car' was a new MG; the MG brand was unquestionably the strongest in the Austin Rover portfolio (Jaguar having been split off in 1984).

Although some exploratory studies into a new MG sports car had been carried out, there was nothing in the business plan. However, Axe could see the appeal of publicly advertising the talents of his new design team, and at the same time developing further the innovations of the MG Metro 6R4 rally car. 'The idea was to provide a showcase of the talents within the company ahead of the new Rover 800' Axe recalls. 'We wanted to avoid a direct conflict with the Rover 800, but we also wanted to generate some interest and excitement ahead of its launch.'

Work on the project, in conjunction with various outside suppliers, was carried out in great secrecy during the summer of 1985; nobody outside the small circle involved knew of the surprise in store for the press at the Frankfurt Motor Show on Tuesday 10 September 1985. Austin Rover chairman Harold Musgrove unveiled the full-size model as the MG EX-E, and said to the press:

> I believe that the EX-E is a superb illustration of the talent and technology within Austin Rover, qualities upon which our future as a significant world car manufacturer

depend: will we put the car into production? As a car enthusiast I would dearly love to build it. But as a businessman – well, that could be a different matter. At this moment, I don't know the answer, but it does have manufacturing feasibility. One thing I will confirm is that our future studies with the car will include further assessment of its production viability. We must consider whether to make some prototype runners.

The level of interest was great, and the publicity superb; but naturally the press reported the car as a real project, and the BBC television news suggested naïvely that EX-E was 'the new MG sports car'. Sadly EX-E never went much further than that. According to Axe: 'The EX-E project officially died because of lack of funds, but there was more to it than that. The paymasters – the government – would, it was felt, have thought such a car frivolous, particularly when they were hoping to sell the company.'

When Austin Rover was later bought by British Aerospace in the spring of 1988, EX-E was mooted as a potential project on which, it was suggested, the very different aerospace and automotive sides of the business could work together. According to Austin Rover senior designer Richard Hamblin:

Seen here at the Earls Court UK debut, a month after its world debut at Frankfurt in September 1985, the MG EX-E was the star of the whole show. (Author)

The MGB GT V8 was largely a factory response to the enterprise of MG conversion specialist Ken Costello – although its launch just before the Middle East conflict of autumn 1973 was a case of unlucky timing. (Author)

We tried to find some common ground with the people at BAe, but they were involved in small numbers of hand-built high-budget bespoke aircraft, whereas we were involved in mass-produced products. My idea – although never pursued with much effort on my part – was for a small number of EX-Es to be built by BAe to aircraft standards and technology.

The car that would have resulted would have been very expensive but almost unprecedented in its technical prowess – the sort of philosophy that McLaren would later adopt for its seminal 'F1' supercar.

Even though EX-E had never gone into production, it had successfully sent the message that Austin Rover was emerging as a design-led company, and for many years afterwards, the single full-size fully trimmed plastic display model toured the world as a demonstration of Austin Rover design excellence, before eventually being 'retired' to the British Motor Industry Heritage Trust Collection. Looking back at EX-E with the benefit of nearly twenty years of hindsight, the design is still stunning. Peter Stevens agrees that the EX-E was a very good piece of work: 'I think that echoes what I feel about the MG R-type, because if we have that in mind it would allow us to do much more advanced MG sports cars, including re-organization of the mechanical bits and the way the car is made.'

THE MG V8 CONNECTION

As explained earlier, the MGB GT V8 of 1973 was the first production use of a V8 engine in an MG, although the idea of slotting a big V8 – typically a side-valve Ford unit – into an MG goes back at least to the North American tuning scene of the early 1950s, when US sports car enthusiasts shoehorned V8 engines into their

TC and TD Midgets, with varying degrees of success. However, after the MGB GT V8 was withdrawn in July 1976, the idea of a V8-engined MG was a long way from the thoughts of anyone directly concerned with MG affairs. By the beginning of the 1990s, however, the situation was becoming somewhat different, the MG EX-E having proved something of a dead end, although it had helped generate further research into more realistic sports-car studies. Even so, there was always something more pressing to spend time and money on, and so the idea of a new MG sports car remained a nice dream for the wish-list. Then in 1989 the Mazda 'Miata' (MX-5 in other markets) was launched, and the picture changed: suddenly the market for small sports cars was alive and kicking again.

In the meantime, Austin Rover had been purchased by British Aerospace and had become 'Rover Group', and while the relationship with Honda continued to flourish, the company was encouraged to explore new market niches – sports cars being an obvious example. Under the enthusiastically watchful eye of 'small cars' director Nick Stephenson, studies began into new sports car concepts. As these studies were getting under way, a separate project was being developed by British Motor Heritage to build replacement bodyshells for the MGB; a subsidiary project was to investigate the idea of building the car that Abingdon never did – an MGB V8 roadster.

Before long the Heritage project was subsumed within Rover's main sports car programme, and it was decided that a restyled MGB V8 could mark the thirtieth anniversary of the MGB and form a vanguard for the all-new MG sports cars that were planned to follow. At one point this new family of sports cars was to have included a new MG V8 aimed at the US market, and the new MGB V8 – codenamed 'Adder' – would

The MG RV8 of 1992–1995 was a surprising reprise of the MGB, conceived by Rover Group as a prelude to planned all-new MG sports cars. (MG Rover)

have made a logical first act for that car to follow; however, plans for the all-new car evolved into a V6, and were then dropped altogether when Rover withdrew its Rover 800-derived Sterling saloon from the North American market in 1991.

Project Adder – the name intended as an allusion to the Cobra – eventually emerged in September 1992 as the 'MG RV8', and married a much-modified MGB-derived monocoque with a current Land Rover-sourced 3.9ltr V8. The RV8 was hardly the last word in sophistication, but in its way, like the EX-E, it promoted fresh interest in, and awareness of, the MG sports car

– paving the way for the MGF that followed in 1995, and making the case for a future MG V8 easier to justify.

By the time the MGF emerged, Rover Group had been bought by BMW, and even then, in an interview for *Automobile* magazine, BMW chairman Bernd Pischetsrieder suggested that he 'could see a V8 in MG's future'. In the event, such a car never emerged, and MG was forced to be a one-model marque from the MGF's launch in 1995 right through the remainder of BMW's period of ownership; and even if Dr Pischetsrieder voiced enthusiasm for a bigger MG sports car, some of his colleagues within BMW seemed less keen on a concept that threatened to step on the toes of their mainstream BMW sports car plans. It was obvious that another MG V8 was not high on the agenda for the time being.

chapter three

The Italian Connection

THE ITALIAN TVR

The engineer at the heart of the MG XPower SV – and the Qvale that spawned it – is Giordano Casarini, a former Ferrari and Maserati engineer with many years of experience, a man imbued with that special blend of motoring passion and talent that is endemic in the area of northern Italy centred on Modena, spiritual home of Ferrari. Casarini told me that Peter Stevens once joked that 'Giordano comes with a lot of experience of mistakes', the clear implication being that experience of the sharp end of the low-volume car industry can be painful but invaluable. Casarini's response is that philosophers often say that history repeats itself, but that this is only when people don't learn from history.

Casarini was technical director at Maserati, and throughout 1993 and 1994, found himself making frequent visits to the UK in connection with airbag development work for the Maserati Quattroporte. Being a car enthusiast as well as an accomplished engineer, Casarini was naturally interested in the different cars that he saw on the roads in the UK: 'I was particularly impressed by this small thing that would zip around me making a wonderful noise but which looked like a Mazda: I soon found out that it was a TVR Griffith.' Casarini's fascination with the TVR would prove instrumental in the development of new ideas back home in Italy.

At that time Maserati had a major problem with the final-drive differentials on their cars, which used proprietary axles from a well known supplier: 'They were the main source of problems in our warranty system,' Casarini recalls with a shudder. 'We could change at least two differentials on each Maserati Biturbo, and they were incredibly noisy – and there was always some good reason why they should be better next time.' But Casarini had investigated the TVR in

TVR had undergone a renaissance in the early 1990s – and served as inspiration for a new concept of De Tomaso. (TVR)

Modena – The Italian Connection

In the Piazza Grande, in the heart of the Emilia-Romagna town of Modena, stands the cathedral that has watched over the souls of the local populace since it was consecrated by Pope Lucius III in 1184. The building of the great edifice started in 1099, just thirty or so years after England's King Harold had a spot of trouble with the Normans. This beautiful white building has been declared a historic treasure of such value that since 1999 a UNESCO charter has protected it. A casual visitor to this classic work of Italian architecture might not notice, however, some peculiar geometric carvings in one face at the end of the cathedral, within easy reach from the ground. Their purpose becomes clear when their origin is explained, and gives a small clue as to the whole nature of the Modenese economy and way of doing business.

Even before the great cathedral was raised from its mighty foundations, generations of craftsmen and tradesmen had congregated in the area of the Piazza Grande to sell and barter their wares, much of which were based on even older traditions of local manufacture: roof tiles, bricks and fabrics were all ancient parts of Modena's past long before 1099. However, the roof tile that one man made in his little family kiln might not have matched one made by a distant cousin on the other side of the Po valley, and a bolt of fabric from one loom might have been smaller than another. So the educated wise men of the Church decided to intervene. Precisely carved in the lower face of one wall of the cathedral are four small, regular, recessed shapes: they are respectively templates for a yard of fabric, a brick, a roof tile and a land measure, and each shows the wear and tear caused by generation upon generation of artisans who have tested their wares and shown them to prospective clients. In this way hundreds, maybe thousands of small, outlying family workshops could all

A Qvale Mangusta at home in the picturesque Italian countryside. (Qvale Automotive Group)

produce work to a common standard.

For hundreds of years ever since the town of Modena, and the province at the heart of which it lies, has been home to vast numbers of small businesses. Even now, it is said, the average number of employees per company throughout the region is no more than ten – but with such clever foresight as the churchmen of 1099, those many small companies can together be a powerful force to be reckoned with. Quality control and efficient sub-contracting is therefore not a new idea – it was alive and well in northern Italy in the eleventh century…

more detail, and as soon as he learned it had a V8 engine and rear-wheel-drive, he realized that it had to have a differential similar to the Maserati one. On one of his frequent visits to the UK, Casarini was staying near London and, taking the part of an Italian enthusiast, located a local TVR dealer:

I was waiting there to talk to a salesman, and I was leaning under the car to look at the differential, and this guy came round – it was the proprietor himself – and he asked me what I was looking at: 'Are you interested in the differential?' he said. I answered that, as a matter of fact, I was, and he said 'Did they tell you it's no good?' I said no, although I recognized that it was the same one that we used on our Maseratis; and he said, 'Well, whatever they tell you it isn't true, because this differential is so good that Maserati uses it!' I said 'Thank you very much – that's so reassuring to hear!'

Casarini found himself becoming more and more intrigued by the TVR:

I learned a lot from the salesman; he took me around the car, and although I had already seen some defects that were reasonable to expect in a hand-built car in that price range, he kept showing me other defects, even ones I couldn't see: 'This is uneven … when the car comes in, we have to disassemble this …' and so on – and then he said 'Here is the key – take it for a drive!

Even before he fired the engine, Casarini could see the appeal – and why customers and dealers alike were evidently so forgiving: 'There was this marvellous noise, the environment was pleasant, and when you were going at 90mph [55km/h] it looked as though you were going at 200mph [125km/h]. I wanted to have one!' Then Casarini learned that at that time (in 1993) TVR was making and selling 800 Griffiths a year – 'That was tremendous!'.

A lifetime of working within the close-knit Modena community meant that Casarini both knew, and had worked with, many of the famous faces in the industry; for instance he had been on first-name terms with 'Commendatore' Ferrari himself, who in years gone by would amuse himself on a Saturday morning sitting in his office chatting and playing with Casarini's small daughter while her father was out in the workshops ensuring that the Ferrari race cars would be ready for shipping out on Monday. A close bond also existed between Casarini and the Argentinean industrialist Alejandro De Tomaso, who for several years owned Maserati as well as his own De Tomaso business.

In 1993, De Tomaso suffered a debilitating stroke, from which his recovery was long and slow. Giordano Casarini was one of the trusted few with whom De Tomaso kept close counsel. 'I used to go and see him as a friend,' Casarini recalls; 'after all, we had been working for nineteen years, bitching at each other day and night.'

Eventually, when De Tomaso had recovered sufficiently, Casarini was summoned by his old boss:

> So I went to see him. His speech was a little difficult to understand because of the effect of the stroke, but his mind was still sharp and he said to me: 'What do you think I should do with De Tomaso?' then a small company of thirty-five people: 'Should I sell it, should I close it – what should I do?' I almost instinctively said: 'Why don't you make an Italian TVR?' We were selling twenty Maseratis a year – at that time the right sort of quality had finally been achieved – and while we would only sell a handful of Maseratis in England each year, these people at TVR were selling 800 cars a year, and from a quality perspective, our car was in a different league!

Casarini put it to De Tomaso that he should create a car with the same raw emotions conjured up by the TVR, but 'do it the Italian way – improve the quality and style and aim to get that same emotional load to the customer'. Without hesitation, De Tomaso agreed, and within days had begun negotiating with the Maserati chairman to release Casarini to allow him to lead the De Tomaso company in order to develop such a car. Sufficiently intrigued, De Tomaso himself wanted to look at the Griffith – something that Casarini arranged – and so the planning process began, with discussions starting with designers and engineers to develop the basic concept. Giving up his position at Maserati was not a simple decision; Casarini laughs: 'I left a big boat for the raft!' – but by way of compensation for the risk, De Tomaso gave him complete freedom to develop the car conceptually.

SPORTS CAR MANUFACTURE IN THE PO VALLEY

Modena is the original home not only of Ferrari – unquestionably the pre-eminent Italian sports car marque – but also of a veritable hive of industrious

smaller businesses that have, over the years, supported the enterprises of Enzo Ferrari and his contemporaries. Even today, many of these factories – often no more than a small building with a handful of skilled artisans – continue to form a vital part of the Italian supercar food chain. Although Italian prowess in motor racing goes back well before World War II, it was during the fifties and sixties that an explosion of activity took place in the Modena district; entire genres of Motorsport crystallized on various epicentres throughout the town, ranging from Formula Junior to F1, while the leading names locally included Bugatti, De Tomaso, Lamborghini, Maserati, Serenissima and Stanguellini, as well as Ferrari.

At that time, as now, Italian engineers and entrepreneurs combined their love of race cars with an appreciation of fine food, and from as early as the thirties, the Fini Restaurant in Piazetta San Francesco became a meeting place for everyone including drivers, engineers, mechanics, manufacturers, owners and wealthy aristocrats who, over meals of the finest local cuisine, would decide strategies and arrange deals that would help shape destinies on and off the race tracks. Enzo Ferrari himself first set up shop at 11 Via Trento Trieste on 16 November 1929 with the purpose of developing and racing Alfa Romeo cars. For

The original De Tomaso Mangusta was a truly exotic marriage of Italian style and American power. (De Tomaso spa)

the following nine years, Ferrari had a remarkable run of success under his own steam, until in late 1938, Alfa Romeo took the racing division back in house. Ferrari continued his activities, and on 12 March 1947, the very first Ferrari motor car was fired up in his workshops. Two years later, in 1949, Ferrari was in command of his own company – 'Auto Avio Costruzioni Ferrari' – and thus began the exciting history of the Ferrari marque.

Meanwhile in 1939 Modena became the headquarters of another of the great Italian sports car marques: Maserati moved to Viale Ciro Menotti, with the factory situated down the road at Ponte della Pradella. Although the firm raced with great distinction during the fifties, it is nowadays better known for the series of luxurious road cars that emerged from the company from 1960 onwards. Within another three years, tractor manufacturer Ferrucio

The De Tomaso Story

Argentinean Alejandro De Tomaso was born in Buenos Aires on 28 July 1928 to a wealthy politician father of Italian origin – he died when Alejandro was just five years old – and a landowning mother from one of Argentina's oldest Spanish-descent families. By the time he had finished his studies, De Tomaso was already an accomplished race driver who, seduced by the Italian motor-racing scene, arrived in Modena aged twenty-seven in 1955. In 1956 he took part in the famous Twelve Hours of Sebring race with an elegant female blonde co-driver – the wealthy New York heiress and society lady Elizabeth Haskell – who later became Mrs De Tomaso.

Between 1957 and 1959 De Tomaso worked with, and raced for, OSCA – the race car company formed by the Maserati brothers when they split from the Orsi family business that had previously bought out their company. At around the same time De Tomaso raced for the Centro Sud Racing Stable, also based in Modena. Setting up on his own at via Albereto in 1959, De Tomaso developed his business from building a Formula Junior and F1 race car, until eventually it encompassed the manufacture of complete cars. His reputation at the time was as a brilliant innovator, but also – perhaps unfairly – of a man who flits from one unfinished project to the next.

In October 1963 De Tomaso exhibited his Vallelunga Spider (named after a race track near Rome) at the Turin Motorshow, marrying GRP bodywork and a Ford Cortina four-cylinder engine; he went on to build fifty-six cars for customers. One of the striking features of the Vallelunga was the backbone chassis frame, which made the engine part of the structure of the car itself. The link with Ford seemed a promising one, and De Tomaso could see the success that Carroll Shelby had been having with his Ford V8-powered Cobras. Soon, therefore, the two were in touch, and Shelby sent a sketch by designer Pete Brock to Ghia – of which De Tomaso had control – and asked them to build a mid-engined, Ford V8-powered sports racer.

The result was dreadful, and so Brock himself came and supervised the construction of another car, which eventually emerged as the Ghia De Tomaso 5ltr (although Brock managed to coerce *Road & Track* to refer to it as the 'Brock-De Tomaso'). The car looked promising, but Shelby lost interest and decided not to proceed. Then in 1965 a young designer at Ghia, name of Giorgetto Giugiaro, drew up an exciting mid-engined body shape intended as a sister car to his earlier Iso Fidia saloon. The intended purchaser of this body – believed to have been either engineer Giotto Bizzarini or his usual customer, Renzo Rivolta – decided not to proceed, and so Ghia found itself with a body in need of a chassis. De Tomaso was keen to show off his wares at the 1966 Turin and Geneva shows, and so he decided to have the car built as a 'De Tomaso'.

Alejandro De Tomaso. (De Tomaso spa)

Possibly as a slight dig against Shelby, De Tomaso also chose to name the car the 'Mangusta' – Italian for 'mongoose', the deadly enemy of the cobra.

Although he was heavily involved with Ghia, it was not until 1967 that De Tomaso managed to engineer a complete buy-out – through his wife's family business, Rowan Industries – of the remaining interests in Ghia, at that time owned by one Rafael Trujillo, son of the Dominican Republic's dictator. Trujillo Jnr happened to be languishing in gaol and so was presumably receptive to the overtures from Mr De Tomaso and his associates. For the 1967 Turin show, the production version of the Mangusta appeared. Early US sales literature for the Mangusta – like the Cobra 'Powered by Ford' – had Shelby's details printed in as the contact for further information, but evidently the Texan thought better of the deal, or equally probably De Tomaso found the offer from the Qvale family more lucrative. Two production versions of the Mangusta were sold – one for Europe with a 306bhp 4,728cc Ford V8, and an American version with a 230bhp 4,949cc engine. It was a great success for De Tomaso: 280 of the 402 cars built went to the United States, and this success prompted Ford to purchase an 80 per cent stake in De Tomaso.

By 1968, business had expanded sufficiently to warrant a move to via Emilia Est, and the 'De Tomaso' name was immortalized by further cars such as the Pantera supercar – styled by American Tom Tjaarda – alongside the various Deauville and Longchamps saloon models. In March 1970 Ford bought out Rowan Industries' shares, and Ford's Lee Iaccoca was listed as Chairman of De Tomaso Inc. Also in 1970, De Tomaso finally realized his dream to take part directly in the Formula One Grand Prix with his own single-seater. The last De Tomaso Mangusta was built at Modena in 1971.

Meanwhile, however, the relationship between De Tomaso and Ford became strained, and divorce finally came in 1972, Ford acquiring the responsibility for keeping the Pantera engineered to meet US standards and on sale in that market. Pantera production continued but on a dramatically smaller scale, before being dropped from the US market in 1974. In the split from Ford, De Tomaso lost control of Ghia and Vignale where the Pantera was originally built, but he was nevertheless able to expand his empire, and acquired the famous Guzzi and Benelli motorbike concerns, as well as the Innocenti car-making business.

Maserati, meanwhile, had been owned for a turbulent period from 1968 onwards by Citroën, until the opportunity arose for De Tomaso to acquire it in 1975 – adding it to the De Tomaso-Benelli-Guzzi-Innocenti Group. In 1984, Lee Iaccoca left Ford and joined Chrysler, and he soon came calling on De Tomaso at Modena, the

The De Tomaso Story *continued*

relationship leading to the Chrysler-Maserati TC that was built between 1987 and 1989. This was not the first Chrysler-based tie-up: in 1980 there had been the best forgotten Dodge De Tomaso hatchback. De Tomaso maintained his overall control of Maserati until 1989, when he sold 49 per cent of the company to Fiat, who subsequently bought the remainder in 1993. Meanwhile the De Tomaso Guarà was released in 1992 – the first significant new De Tomaso road car in many years. The Guarà married composite bodies with fully independent suspension, and a torquey mid-mounted V8 – but this time the supplier was BMW rather than Ford. With his health failing, De Tomaso found both himself and his beloved company at a cross-roads, and the De Tomaso Bigua concept shown at Geneva in March 1996 was born out of his discussions with his trusted advocate, Giordano Casarini. The subsequent story of what became the Qvale Mangusta is covered in the main text.

For the De Tomaso company, the split from Qvale did not prove the end of the road, because the Guarà Coupe and Barchetta remained in low-volume production. De Tomaso also reached agreement with the Russian automotive firm UAZ for the production of an off-road vehicle called Simbir, to be built in a new industrial site in Calabria, in the south of Italy. For the great man himself, however, time was running out, and he finally lost the battle on 21 May 2003. With a final sad twist of irony, his company went into liquidation almost a year later.

Lamborghini began to produce his own supercar, the Lamborghini 350GT, and from 1965 this car was being built at a new factory at Sant'Agata Bolognese. Within a few more years, Lamborghini created seminal greats including the Miura, Countach and Diablo, the latter two both styled by Marcello Gandini. The Miura evolved into the legendary 'SV' version – those two familiar letters standing for 'Spinto Veloce', which literally means 'tuned fast'. Even before Lamborghini made his mark, however, another entrepreneur with motor racing in his blood had set up shop in Via Albereto: that man was Alejandro De Tomaso…

De Tomaso had long been different to most of the other Italian supercar specialists, who generally built their own high-revving, exotic semi-race engines. The De Tomaso approach was to mirror the Italian style and flair seen in Ferrari and Maserati thoroughbreds, but to use virtually off-the-peg, large capacity, overhead-valve American V8 engines under the bonnet. This meant that customers had more or less the same sense of occasion, but fewer of the costs – either of purchase or maintenance – normally associated with an Italian road rocket. As Casarini explains: 'If you buy a De Tomaso, you don't expect it to have a "De Tomaso" engine: it could have any engine, which we could buy in, along with other mechanical components.'

It had not escaped Casarini's or De Tomaso's attention that at the time, TVR used Rover engines. De Tomaso, however, had historical leanings towards Ford, and the US manufacturer in turn was used to supplying V8 engines to a number of specialist companies. However, at this stage – around mid-1994 – Casarini found that Ford was not yet ready to sell its new modular V8 engine. Casarini therefore traced his steps back to the earlier discussions about differentials, and TVR let him know that they were investigating a new differential from Australia – BTR (now part of Dana) – with which they experienced no problems.

Before long, Casarini got in touch with the representative in England and managed to obtain a supply of differentials suitable for a range of models and without any of the problems that he had experienced with the previous units. 'I called him up and I said "Look – you make a differential like that, capable of handling 400bhp – what is it used for? I need an engine!"' Casarini was pointed in the direction of HSV, a performance-oriented offshoot of General Motors' Australian Holden Division. Holden is responsible for some large and powerful Corvette-engined, rear-wheel-drive, outback-proof family saloons in the best Australian tradition, and soon after Casarini established contact, he was being offered engines, powertrain, transmissions – 'everything we needed' – and they helped to support the fledgling 'new De Tomaso project', dubbed 'ETX' at that stage.

No sooner had General Motors begun to take an interest in De Tomaso's project, however, than almost by magic, Ford Motor Company managed to get wind of the venture, and within a remarkably short period of time, Casarini and his colleagues suddenly found that Ford – no doubt sensitive to the historical links between Ford and De Tomaso – had somehow discovered a way to supply the latest 4.6ltr Ford V8 and ancillaries: 'They told us to come over as they had an engine available for us – we started dealing with Ford, and got Ford powertrain, transmissions and everything – the electrics and ancillaries.'

For an Italian car, there was perhaps little question that the design should be in the accepted mould, with an Italian designer – or design house – responsible for the aesthetics. Casarini looked at various possible candidates, but to some extent the choice was made for him by Mr De Tomaso himself, who loved the work of one particular designer: Marcello Gandini, architect of the Lamborghini Diablo. 'So we called Gandini to Modena, we explained to him what we wanted, and we took him around in a TVR Griffith and tried to give him the feeling of what we wanted.' So it was that Gandini was commissioned to develop the style of what would eventually become the Mangusta.

At Casarini's insistence, Gandini took one specific cue from the TVR Griffith: 'I particularly loved the ease

The origins of the new Mangusta lay in this 'Bigua' concept, shown at the 1996 Geneva Motor Show. (De Tomaso spa)

of lowering the roof on that TVR, and so we told Gandini that our car must go from a closed to an open car very easily.' Gandini's answer was the swivelling 'roto-top', a clever arrangement whereby the rear window unit would tilt into the passenger compartment and allow open-top motoring. 'Despite the many things that were not perfect on the car, that was one of the things that did work, and it was watertight!' Casarini remembers.

THE QVALE CONNECTION

With Gandini on board, and a full-sized running prototype ready for display at the 1996 Geneva Motor Show as the De Tomaso Bigua, the project was still very much at the formative stage; but De Tomaso was now faced with a rather fundamental obstacle, according to Casarini: 'When we were ready to start on developing the prototype and trying to make a car, there was no money!' Even when there is a viable prototype, a manufacturer is still several millions of dollars away from the production car. 'So we started to look for money, and the first choice was to look at the government. The Italian government and the European Union had provisions for creating employment in areas where there were employment problems, and we identified a place – a former steel plant – at Massacara in Tuscany.'

At the time, the Italian steel industry was wilting under the pressures of recession, with many plant closures and consequent loss of jobs. At first it seemed that the Italian government was keen to help fund the venture, but an unfortunate sticking point was the by-now wheelchair-bound Alejandro De Tomaso's personal state of health, which was certainly not improving. Naturally this was a sensitive subject, but the simple fact remained that eventually, De Tomaso was politely

told – and with regret – that the money would no longer be available from the public purse. 'So we went out hunting for money, and came up with the idea – quite independently, by the way – of our former Maserati importers in the United States, the Qvale family.'

The Qvale family – in particular, father Kjell and his son Bruce – were long-standing friends of De Tomaso, and according to Casarini there had been 'a wonderful relationship' in the past. De Tomaso and Qvale initially crossed one another's paths over the first De Tomaso Mangusta:

> Kjell Qvale was already a very successful businessman in the 1960s, and there was this Argentinean with his car, which he brought to New York. As soon as Qvale saw it he said 'I want it!' – and so he became the distributor for De Tomaso at that time. Then in due course this led to him becoming the distributor of Maserati when later De Tomaso bought that company.

This historic link between the businessmen was a strong emotional bond for both of them. A link was also forged between De Tomaso and the younger generation of Qvale, as Bruce later reminisced to *Motor Trend* magazine in October 2002: 'De Tomaso used to test its cars at an old airport track in Modena, and Mr De Tomaso – a creditable race driver in the 1950s – took me for ten fast laps in the very first Mangusta. My life changed, right then.'

Accordingly it was not long after their initial approach that the Qvale delegation came to Modena and began enthusiastically to talk about the potential of injecting some capital into the De Tomaso business for the express purpose of developing the Bigua for production. De Tomaso was, however, determined that while he needed the Qvale's money, one thing was non-negotiable: the car that emerged from the venture

Kjell Qvale

Norwegian-born Kjell Qvale began his long association with MG sports cars in 1947, right at the start of the post-war boom when America adopted the MG TC as something completely different from anything else on offer. Before long, the entrepreneurial Qvale had founded what would become the basis of a substantial empire known as British Motor Car Distributors, or BMCD for short: with its head office in San Francisco, followed in due course by various satellites including Los Angeles, it soon handled most of the west-coast import of MG and other British marques. Qvale was a great salesman, often giving personal demonstrations of the MG sports cars he was selling, and his reputation grew rapidly. He also helped foster the west-coast Motorsport scene, and was an influential member of the Sports Car Club of America, running under their auspices the original road races through the pretty forest roads above Pebble Beach near Monterey,

The Qvale dynasty. Left to right: Bruce, Kjell and Jeff Qvale. (Bruce Qvale)

and helping to design the famous Corkscrew turn at Laguna Seca Raceway at Monterey itself.

During the fifties and sixties, the BMCD business grew substantially, to the point where eventually the company became the largest single distributor in the United States of Austin-Healey, Bentley, Jaguar, Jensen, Lotus, MG, Rolls-Royce and Triumph. Meanwhile Qvale embraced other franchises, and when, in 1953, he established Riviera Motors as the first Volkswagen distributor in Northern California, he began another highly lucrative association with what at first must have seemed an eccentric choice of product. Riviera Motors went on to deliver over 400,000 vehicles through up to seventy dealers over a thirty-year period. In 1968, BMCD was granted the importation rights for the whole British Leyland franchise throughout the massive Los Angeles, Arizona, Nevada and Utah territories, selling through fifty specially selected, dedicated dealers. Giordano Casarini first came across the Qvale business when at Maserati:

> I remember in the early 1980s when I used to go and see him – they had this facility in Compton, south of Los Angeles, where he had a continuous line of trucks unloading cars into the 'PDI' facility – Jaguars and TR7s – and they would 'PDI' these cars and put them back on the trucks and distribute them all over western America.

Through BMCD, British Leyland found a very successful partner, and the relationship continued until Jaguar exercised its option in 1991 and bought back the entire south-western territory. With the end of the Austin-Healey 3000 sports car in 1968, Qvale had seen a gap in the market that would soon begin to be filled by the Datsun 240Z, and before long he co-operated with Donald Healey on what would become the Jensen-Healey sports car project. In fact Qvale became so enmeshed in the process that he bought Jensen Motors in 1970, and so began a turbulent six years as the man bankrolling one of Britain's troubled but noble marques.

By this time Qvale had also forged a friendship and business arrangement with Alejandro de Tomaso, to import the latter's cars to the United States. When Jensen folded in 1976, Qvale maintained an interest in Jensen Parts and Service, which evolved into International Motors, and helped establish both the Subaru and Hyundai marques within the United Kingdom. At the same time, Qvale brought his son Bruce into the business and established Maserati Import Company back in the United States: he appointed some sixty dealers to sell the contemporary Maserati models, including the Bora, Merak, Quattroporte and BiTurbo. This business functioned for around ten years until Maserati bought back the importation rights. Over the same period, Qvale had built up lucrative parallel businesses through Porsche, Audi and Subaru franchises, and many other successful business ventures; but the Jensen business had left a taste for entrepreneurial automotive adventure...

should be a De Tomaso. The fact that the original car that had seen the two men begin their association was the De Tomaso Mangusta made 'Mangusta' a natural choice of name for the new car – in Casarini's words 'it was a romantic link'. (As an aside, the Bigua prototype itself was later crashed by a Ford component engineer in Modena; according to Casarini: 'The car survived but it damaged the kerb, and we had to pay a fine to the City of Modena – and do you know, for years afterwards they never bothered to repair that piece of kerb!')

At first there were tentative thoughts about De Tomaso building the car using his existing facilities, but it swiftly became apparent that this would not be adequate for the big push into North America that everyone wanted. The decision was therefore taken to establish a wholly separate facility, principally underwritten by the Qvale family. 'The Qvales agreed to finance the project, we made a big business plan, and it was foreseen for the car to be a De Tomaso; we established a dedicated company to manufacture the car, and we would pay a royalty to Mr De Tomaso for each car,' Casarini explains. On the face of it, this seemed to be the best of all possibilities: a wealthy American industrialist who would bankroll an Italian sportscar company with a highly marketable name, and one that he would then sell in the United States through his impeccable distribution network: what could possibly go wrong?

With Bruce Qvale overseeing the project, the De Tomaso team – headed by Casarini – began putting together the Qvale Modena facility. By the time the Qvales had finished remodelling it, the ten-year old

building was an eye-catching piece of architecture in itself, and quite unlike the average car factory, even in the heart of the Italian supercar industry.

The Qvales never saved their pennies – we told them we needed something, and we got it, and more! The factory was beautiful, and people would stop in front and say, 'If this is the building and everything inside is consistent, then what a car it will be…' All the offices were elegantly and comprehensively furnished, and there was marble everywhere – the most sophisticated electronics system you could imagine – for dealing with orders, purchasing, aftersales, all on AS400 computers. We got the top level of ISO9002 certification – everything was near-perfect. I had BMW people in there praising the precision of the organization – and we set everything out in a manual of all our systems and procedures.

QVALE MANGUSTA CHASSIS AND BODY

The Mangusta used a combination of modern technologies. The chassis was designed by former F1 designer Enrique Scalabroni; it was jig-welded (from laser-cut steel pieces) and galvanized by Vaccari & Bosi, while the body was made from 'Resin Transfer Moulding' (RTM) plastic panels supplied by Stratime

Seen here at the 1996 Geneva Motor Show are (L-R) Bruce Qvale, Giordano Casarini (chief engineer) and Santiago De Tomaso (son of the founder). (Frank Mandarano photo)

ABOVE: The special 'Antera' wheels offered on the Qvale Mangusta. (Qvale Automotive Group)

Cappelo Systems of Villers-Cotterêts in France, and then pre-painted prior to assembly using special paint supplied by Scott Warren/Rovercoat of Rome.

An Argentinean engineer who had been a technical director at Ferrari (see below), Scalabroni was also an old friend of De Tomaso, and Giordano Casarini knew him from their Ferrari links. 'When we started the project, we called him up for ideas' Casarini explains, 'and although we did have some thoughts about making the chassis from tubes – like TVR – we found that we could only get the stiffness about a third of what we wanted. So Enrique and I began to plan out the chassis, using cardboard cut from packaging to mock-up our first layout!' The effort was clearly worthwhile, for the chassis of the Mangusta – an open car, remember – is both strong and stiff. Scalabroni confirms the story of the cardboard Mangusta:

BELOW: The interior of the Qvale Mangusta was an intriguing blend of Italian craftsmanship and off-the-shelf Ford componentry. (Qvale Automotive Group)

Vaccari & Bosi: 'Il Tubista'

In the mid-fifties – around the time, coincidentally, that Alejandro De Tomaso first arrived at Modena – the small Vaccari workshop was established in Via Barchetta on the outskirts of the city. By this time Ferrari was already a household name, and to become a supplier to the famous Maranello factory was a considerable privilege enjoyed by few. William Vaccari was one of those few, and in 1956 he became the sole supplier of chassis for Ferrari, often using his firm's unique oval-section steel tubing. Vaccari was known as 'il tubista' ('the plumber') on account of the tubular construction of his chassis, used in such legendary cars as the Ferrari 250 GTO, and many other great Ferrari, Lamborghini and Maserati models.

In due course Vaccari's daughter Lucilla married Paolo Bosi; working together as Vaccari & Bosi, the two families brought under the same roof not only chassis frames, but suspension members, exhaust manifolds and silencers. Vaccari & Bosi have always moved with the times, and by so doing have ensured that their crucial part in the Italian supercar business has remained central to modern design and manufacture; recent Ferrari models have also featured the company's chassis, and many of the wishbone suspension

systems in Ferrari and Maserati products still owe much to Vaccari & Bosi. State-of-the-art software is used for structural analysis of suspension and chassis alike, and the company has adopted IBM CAD/CAM workstations with CATIA 3D software.

When it came to the Qvale Mangusta, Vaccari & Bosi was a natural choice to manufacture both chassis structure and the wishbone suspension, and as these components were among the more successful parts of the Mangusta as a whole, it is perhaps not surprising that the relationship has endured beyond the end of the Qvale project. The Vaccari and Bosi families are still both heavily involved in the running of the business: Lucilla's brother Marco Vaccari runs the Modena factory where the MG SV rolling body is built, while Paolo Bosi runs the factory where the SV chassis originates in Pievepelago, on the Modenese Apennines not far from Bosi's village of birth and his present-day home.

Seen at Vaccari and Bosi's Pievepelago factory, MG X80 Project Manager Ian Moreton (left) is seen examining one of the dedicated jigs for the SV chassis with Paolo Bosi. (Dave Woods)

Oh yes! That was at the beginning, to try and organize all the packaging of the components; we put everything inside the body perimeter, but also calculated the moments of inertia and polar moments to ensure that the steering balance would be good – to the best standards possible, in fact. It is often difficult to visual the 3D just in drawings, and the model was a good way to help this process.

Scalabroni is based in England, but his work takes him all around the world; when I spoke to him, he had just flown in from South America where he had been working on a project for a major manufacturer. He recalled being contacted by Casarini, and went to see him in Italy; afterwards he came back to England in order to begin to analyse the problems and see what should be done. He explains:

We started to work directly together. They hadn't got the Gandini body shape at that stage, and so we created the basis of the shape ourselves to allow the best arrangements of components to provide the optimum balance – considering the moment of inertia as well as important aspects such as comfort and ease of access.

We created a very precise mock-up to get the package right. We worked hard together, and did all the design. I wanted to use a new design for the chassis as it had no structural roof, and that can lead to poor torsional stiffness, which has a detrimental effect upon the performance of the suspension. I also had to consider the frontal impacts – both asymmetric and straight-ahead. An asymmetric impact will move the engine to one side – which is good; one of the things that kills so many people in car accidents is cockpit intrusion, and we proved that the Mangusta was particularly resistant to that in testing.

Scalabroni remembers talking to some engineers from a major car manufacturer at that time: 'They told us that they had needed twelve tests with their car to get the results they wanted; we succeeded on the second try!' Scalabroni is an expert in the field of body and chassis design, which has to cater for the extreme forces experienced during crashes:

You need to dissipate energy in an impact, and hard points cause difficulties with that – you can get accelerations of up to 60g when there is no progressive collapse. In our case, we managed to dissipate most of that energy through the sideways displacement of the engine – so the cockpit in a Mangusta [and therefore an SV] is a very safe place to be.

Back in England we worked using finite element analysis to reduce the weight while keeping the strength. It was a nice project to work on – we were able to be very precise with the model and the finite element analysis. A typical open car would have 350kg per metre per degree of torsional stiffness. For a BMW, it would be 750kg/m/deg – but for our car it was 1,450kg/m/deg – like a Mercedes Benz with a roof! The torsional strength is very high – and the structure of the car is a very good basis for a competition version, as it is so strong to begin with. In addition, the vertical stiffness of the Mangusta was also very strong – so you wouldn't see the doors sticking as a consequence of the body sinking with age.

The choice of RTM bodywork was a fairly bold departure within an industry that had a tradition of steel or aluminium, but the Mangusta was not the first exotic car that Stratime Cappelo Systems had worked on: the eccentrically styled Alfa Romeo SZ had used their bodywork technology, as did the 1989 'M100' Lotus Elan. Among the stated advantages of RTM mouldings were the high quality finish straight from the mould – with good finish on both sides of the panel – and the relatively small amount of finishing needed prior to painting.

Interior trimming was carried out by Italian artisans in the traditional manner, with leather swathing every visible surface, while the patented 'roto-top' was a novel approach to Giordano Casarini's desire for a simple folding roof. The interior electrics were supplied as a complete package by Visteon Automotive Systems. No one at this stage seems to have ventured to suggest that the appearance of the car was anything less than lovely – they presumably held to the maxim that to be successful as a small company meant inevitably to be 'different' and 'challenging' – but with the combination of new-generation manufacturing, an enviable quality system and the De Tomaso name, the prospects looked more than reasonable.

The first production Mangusta rolled off the line at Modena on 10 November 1999, an event at which Giordano Casarini's heavily pregnant wife Fiona was present, to see the results of her husband's labours: 'That very night she delivered my son Luca,' Casarini recalls fondly.

ENRIQUE SCALABRONI

The chassis design of the Qvale Mangusta – and hence the MG that evolved from it – owes a great deal to the talents of one man, Enrique Scalabroni. An Argentinean, like Alejandro De Tomaso, Scalabroni graduated from the University of Buenos Aires, and in 1982 moved to Europe where he joined the Dallara team for three years. In 1985 he moved to the Williams F1 team, working alongside Patrick Head as his assistant designer for four years; he then switched allegiance to Ferrari, where he took over as the head of chassis

Enrique Scalabroni. (Enrique Scalabroni)

development. The following year – 1990 – he moved to Team Lotus; two years later he was announced as chief designer of the 'Il Barone Rampante' F1 team. By April 1992 he was engaged on the sportscar programme at Peugeot Sport, where he started working on the Peugeot 905 GT project, managed by Jean Todt. Todt put forward the idea of a full F1 programme, but the Peugeot board of directors would not sanction such a venture, and so Scalabroni left for Williams.

In the middle of 1994 Scalabroni was noted as the designer of an F1 car for 'Ikuzawa International'. Sadly that venture proved to be another blind alley, but Scalabroni kept his F1 ambitions burning, and to keep himself gainfully employed offered his talents as a freelance designer in the junior formula and also in road car design. This brought him to Modena, where he worked with Giordano Casarini and the Mangusta project team. Casarini says that like many passionately driven, creative engineers, Scalabroni is an inveterate scribbler of ideas: 'You would want to keep and frame many of his sketches!' Following his involvement with the Mangusta, Scalabroni was linked with Alain Prost's team as technical director before moving on again to work with Asiatech to help them in their plans to acquire the Peugeot Sport engine programme; he became technical director, though sadly the events of '9/11' caused that project to collapse.

Asiatech laid tentative plans to launch a full F1 team, but funds were never sufficient and the company closed down at the end of 2002. After that, Scalabroni joined Barcelona Competicion, a new Formula 3000 team, testing with experienced F3000 race winner Enrico Toccacelo.

PRESENTATION OF THE MANGUSTA

Meanwhile, on 6 January 2000 at the Los Angeles Motor Show, the return to the US market of the De Tomaso marque after a twenty-five-year gap was heralded with the presentation of the Mangusta. Bruce Qvale proudly claimed that:

> In building the Mangusta for the US market we did not compromise in any way. The Mangusta underwent crash testing at MIRA in the United Kingdom, and has been integrated with all United States-mandated safety features, including driver and front passenger airbags. Although we are not a volume manufacturer, we felt it was necessary to offer a vehicle comparable in every way to those of larger volume automakers. Therefore, we chose not to rely on waivers for systems like airbags.

At the same time, Qvale announced that the coming year would also mark De Tomaso's return to United States motorsports competition:

> The Mangusta, in racing trim, will make its debut in the BF Goodrich Tires Trans-Am Series, campaigned by Huffaker/Qvale Motorsports. The Tommy Bahama-sponsored Mangusta will be the only official factory team competing in the Trans-Am series: with our returning sponsor Tommy Bahama, we're ready to take on the challenge of being the factory De Tomaso Mangusta Team; we have an exciting new car, a proven Huffaker/Qvale crew, the outstanding technical expertise of Huffaker Engineering, and a chassis that is the match of any. We're going to set the standard for the Trans-Am series in the year 2000.

FIGHTING TALK INDEED!

The De Tomaso Mangusta was officially placed on sale in North America with effect from 20 January 2000, priced at $78,900 (US) totally equipped, including a full leather interior. At the launch, the only available option was 18in alloy wheels and tyres. The Qvale press release proclaimed:

> The Mangusta is an all-new, exotically styled, 2+2 front-engined sports car featuring a unique three-position roof that converts the car from coupe to targa to roadster. With a top speed near 160mph (260km/h) and 0–60 times in the 5sec range, the Mangusta delivers reliable performance from its 4.6ltr, double overhead-

The Huffaker Engineering-developed 'Tommy Bahama' Qvale Mangusta was a force to be reckoned with in the 2001 Trans Am championship. (Qvale Automotive Group)

cam Ford V8, plus innovation and exclusivity in a package that evokes the best of Italian style and design.

One imagines that a certain Italian ego may have been mildly perturbed by the notion that 'the Qvale Automotive Group was the catalyst for the De Tomaso renaissance', although the fact was indisputable that only through the Qvale's money had it been possible to bring this project to fruition, let alone within two years of signing the licensing agreement with De Tomaso Modena S.p.A. in March 1998. 'At that time the Qvale Automotive Group acquired rights to manufacture, distribute, and market current and future De Tomaso products,' the release continued, without seeking to elaborate in too much detail on the finer points of those distribution rights.

However, while the public face presented by the De Tomaso-Qvale partnership was a united one, rumours were already circulating during the winter of 1999–2000 that not all was sweetness and light behind the scenes, and matters were probably not helped when Mr De Tomaso unveiled his own prototype – which he dubbed the De Tomaso Pantera – without, it would seem, any input whatsoever from the Qvale family. As with Ford in the past, it looked as if Mr De Tomaso was trying to continue to plough his own furrow while someone else bankrolled his company.

Matters came to a head when, as Casarini succinctly puts it, 'We had a crash, and everybody wanted back his toys!' Kjell Qvale, watching a constant stream of capital flowing out of his bank account and with no early sign of return, began to think that Alejandro De Tomaso's insistence on having his name over the door was no longer tenable. Qvale senior certainly had finance (if not managerial) experience in the car manufacturing field through his involvement with Jensen over twenty years previously; on the basis that his other motor distribution businesses were extremely successful enterprises on the west coast of America, he decided that his name was sufficiently strong to go on the car and the factory door. This unsurprisingly led to a major clash with De Tomaso – but Mr Qvale would not be dissuaded.

Every production Mangusta was fitted with this special chassis plate bearing the signature of chief engineer Giordano Casarini. (Courtesy Giordano Casarini)

Giordano Casarini found himself in the eye of a storm, and knowing both parties, did his best to intercede.

> We explained several times that with a De Tomaso, the customer already knows what he is buying; it is not a Ferrari – it is not, by itself, a car that is very precise – it is more brutal and does not have quite the same finesse. So we explained to him that if you are marketed as something completely new, people will expect everything from you – if you want to be in there you must have the best of Ferrari, the best of Maserati – high performance, high finish and everything the very best – otherwise they would not buy it.

Casarini and his colleagues tried to point out that outside the car distribution business, Qvale's name was not a household one, but all this was to no avail. Within weeks came the formal announcement in March 2000 that the two parties had agreed to separate.

By spring 2000, the Mangusta – now rebranded as a Qvale – was ready to appear again on the world stage, and production began to ramp up for sales in the United States. Homologation followed, with the manufacture and crash-testing of no fewer than twenty-nine cars, and leading US motoring journalists were invited to test early pre-production specimens. Most testers enjoyed the Qvale Mangusta; they revelled in its sporty handling, loved the performance, and appreciated the quirky but effective folding top. What they were less convinced about were the apparent early quality glitches – the fact that, good though it was, the engine was an unreconstructed Ford Mustang unit; the rather oddball styling; and last but not least, the unfamiliar

Giordano Casarini

Giordano Casarini was born on 10 February 1946 into an Italy determined to put the war years behind it, but wracked by political tensions. As far as the sports car world was concerned, however, it was soon business as usual, and the young Casarini showed great interest in and aptitude for all things mechanical. During his mechanical engineering degree at the highly respected Bologna University, Casarini spent valuable time at Ferrari, joining the famed racing department in 1969.

Six years later he moved to the United States where, in partnership with a friend, he started 'MIR Racing' – a specialist Formula 5000 race team that built its own engines using General Motors 'short-block' engines. Through sponsorship from a novel quarter, MIR Racing's main attraction became the 'Evel Knievel Special', although this happy arrangement was blighted somewhat when one of Mr Knievel's accidents led to a cash-flow problem for the team.

After two years in America, Casarini came back to Italy and joined Maserati in Modena, where he stayed for the next nineteen years. 'I started in the 'dyno' rooms, and moved on to take over homologation and the experimental shop – and by the end of my time there I was the technical director in charge of engineering' he explains. Then, as we saw earlier, Casarini was persuaded to leave Maserati to join Alejandro De Tomaso and sow the seeds of what would become the Qvale Mangusta...

Giordano Casarini seated in a pre-production MG XPower SV. (Roger Parker)

name. Many articles had to start by explaining how to pronounce the Qvale name (Kah-vah-lee, by the way) and one magazine even dubbed the car the 'Q-what?'.

Car and Driver perhaps best summed up the views of many observers by suggesting, at the end of a mixed review of the Mangusta in its October 2000 issue: 'With so much fine machinery at this price, it's hard to justify.' It was something of an ominous beginning.

The trouble of the name kept haunting the car, as Casarini had said it would: 'A car with a good name is something that can be accepted by its customers, but a car with a new name, nobody wants! We made 280 of these cars – beautiful factory, beautiful project, and beautiful engine – but no customers!'

BELOW: The Mangusta styling was not derivative, but perhaps an acquired taste. (Qvale Automotive Group)

ABOVE: The unique 'roto-top' folding roof meant that the Mangusta could easily switch from coupé to convertible in a matter of moments. (Qvale Automotive Group)

chapter four

New Frontiers

EXIT STRATEGIES: THE LINK BETWEEN QVALE AND MG

Just as the Qvale Mangusta was emerging into the critical American spotlight, across the other side of the Atlantic another remarkable story was unfolding – or perhaps one should say, unravelling. Compared to the falling out between Qvale and De Tomaso, the tortured relationship between BMW and Rover Group was of epic proportions: everyone – friends and rivals alike – could see there were problems, but just how terminal they were only became public in April 2000 when BMW announced that it intended to dispose of its Rover Group subsidiary, ending a six-year British affair.

The cracks had been showing for some time: when the German company began to exercise much greater direct control from Munich of affairs that it had previously been content to manage at one remove, it was clear that all was not well. There are various reasons for this state of affairs – too many and too complex in total to warrant detailed discussion here – but basically BMW had been pouring billions of Deutschmarks into a business whose market share and export prospects were shrinking, due partly to the strength of the pound sterling; it had become like the classic conundrum of the irresistible force and the immovable object – something just had to give.

When the news broke, there was just one party who was, as it were, named in correspondence, and that was Alchemy Partners, managed by Jon Moulton. Moulton had set the agenda cleverly when he had started negotiating in the autumn of 1999, and one of the key assets he was determined to prise out of BMW – in fact the single commodity that, in his eyes, made the proposition tenable – was the MG name. Before long there would be other interested parties, among them the Phoenix Consortium, but notable by their absence were most of the big car manufacturers; these took an understandably jaundiced view of BMW's problems, and anyway had their own problems to address concerning industry over-capacity. Ford was the honourable exception, and took the opportunity to purchase Land Rover and add the premier off-roader brand to the blue-chip Jaguar and Aston Martin names already in the corporate cupboard.

IN SEARCH OF AN MG SUPERCAR

From the very beginning of their plan to acquire the MG brand and to rebuild it for the future, Nick Stephenson and his colleagues at the fledgling Phoenix Consortium pencilled in the idea of a special flagship supercar project to serve as a talisman for the expanded MG range they were planning. They had not been the only people to see the merit of this idea: their rival bidder for MG, Jon Moulton's Alchemy Partners, had also proclaimed a desire to build some extra-special MG sports cars. While Jon Moulton was contemplating new sports cars to be designed and built with Lotus input –

MG Rover entered a brace of 'MG Lola EX257' race cars in the Le Mans 24 Hour races of 2001 and 2002 – but sadly early promise failed to follow through to the hoped-for class victories. (MG Rover)

The MG K4 concept

Before the deal with Qvale led to the creation of the MG X80 project, the Phoenix Consortium had considered creating a more extreme MG supercar, which would have been developed in conjunction with their partners at Lola. These concept sketches of an exotic mid-engined supercar using start-of-the-art motorsports technology show the style of the car – dubbed the 'MG K4' in a nod to the mighty MG K3 Magnette described in Chapter One. In the event, however, other issues in the relationship with Lola combined with the creation of the MG X80 led to the abandonment – for the time being – of the MG K4. (Images: Peter Stevens)

coupled to a Le Mans entry – the Phoenix Consortium were also thinking along the lines of something more exotic; before long, their new motto for MG would be 'Outrageous Fun'.

The Phoenix Consortium

Before the events of spring 2000, two people in particular – namely John Towers and Nick Stephenson – probably thought that their days of working within the Longbridge complex were well and truly over. Both men were originally engineers by profession; they had worked their way to the pinnacle of what had become Rover Group, and had then moved on to pastures new during the period of ownership of BMW. Towers had risen from a position as managing director of Land Rover, through directorship of Rover Group's entire supply chain, and then upwards, during the period when British Aerospace owned the company, to 'Group Managing Director, Rover Group Ltd'. With the takeover of Rover Group by BMW, one might have expected changes at the top (as so often happens in such situations), but BMW's avowed intentions in 1994 were to maintain the existing management whilst bolstering it with more funds and resources where needed. Towers therefore became 'Chief Executive, Rover Group Ltd', a post he held until he left on 1 June 1996. By that time, the dynamics of the relationship between BMW and Rover Group were changing, and Towers had decided to move on.

Stephenson, meanwhile, had also been moving up the corporate ladder, assuming the role of vehicle director (small and current cars) in 1986, forward programmes director from 1991 (in time to become intimately involved in the studies that led to the MGF), and from 1996 as a member of the Rover Group board. Stephenson stayed at Rover Group during the period of increasing BMW influence, after Towers had left, began to percolate throughout the company, and was even an enthusiastic participant in the more effective aspects of BMW-Rover interrelationships, such as the new generation 'NG' engines that were being developed for both Rover and BMW use. However, by spring 1999 Rover Group's subservient role within the Munich control structure had reached such a pitch that the position of Stephenson and a number of his fellow board members had become all but untenable, and so he, too, moved on to explore other avenues.

In Towers' case, a non-executive directorship at Concentric Group was seen by him as a stepping stone towards an early retirement, for as he told his audience at a lecture in April 2002, he and his wife had 'decided to go for a sort of modest semi-retirement in the sun. We'd already bought a little place in Quinta in the Algarve – so all that remained was to get the dog his microchip and passport and give the kids our new address in case they wanted to continue popping home at weekends'. Then

John Towers. (MG Rover)

came the news that BMW was preparing to dispose of Rover Group to Alchemy Partners, and: 'Tens of thousands of people's lives were literally turned upside down. We all expected the business was going to close. And the emotion that flowed from this was understandable'.

Towers felt strongly that Rover, a pillar of the West Midlands manufacturing community, needed to be saved in order to avoid what he called 'economic meltdown': 'You don't have to have a degree in economics to recognize this – we can't all cut each other's hair or give ourselves financial advice. Somebody has to generate wealth and create exports in the first place.' As is now well known, Towers soon recruited Nick Stephenson to his cause, followed by others – including Rover dealer John Edwards and accountant Peter Beale – and they were successful in wresting Rover from BMW in a deal involving payment of a symbolic £10 note. However, even then Towers was under no illusions of the magnitude of the task ahead:

I'll be completely honest with you – when we drove through 'Q' Gate [the main reception at Longbridge] on 9 May 2000, I was naturally proud that we got the reception that we did, but I was also a bit worried – worried because it looked as though everybody thought it was all over when actually it had just started...

A Possible MG/Lola Collaboration

Among the initial consortium members was former Rover man David Bowes, at that stage ensconced at Lola Cars, the famous motorsport race-car builder that had only recently been rescued from commercial oblivion by wealthy Irish industrialist and race-course owner Martin Birrane. Bowes was naturally keen to expand Lola's business base beyond the wealthy but commercially fragile race-car industry, and in discussion with his colleagues in the consortium it swiftly became apparent that there could be an opportunity to develop a new carbon-fibre supercar to bring together the technologies and marketing benefits of the MG and Lola names.

The first step along this path was to develop Lola's latest race-car chassis, equip it with a new AER-

developed engine (to be rebranded as an 'MG' unit), and mildly tweak the styling to give it some MG cues. The end result was a new-generation Lola race car: within MG it became known as EX257, drawing on MG's old experimental project number series, and the two proud parents announced that it would be participating in the famous Le Mans 24 Hour race in June 2001. Exciting though it undoubtedly was, the EX257 was obviously a long way from being a feasible road car – even a supercar – but it demonstrated the possibility of further MG-Lola collaborations to that end. At the same time there was ambitious talk of establishing a joint venture between Mayflower (suppliers of the MGF bodyshells) and Lola, which might have used vacant space on the vast Longbridge site. However, Stephenson told me that 'while the possibility of a Lola supercar was a real project, it didn't flourish and was of course ultimately replaced by another programme.'

Some may ask why a small but disproportionately high-profile company such as MG Rover, with many burning issues to tackle, should concern itself with costly pursuits such as Motorsport and related highly specialized – arguably peripheral – exercises. But Stephenson's resolute view was that:

We couldn't afford not to do it. Absolutely key to us has been the task of reinventing ourselves, relaunching the [MG] brand and adding excitement to the business. Competition does this internally, it has done it externally, it introduces us to a whole new set of deadlines – the motorsport world is unbelievably fast-moving – so it is healthy for a company like ours to be exposed to organizations that do set the pace in terms of car production around tight deadlines.

There is certainly truth in this philosophy, for nothing focuses the mind as much as the simple fact that races are not held up to benefit latecomers to the grid; as Stephenson succinctly puts it: 'The race starts at a certain time, and if you don't get there, you don't race...' It has often been said that 'racing maintains the breed', and Stephenson feels that this slogan is also very appropriate to MG; as he explains:

New technologies often exist in race cars first – often they develop over many years, and then find their way slowly but surely into the production scene; and so this motorsport effort is our fast-track towards that. So part-and-parcel of the MG Sports and Racing organization isn't just managing the race car programme, but it is – and it will be – making low-volume cars that will be 'cross-over' types of product.

In our business plan we said that we obviously had to build up the brand, and we put a supercar in there to help with that. To be perfectly honest, the idea then was that we'd do it with Lola, but although things didn't quite turn out that way, we nevertheless always kept a supercar in the plan – and so what happened is that what eventually became the SV assumed that role. We always believed that a supercar would be a good investment – purely for the PR advertising and brand-building benefits so that if, in addition, we could make a few bob on the car as well, that would be a bonus. Supercars are fantastic value. You're talking about a small company, and we knew we'd have to do radical stuff to get ourselves noticed in re-launching.

The Qvale Mangusta

It is not commonly known that one of the parties to show an interest in MG was the Qvale family. Giordano Casarini had good business connections within BMW, gained from his experiences with the De Tomaso Guarà, which used BMW engines:

So we had maintained a very good relationship with them – incredibly good. And then Bruce asked me to find out through our BMW contacts whether within that turmoil it would be possible to buy the MG trademark. So the Qvales – just when the Phoenix thing was happening – tried to buy MG, too....

With the exclusive negotiation arrangements that Alchemy Partners had secured, it seemed at the time that there was no real room for manoeuvre, although in a short space of time the Phoenix Consortium successfully lobbied to get a chance to bid for the Rover Group assets.

While the Phoenix Consortium was eventually successful in its efforts to buy the Rover Group, the Qvales continued to roll out the production Qvale Mangustas, and in particular to prepare to market the car in Europe and elsewhere. At the October 2000 British Motor Show, Qvale exhibited a right-hand-drive Mangusta prototype (which was, in the event, a partially engineered one-off), and a few journalists were encouraged to try Mangusta demonstrators. At around the same time – 13 October 2000 – Qvale reacted to slow sales back home by announcing there would be a price cut of nearly $10,000 for the 2001 model year cars, on sale from the beginning of the following month; the company explained:

Because the Mangusta is built in Modena, Italy, and aside from its Ford powertrain, is almost 80 per cent European content, we have been able to take advantage of the recent downturn in the Euro and pass on a large part of this difference to the consumer.

Nick Stephenson, deputy chairman of the by now successful Phoenix Consortium, was well aware of the Qvale family, and of their reputation and standing in California. 'I'd known Kjell for several years,' Stephenson told me; 'I'd met him some years before we were doing the MGF, in fact.' So it was not too surprising that the Qvales should soon be in touch with MG Rover to see what they were doing, particularly with regard to the North American market. 'It was at that time that we appreciated that Bruce had this venture in Italy, with his Qvale Mangusta sports car – and he sent us some information on it for casual interest purposes,' Stephenson recalls. Bruce Qvale told Greg Perigo of *MG Magazine* that:

...as they developed their business plan, it became clear to MG Rover that while they certainly may have had the funds to build a new product line-up, they lacked some of the other necessary resources to distribute them. We discussed things a bit, and we both realized that it made sense for us to co-operate.

Nick Stephenson recalls this first tentative approach, which his diary records gave rise to a meeting with him on 20 July 2000: 'That was Bruce and David Sharples, about distribution, as David was our overseas marketing man at the time – so this was the kick-off.' August 2000 saw various exploratory discussions about distribution, and Sharples himself has confirmed that most of his talks with Bruce Qvale centred on that aspect. Then, Stephenson continues, the idea emerged to take things further:

I can remember that Bruce got in touch with me and asked me if we would be interested in distributing the car – which was not a crazy idea, by any means – so we said that we'd give it some serious thought. You might imagine that those were still very hectic days and new ideas were popping up left, right and centre, but it was also the period when we were trying to bed down the company – this was of course still fairly soon after acquisition.

From the initial idea of simply distributing the Mangusta came a 'Eureka' moment; Stephenson is not sure now who first thought of it, but 'somewhere in there was the notion that rather than just distributing it, could we not do something more radical?' Having mulled it over, Stephenson knew that he would need to

Nick Stephenson. (MG Rover)

Peter Stevens

On one of the many web sites dedicated to the McLaren F1 supercar, Peter Stevens is referred to as a 'celebrity designer' – a description that is certainly not inappropriate, but is the sort of thing that makes the man himself laugh. Quiet, unassuming but supremely talented, highly respected and universally liked, Stevens has tended to work at the fringes of the car design industry rather than seek the glaring limelight and high-profile lifestyle of some of his peers – many of whom, however, have benefited from his advice and coaching. Stevens was born in Cheshire in 1943; his parents were artists, but by the time he was ten years old he was already hooked on the hot-rod scene, picking up his first copy of *Hot Rod* magazine in 1954. The following year Stevens' uncle, the late Denis 'Jenks' Jenkinson, famously navigated for Stirling Moss in a Mercedes SLR in the 1955 Mille Miglia.

By the end of that decade Stevens had acquired his first car – an MG, as it happens – at the age of sixteen; laughing, he describes it thus:

It was, when I bought it, an extremely sordid MG M-type! I had to hide it round the corner; I'd just sold my pushbike and couldn't legally drive at that stage. In fact it was rather funny, as I couldn't get anyone to go with me to Cambridge for my driving test, so I had to drive up there on my own, and when I got there, put the L plates on to do the test. After it was over (and I'd passed!), the examiner said 'Where's your mate you came up with, then?'; and so I said 'Oh, I s'pose he's gone for a cup of tea or something, and its great, 'cause now I can drive round and pick him up!' I then had a J4 replica and KN Magnette with a University Motors 'MG' registration number, as well as a J2 and a TA that was also a bit sordid. The KN – previously owned by my godfather from new – was a lovely car, but ended in disaster when a drunk came out of a side turning in Chelsea, right into the side of it. At the time, old cars weren't particularly valuable; they would give you something like £200 and then scrap it – it was a tragedy, as I couldn't afford to restore it, which was a darned shame. The J4 replica eventually had a Zoller supercharger fitted to it, along with a pre-selector gearbox.

After the accident with the KN, Stevens' dalliance with MG sports cars ended – he bought an ex-Eighth Army Jeep, which, he reasoned, would be better able to cope with the trials and tribulations of city traffic.

In 1965, Stevens began an industrial design course at Kensington's Royal College of Art (RCA), and three years later enrolled on a new Ford-initiated post-graduate automotive design course. He became one of its first two students; he even helped to devise the course, suggesting who should give lectures, and what equipment was needed. After graduating from the new RCA course in 1969, Stevens joined Ford's Dunton design studios, finding himself working mainly on car and van interiors until 1972. Amongst his early claims to fame was the interior of the first Ford Granada, while he also worked on the Escort Mexico and Mark 3 Capri.

Even in those early days, Stevens did not find the corporate life particularly conducive to creativity: he was offered a junior management post, but saw it as the first step to a lifetime at Ford, and so branched out into freelance design, aided by regular work from Tom Karen at Ogle Design. Among his clients in the ensuing years were ERF trucks, Cougar Marine (designing catamarans and helping on the Virgin Atlantic Challenger), Brabham-BMW (where he met and became firm friends with Gordon Murray), and Alpine-Renault (working alongside Trevor Fiore on the A310 and the original Renault R5 Alpine/Gordini). At Richard Lloyd Racing, Stevens worked on a range of projects including a Group 1 Chevrolet Camaro and a re-bodied Group C Porsche 962; while at the other end of the spectrum, he worked with the World Bank on a tractor project that was subsequently cancelled.

During the 1980s, Stevens began a long association with Tom Walkinshaw Racing (TWR), where he worked extensively on performance versions of Mazdas and Jaguars. By this time he was already combining freelance design work with part-time work as a tutor at the RCA; and he also found time for a bit of fun working with Britain's *Custom Car* magazine, designing ideas for custom specials – some of which upset the purists, much to his amusement. Meanwhile, in 1982, Stevens began a long-term relationship with Lotus Cars – which actually began just a week after Colin Chapman's death; Lotus' Colin Spooner had asked Stevens to work on the Excel styling update. As Stevens later told *Autocar*: '[Spooner] saw that an immediate programme would be good to get the place moving again, and that was the impetus behind the Excel update – but to my lasting disappointment, I never had the opportunity to work for Chapman.'

In 1986, Lotus was acquired by General Motors, and with their funding, plans went ahead for a new front-wheel-drive project, 'M100': this would emerge as the Lotus Elan, and as a consequence, Stevens was taken on full time as the design director. The design of the Elan, with a short nose or 'cab forward' look, was developed by Stevens, who won a British Design Council award for his efforts. Also to Stevens' credit was the 1987 facelift of the Guigiaro Lotus Esprit; the result had softened, fresher lines, and served as the basis of an enduring design that lasted more or less unmolested (barring minor changes) until the Esprit was finally discontinued at the end of 2003.

During the late 1980s, Stevens' involvement with the growing business of TWR flourished, along with the good fortune of Tom Walkinshaw, who had developed a close and lucrative relationship with Jaguar. In late 1990, Jaguar Sport – a joint venture between Jaguar and TWR – announced the stunning Jaguar XJR-15 supercar, with thirty cars available for sale, each at a price tag of half a million pounds, for an exclusive race series. The design of the XJR-15 – body exterior, interior and aerodynamics – was attributed to Peter Stevens, and today the car is seen as one of his seminal works; no doubt it helped to pave the way for subsequent work on his next supercar, the McLaren F1.

In 1993, the McLaren F1 emerged as the realization of a dream by engineering designer Gordon Murray to produce an ultimate supercar – and Stevens was the man who shaped the

Peter Stevens

stunning carbon-fibre bodywork. The F1 is an elegant, petite car with clean, unfussy lines in a sector not usually noted for subtlety. Stevens' interest and expertise in aerodynamics meant that the McLaren F1 did not need to be covered with add-on spoilers – the whole shape contributes to a car with a remarkable top speed of 240mph (390km/h), unrivalled even ten years later. The McLaren also went on to win the 1995 Le Mans 24 Hour race – the last road-car-based car to win this classic race.

Maintaining his successful relationship with Le Mans, Stevens was responsible for many aspects of the design of the 1999 Le Mans-winning BMW Motorsport LM99 sports car, including the design of the interior, as a consultant on the exterior design, as well as directing the aerodynamics, homologation, model making and tooling of production components. In the midst of this process, Stevens worked at Automobili Lamborghini, where he was responsible for the Diablo Jota, SV and SV-R; but his time at Lamborghini was short. More enduring was his relationship with Subaru, where he helped to transform the image of this marque from that of farmer's hack to performance icon.

As soon as the Phoenix Consortium successfully acquired Rover Group in May 2000, Nick Stephenson was particularly keen to tap into the years of design and practical low-volume experiences possessed by Peter Stevens:

Peter Stevens and the MG XPower SV. (MG Rover)

I had my chat with Peter very early on to see if we could get him on board at MG Rover. The history of getting Peter on board was not a long and involved one – I had long admired and respected not just Peter's work but his own personal style, and so my first thought was that he would be ideal for us – he was an obvious candidate – but I thought we'd have to be really lucky to get him, because he has a very high standing in the business.

Involvement with what became MG Rover Group was an intense activity, perhaps bringing Stevens closer to the corporate mainstream than he would normally like; but in between determining design directions for the MG and Rover brands, and managing the X80 project, he has kept his finger in other pies, penning the 2001 Maranello 550 Ferrari race car, and working on more projects with Subaru, Prodrive and Toyota Team Europe, to name but three.

Somewhere in that busy schedule he still finds time for his family and his hobbies, the latter including his continuing following of the hot-rod scene: at the last count he owned a number of mainly Ford-based specials – a 1915 Model T Ford-based dirt-track racer; a 1930 'Alexander Special' dry lakes racer (also Model T based); three more assorted vintage Fords; a couple of Fiat 500s; and an old Ferguson tractor. In between his consultancy work for MG Rover and others, Stevens is still helping nurture fresh design talent in his role as visiting professor at the RCA, and in his time in the business – when he has helped many well known leading designers on the path towards enlightenment – he has seen enormous progress. He told his old friend Tony Thacker, for a recent issue of *Custom Car*, that:

Around 30 per cent of design work is now done on computer, although first ideas are still sketched. We have five-axis milling machines that turn CAD images straight into 3D models. Presentations are often done using Powerpoint on laptop computers. Photoshop is used for putting portfolios together – so it is very different, but being able to draw is still crucial.

However, Stevens is keen to stress the importance of drawing talent, for, as he told Peter Dron of the *Daily Telegraph*:

Computers are just boxes full of wires and sand. They contain neither ideas nor inspiration, but can contribute efficiency to some jobs. I have yet to see much evidence of time-saving during the design and modelling stages of a project, but things seen on the telly are perceived by some to be the truth. The gloss that computer-aided design presentation can give to a project could suggest a talent that is possibly not present.

There is no question that talent is present in abundance in Peter Stevens' case, along with enthusiasm and good humour, characteristics that are not always prevalent in the same person.

become more acquainted with the Mangusta as it stood: 'I started to get more involved in understanding the car technically,' he explains. He could see that there was some sound engineering behind the Mangusta, but he could also see some of its deficiencies:

Not to be unfair or unjust to the Mangusta, but beauty was not one of its strong points! But the more I assessed the car, the more I became convinced that fundamentally it was a really excellent sports car: the chassis, the approach that the Modena team had taken to the car, was very good. Everything we looked at – suspension, chassis, powertrain, the approach to the interior and so on: altogether a very professional job had been done.

Having satisfied himself that the key engineering aspects of the Mangusta were particularly sound, but that some aesthetic changes might be needed, Stephenson began to review the most appropriate level of production:

I would describe the Mangusta in terms of 'low volume', and I believe that you can 'do' low volume in several ways. You can do it in the lowest of low volume ways, when the car is virtually hand-built, and at the other end of the scale you can have a fairly highly tooled car – and by that I mean appropriate tooling, and not the kind of stuff that is used to make tens of thousands of cars – but nevertheless a fairly highly tooled approach to low volume. And with that comes good quality, and that was the approach that the Modena team had taken to the car – and these aspects particularly attracted me to it.

But having said that, we didn't think much of the appearance of the body. The idea then emerged – and there were others involved in this, in particular my co-director Peter Beale – that we could take the project further. I think the first sojourn was when we went to see and touch the car and the factory in more detail at Modena – that was Peter and me. The concept of us taking the project and re-engineering it as an MG, which we felt we could do quickly and for a low cost – but more specifically changing the body style – gathered momentum really quickly.

My recollection is that we then moved fairly quickly from playing around with it as an idea, to saying to Bruce 'What might a deal look like? How much value do you think you have in this venture of yours?' and similar questions. We moved fairly quickly through some fairly

Peter Beale, Nick Stephenson's colleague who led much of the negotiation with the Qvale Automotive Group. (MG Rover)

short, sharp and intensive business discussion periods, and we struck a deal. The key players at the centre of that included Peter [Beale] with his business experience – he has an accountancy background – but obviously also by then the other members of our team had been drawn in – Rob [Oldaker], Peter Stevens, Kevin [Howe] – and we sent some of our manufacturing guys over to assess what was there.

The First Formal Business Meeting

The first formal business meeting – the point when Peter Beale became involved – was when it became obvious that it wasn't just a distribution deal, and was probably going to be an acquisition. 'Bruce came over to see us here at Longbridge on 12 and 13 of February 2001, and after fruitful discussions we prepared to fly over to Italy later in the month, after drawing up Heads of Agreement.'

The Geneva Motor Show is one of the most important outside North America; held at the Palexpo complex right next to Geneva Airport around the end of February or beginning of March every year, in a country that is centrally placed in Europe and yet is 'neutral' in car-manufacturing terms, the Geneva Salon is popular with the 'movers and shakers' as well as the international motoring press. For MG Rover, the main public event on Press Day, 27 February, at the 2001 show was the unveiling of a prototype of MG's first production estate car – the Rover 75-derived MG ZT-T. There was a fair level of corporate presence from MG Rover at the show, although the reasons for this are only now apparent. Having seen the ZT-T unveiled, the team of Kevin Howe, Rob Oldaker and Peter Stevens headed south from Geneva into Italy, their destination the Qvale facility at Modena, where they would meet up with Nick Stephenson and Peter Beale, who had flown straight there. According to Peter Stevens:

Initially there was the idea that maybe we could just re-badge the car as an MG, but it was pretty apparent from the way it looked that we'd have to start again. Because, with the best will in the world, they had gone to what they had thought was a top designer, Marcello Gandini, and he'd done another 'Gandini' – and not a very good one; so it was obvious that we had to start again. It was also clearly difficult to build, and hard to get the quality that was needed, and so generally we didn't think [the body style] was what we wanted. But the feeling was that there

The main focus of attention for the media at the 2001 Geneva Motor Show was the unveiling of MG's first ever production estate car: the MG ZT-T, seen here in concept form as revealed on the stand. (MG Rover)

was some interesting technology that we could tap into. The crash testing had already been done – homologation had been properly done for North America.

Although there was little doubt which badge the car would wear, Nick Stephenson admits some brief thoughts about alternatives: 'I'm sure we had a very small excursion that said "Is this an Austin-Healey?" for about ten minutes; but we thought, "no", MG is our core sporting brand and we can't manage too many brands – let's not get carried away.'

Meanwhile Stephenson identified the need for some practical pragmatic back-up from his technical colleagues to support his initial enthusiasm: 'I'd derived my view from a fairly casual "look-see", but that needed to be validated with such things as visits to the key suppliers to verify that what we'd initially seen had substance behind it – which indeed it had.' At this point Stephenson admits that there could have been more to the link with Qvale:

We definitely had in our mind the possibility that there could be a strong bond for us if we went back to the States – and of course the Mangusta was certified for

the USA – and so then there was the thought that Bruce and his team could also play a central role in possibly re-entering the US market.

According to Peter Beale, the Phoenix board, like many other businesses, tries to give a sensitive project a name that doesn't have any obvious bearing on the actual project at all:

…but with projects like this, which are not a great state secret, we try to give them a name that has some meaning in it. So we came up with the name 'Project Icon', since that was the idea of the SV project – to become iconic for the whole brand. Some other projects have had ridiculous names, and if someone asks 'how is project so-and-so going?' you can't always be certain what it was!

For the night of 27 February 2001, Stephenson and Beale stayed not far from the Qvale factory at the quaintly named Mini Hotel La Ville, the Heads of Agreement ready for discussion the following day with the Qvale legal team. Beale recalls:

By then we were really in the teeth of the negotiations; I remember the afternoon well because I discovered that I was sitting with all the solicitors reading through all the documents, and I suddenly thought to myself – where's Nick? It turned out that Nick was out test-driving in the car around the Italian countryside for the afternoon! I then began to realize there was a less than fair division of duties here!

The Qvale family proved ready to negotiate, but the process was at times hard fought; Beale recalls:

> Although Bruce had a small team of people, he was very centrally involved – which was perhaps one of the problems, because to some extent he tried to do everything himself for their team. A few times we were close to not doing a deal, but at the end of the day we did do a deal which we thought for our part was fair and equitable, and we hope it was for them, too.

Unsurprisingly, MG Rover prefer to remain slightly coy about how much the deal cost them – 'It was a few millions' they will admit – but in fact, posted accounts value the assets acquired from Qvale at £7 million, which seems a veritable bargain. Giordano Casarini certainly feels that the Qvale Modena factory was a great shop window for the would-be purchasers: 'I think that when Bruce Qvale finally met with the MG Rover people, it was very easy – it was like going through an open door – they came out there [to Modena] and they saw a beautiful facility with a system in place, people doing the right things.' Peter Stevens points out, however, that (in his words) 'not quite everything was in the box': for example, the promised right-hand-drive Mangusta had not been fully engineered, as was originally thought.

Up until March 2001, Qvale continued hedging its bets, and a draft of the business plan from that month shows that there were already tentative thoughts about either a second model or a facelift – Guigiaro being

The MGF on display at the 'Cobo Center' in March 2001. (Chapman Arup)

referred to. Before long, however, the MG talks would overtake these studies.

Simultaneously, MG Rover was also dabbling with various studies, and visitors to the SAE Show at the Cobo Center in Detroit on 5 March 2001 were intrigued to see a silver right-hand-drive MG TF sports car perched on the small stand of British automotive design consultant Chapman-Arup. MG Rover issued a release that stated:

> [MG] has not been marketed in the USA for over twenty years, yet the market remains the largest in the world for sports roadsters ... this was considered an opportunity to update the company's knowledge of current US perceptions and awareness of the MG brand.

Chapman-Arup staff dispensed market research questionnaires to visitors, but MG Rover cautioned that their five-year business plan 'assumes no planned sales in the US market'. As Project Icon developed, MG Rover's enthusiasm for re-entering the US market actually waned. 'I don't mean by that that we've lost interest,' Stephenson stresses; 'it waned in as much as we've done a lot of work – a number of fairly serious studies – into the costs of taking back product range into the States, in a number of different fashions, and the result was that that element was reluctantly put on the back burner.' Since then, studies have at least continued to percolate on a low gas...

A DEAL IS STRUCK

Although the negotiations continued for some time, it was not until June 2001 that MG Rover and Qvale were prepared to finally ink the contract. MG Rover management focus at the beginning of June was at least partially taken up by the excitement of the company's foray to the Le Mans 24 Hours race – the first MG entry of any description at the famous race since Syd Enever's last long-nosed MGB had raced there in 1965. The board chartered a couple of planes and, together with a few guests, flew to the Le Mans circuit to watch the debut of a pair of green and grey MG-Lola EX257 cars. Casual onlookers who happened to look in at the MG Rover hospitality suite above the MG-Lola pits would be forgiven for failing to identify the handsome forty-something Californian chatting to Nick Stephenson and Rob Oldaker; in fact it was Bruce Qvale, keen to pass on best wishes to his friends.

A few days afterwards – by which time MG's dream of class victory at Le Mans had been dashed – on 19 June 2001, the two partners simultaneously released news of the deal they had struck. Qvale's release stated:

> The Italian subsidiary of San Francisco-based Qvale Automotive Group today announced that it has entered

into an agreement to sell its assets to fabled British luxury and sports-car manufacturer MG Rover ... The agreement reunites the Qvale name with MG, a pairing that began in 1947. ...this transaction benefits both companies, because it combines the design and engineering strengths of the Qvale Mangusta project with the financial resources, brand recognition and production expertise of the MG Rover Group.

Operating though thirteen franchise dealers, Qvale proposed to continue to market and sell the Mangusta in the United States, while service, parts and warranties would be provided by the dealers, with the support of Qvale Automotive Group's San Francisco headquarters. This was understandable, for while the Mangusta itself was about to be overtaken by MG Rover's own plans, the Qvale family still had quite a stock of unsold cars to dispose of in their home market. At the same time we were told that 'Qvale Automotive Group is currently negotiating with MG Rover on a distribution agreement for MG Rover's newly announced X80 sports car, tentatively scheduled to make its debut in 2002.'

On the following day, 20 June 2001, the influential *Forbes* magazine carried a story headlined 'MG Plans American Comeback?'. Forbes spoke to MG Rover's director of communications, Gordon Poynter, who refused to confirm or deny that MG would be coming back to the USA; but he admitted that the Qvale deal meant 'the door is now open much wider. The US is the largest sports car market in the world, and if we were to come back, the X80 would be our halo car.' Forbes expressed the view that this would not be an easy task: 'MG will need far more than a pricey sports car to be successful in the US, especially since many Americans who remember MG from the bad old days wouldn't likely pay extra for the privilege of driving one.'

Forbes also spoke to an analyst at Merill Lynch in New York, John Casesa, who cautioned that although whatever MG brought to the US market would be 'very distinct, being different is not enough any more.' At that stage, it was already known that Porsche was planning to bring what would become the Cayenne 4x4 to the market; Casesa said that 'the market is already crowded with excellent products', adding that if MG Rover did decide to come to the US, 'They'd better bring great cars.' *Forbes* put this to Poynter, who countered 'these will be fantastic, outrageous cars, with all new interiors and great exteriors', and suggested that the X80 would be only the start: 'We'd have a complete line-up of sports cars, and they'd start at just £10,000 [about US$14,000].'

THE MOVE TO MG

As soon as the Heads of Agreement were signed, just after the 2001 Geneva Motor Show, there followed a period of what is called 'due diligence' prior to the formal contract. Due diligence, as the term implies, is the process of auditing the business to ensure that there are no unforeseeable obstacles to it being taken forward by the intended new owners. Within this process would be the opportunity for appropriate technical and financial staff to get to know more about the detail of the product, facilities, suppliers and third-party arrangements and commitments. Naturally while at the higher level, Nick Stephenson, Peter Beale and Kevin Howe had been able to satisfy themselves of the validity of the business case, they nevertheless needed some more robust investigation by people within the MG Rover organization.

Nick Stephenson also knew that Peter Stevens could bring a different perspective to the company:

> Peter had not been on board long at this stage, but he came to us with a nice refreshing view of what MG could be. We were instantly totally aligned – Peter and I find that we agree on stuff almost straightaway – but we do stress that the assessment team was still very important to us in deciding if this deal was right or wrong for us. Thus we were clear in what we wanted to do.

Part of the brainstorming at the outset was to see what the best course of action should be, since there were several possible routes through which 'MG' could evolve. According to Peter Stevens, one early idea was 'let's make a couple of cars and see what they're like, see if we like what we come up with; we'll do them just in GRP and see if the car – the product – has got any future.' The initial work on the styling clay, using sketches by Stevens and his team, was done at the Dove Company in rural Norfolk (not far from Lotus), and the 'couple of cars' would have been built there, too.

The Dove Company

Colin Jones is the quiet but efficient force behind 'Dove', a Norfolk-based specialist whose skills combine pattern-making and top-quality hand-laid composite manufacture, Lotus being a notable customer from just up the road. Colin Jones first met Peter Stevens when the latter was working with TWR in 1978:

> The very first project I did with Peter was when we worked together on the Mazda RX-7 'spa' racing car. Peter was good at suggesting design project ideas to Tom (Walkinshaw), and as a result we did a range of bits and pieces for Mazdas. I remember Peter taking three XJS renderings to Tom and a set of transparencies after Tom had decided which design he preferred. I projected the transparencies on the wall, and did the clay modelling on the floor in our pattern shop.

Steve Hudson

Steve Hudson joined what was then Austin Rover Group in 1985, working in product engineering under Rob Oldaker – nowadays the director of product development at MG Rover Group, but at that time head of chassis engineering. 'I moved around the company, probably more than most,' Hudson explains, 'and one particular move I made back in the mid-nineties was from engineering into manufacturing; at that time we were doing the "portfolio" project – "three into one" – the MGF, Rovers 200 and 400.' The portfolio project was an interesting and challenging exercise in flexible manufacturing, as it was unusual to be launching so many major new projects at one time. This project saw Hudson cross the cultural divide from engineering to manufacturing, two disciplines which, in Hudson's words 'traditionally didn't always cross over – I'm afraid it's the same everywhere – generally you are either an engineer or you are a production person, and never the twain shall meet!'

Hudson's experience in both the key disciplines gave him a good basis for running operations that bridge the divide, and he found himself effectively integrating the two areas.

> With my manufacturing and engineering background I obviously spent a lot of time working with product development at that point, and representing the factory with their product delivery in mind. I was given a couple of directorships by Kevin Howe, the first of which was to look at 'manufacturing integration' – managing a launch effectively and bridging the gap between the engineering project delivery and manufacturing production launch. And

then I went to Munich – I was asked to go there to be the R30 production director, which was for the new medium car intended for Longbridge.

With the split from BMW, the R30 project was cancelled, and Hudson was soon running the production system for the group. This posting, in April 2000, was seen as roughly an eighteen-month job; but ten months later he was called to join the 'due diligence' team that would be looking at the Qvale Modena facility. The story of Hudson's central role in the early stages of the X80 Project are covered in the main text; after that the project changed direction, and Hudson assumed other crucial roles in MG Rover:

> I spent some time [after X80] looking at international manufacturing, and specifically the China Brilliance proposals that were becoming a hot topic at the time. We had to set up some project plans very quickly, and sort out some directions for the China Brilliance activities. So I was asked to go and sit with a project team to do that with the Chinese for two to three months. Then in the summer of 2002 I was asked to take on the quality director's job, which is great – a case of a 'round peg in a round hole' – and I'm thoroughly enjoying it.

Hudson's multi-stranded experience has been of enormous benefit to him in this regard: 'I've got a good CV behind me for this role!' he laughs. 'We've brought aftersales and service in, too, and that allows me to get involved and dabble in a lot of things really, from concept through to servicing of the current product.' Although he moved on and up within the company, Hudson retains many fond memories of his time on the X80 project, beyond even those mentioned in the main text:

> In addition to Aston Villa, I have a passion for motorbikes. I run a Ducati, and the Ducati factory was only fifteen miles up the road from Bologna and the Modena factory; Giordano sorted me out with a visit there. There were also 'ride-and-drive' sessions that we set up in Wales for the board so that Kevin Howe and the other key board members were taken out to drive the Mangusta against many other products such as Porsche 911, Boxster, Maserati, TVR Tuscan – some of my fondest memories are being able to drive and assess some of those cars – fabulous fun!

Hudson reserves his greatest respect for the Italians he found himself working with:

> If you separate out the product just for a moment, the experience with the Italian guys I thought was extremely rewarding. I've worked with Germans, Japanese and Chinese – you name it – but I don't think from a cultural point of view I've found a better fit than the English and the Italians …a good creative and technical mix. At every level, really, our guys seemed to bond, to understand each other and to strike up good relationships very quickly.

Steve Hudson. (MG Rover)

The way that we got into fibreglass was through the RX7; we hadn't been making fibreglass panels, we only did modelling and pattern-making and had the occasional fibreglass prototype made. But the people at TWR said 'We'd like to sell these,' so in effect, we made them 'prototypes' over and over…!

Dove still makes sophisticated prototypes that often turn into limited production runs, and frequently their customers – typically lower-volume manufacturers such as Lotus or Aston Martin – find that while Dove are not 'cheap', the costs involved are nevertheless still more reasonable than the investment required in sophisticated tooling. Peter Stevens is very supportive of Colin Jones's professionalism:

I crudely describe it that you can find lots of people round the back of a barn who will make you a fibreglass chicken to go on a fairground ride, but it is absolutely not the same business that Colin is in: he is making limited quantities of much higher quality bits. And there is a classic discussion where people say 'That's expensive!' and then they go round to the place behind a barn; but three months later they're back again saying 'Can you do it properly for us please, because it didn't work!'

Jones says that his approach comes from his experience of working in Detroit: 'I guess it's my background – I've been in the motor industry most of my life, and we really approach cars now the way I would have approached them in Detroit as a body engineer: we do it professionally.' Stevens says he simply feels comfortable working with Jones:

He doesn't go wrong – it's that straightforward. There has only ever been one joint venture financially between us, when we established 'Simpatico' to build Fiat 500 roadsters – and we built just ten cars! We've always worked together best when we're separate but complementary. Colin did a lot of stuff on the McLaren F1, and it's funny that when I said we'd do the car together, they obviously imagined that there was some kind of deal going between us. And it got to a silly stage, partly because they mistook one supplier for another, and they said to themselves 'Aha! That's where he is getting his profits!' I went to see Ron Dennis and I said, 'I know that some people in McLaren think that I've got a deal going with Colin, and – we can be honest about this – I can tell you that I have got a deal – it is simply that I take the work there and it gets done really well – and that's the deal! There has never been any kickback from Colin's work, and that is why we go back again – and that's what I'm paid for – to make sure that things come out right in the end.' And Ron Dennis didn't really have a response to that!

Colin Jones of Dove remembered that Nick Stephenson had some sympathy with the idea of making just a couple of cars in GRP: 'He said that he wanted to see half-a-dozen cars on the road. He wasn't necessarily too worried about feasibility, in that he wasn't concerned about things such as bumper impacts.' However, the Qvale Mangusta could also form the basis of a quick return to the forefront of prestige sports-car motoring for MG, and as it had been certified for sale in North America, there was the very tempting possibility that an MG derived from the Mangusta could form part of the much-awaited return of the MG name to US soil.

Steve Hudson later went on to oversee quality management for the whole MG Rover Group, but at the time that the Qvale deal was being mooted he had been heavily involved in integrating the mainstream car-manufacturing facility on to one site where formerly it had been spread across several – no mean task. Steve was asked to be part of the due diligence team soon after the Geneva Show; Hudson explains:

Colin Jones (left) oversees the creation of the MG XPower SV show car at his Norfolk premises in September 2002. (Author)

As well as myself, that team comprised Graham Fairhead [director sports cars], Keith Twigg [senior accountant] and Keith Chetwin, among others. Predominantly we thought at the time that we needed our finance, manufacturing and engineering representation to go through the due diligence.

AN MG DERIVED FROM THE MANGUSTA

Steve Hudson was closely involved with the Mangusta project, right from its inception; in his words:

> We set about evaluating the business case of the project and product, and the assumptions running up to the planned acquisition date. That entailed us – through Graham Fairhead's office – fleshing out the product proposal and evaluating the Mangusta, very much from a product development point of view – looking at opportunities, issues, concerns and so on.
>
> [With regard to the Mangusta itself, Hudson soon found that he shared the opinion of most of his colleagues:] It had a good platform – that was obviously why we were interested in it in the first place – and it had an excellent chassis, and we had the opportunity to assess the car from the ride and handling dynamics point of view while we were doing the due diligence work.

Under development prior to the deal with MG Rover was this 'Mangusta SS' featuring chassis and engine enhancements. (K. Ahmed)

Hudson believed that from an MG brand point of view, the Mangusta certainly offered a good opportunity in respect of the performance it already had, as well as the potential that remained for further development:

> The powertrain and mechanical installation with the Ford V8 as well also offered us possibilities: good basic installation, and opportunities that we could look at down the line, such as supercharging, as well as further developing the specification of the powertrain to allow us to grow the MG brand vision that we had from that point of view.

The Mangustas that Hudson recalls trying had 260Ps powertrains, although Qvale had already been looking at higher-powered variants, with studies being carried out into a Mangusta 'S' version by Rousch Industries.

Although he developed great respect for the Mangusta, Hudson thought that in the production versions he tried, it was, in his words, 'a little bit lacklustre in the context of an out-and-out sports car'. When it came to the styling, though, Hudson shared the view of Nick Stephenson, Peter Stevens and many commentators:

> The styling was certainly idiosyncratic! My personal view was that the car had presence on the road – you couldn't ignore it – but the styling for me wasn't the best, given the position that Qvale had the car in, particularly from the point of view of the brand equity they would be struggling with in that sector of the market place. I didn't think it would sell on style, obviously.

[Hudson also had some concerns about the quality of the cars he saw:] The guys were going through a sort of ramp-up at Modena. Bruce Qvale was talking about – I think – trying to sell 500 a year – but they were still very much at an early phase, for they were way, way off that. From a quality point of view, the finish of those cars that we'd been driving – admittedly early cars – was not everything that we'd have wanted.

Giordano Casarini acknowledges that there had been problems:

We did not put enough testing into the car – there was no what I would call 'maturation' of the product – although it was coming. But the cars were hard to sell with that name, and we had a row of dealers from all over the world saying to us 'please go back to the De Tomaso name and we will sell them – and we'll be prepared to have a rattle, a noise, a squeak!' But it was not to be!

Part of the problem was undoubtedly the fact that not far off from the Mangusta's market segment there were some pretty competent sporting cars – such as the Jaguar XK8 and Porsche 911 – and although Qvale had hoped to lure the customer who wanted something different, it was hard to ignore the fact that those other cars might also have been on the potential shopping lists of would-be Mangusta buyers. Hudson suggests:

Of course, there are various niches in the segments that are playing with this sort of product in mind, and if you were comparing it to, say, a TVR, then the quality [of the Mangusta] probably wasn't too distant from where a TVR would have been at that point. But yes, we were looking at the Jaguars and the Porsches, and the trim quality was something we'd have been a bit concerned about. But the decision was that we would be re-engineering exterior and interior trim, and so in the event those aspects of the existing car were never going to be an over-riding factor for us.

Hudson and his team – in particular his colleague Craig Donovan of MG Rover Group Purchasing – found themselves looking at a raft of different suppliers, some familiar and some not, and each posing their own potential difficulties. 'The Mangusta had some "big suppliers" – big players in the supply world, Ford being an obvious example, and there were others – companies like TRW supplying various joints and parts of the steering system, too – and it was of concern to us that we could secure their ongoing supply commitment.' Without this commitment, continuation of the project clearly might either not have been viable at all, or at the least could have necessitated delays and further expense from re-engineering or re-sourcing.

'So we needed to gain some indicative commitment, at least from those suppliers, and particularly Ford, because clearly they might have taken the view that they would rather not have had us dabbling with this sort of product in a segment that was so close to Jaguar.' In discussion with Ford, this in itself did not prove to be much of a stumbling block, for it was clear that the Mangusta – and any closely related MG that might evolve from it – was not in quite the same category as the XK8, even if there might have been some crossover in pricing.

With Ford, it was mainly a case of securing supplies of the Ford V8 engine and transmission and various related components; but if anything, Hudson's bigger concern at the outset was understanding the spider's web of suppliers and contractors local to the Qvale factory who had supported the Mangusta:

There was this bunch of specialist suppliers – the niche low-volume sports car market suppliers that abounded in and around Turin, really – and the issue there was for us to understand who had the 'IPR' (the intellectual property) for the design, whether it was Qvale or the supplier; but also who owned the tooling, and what position the supplier was in with regard to their ongoing ability to supply us with the quality and volume we were considering.

Amongst those key suppliers were Vaccari & Bosi, for whilst MG Rover was formulating its own plans for the bodywork, the Scalabroni-Casarini honed chassis was to remain an enduring part of the picture. 'We went out to see Mr Bosi a few times; he is a smashing bloke, a big bear of a man located in the hills of Tuscany – very emotional, very Italian, and very good to deal with.'

As the due diligence process drew to its conclusion, Hudson and his team finalized the details of their 'project proposal', which led them to conclude that they wanted to move ahead with the acquisition:

The next step then was for us to form a project team to get on and deliver that proposal, and I think it was around July or August 2001 that I was appointed as the 'Programme Director'. We – that is, Kevin [Howe] and the consortium – had a view that we would deliver the product from within the existing MG Rover Group organization … in other words, to build the car at Longbridge.

The idea of taking on an existing project, modifying it fundamentally and in the process moving it lock, stock and barrel to a different factory, might seem too much of a challenge; but then, this was the company that only recently had uprooted both the 'new Mini' and Rover 75 production facilities, bringing the latter into Longbridge from its former home at Cowley. In that context, bringing an Italian sports car to Birmingham seemed almost tame by comparison…

chapter five

Project X80

PROJECT X80: THE NEW BEGINNING

According to Steve Hudson, it was during March 2001 that Project Icon became Project X80. At the time, the recently reinvented MG Rover Group had adopted a two-strand code number system for production car projects, using 'RD' for Rover and 'X' for MG models. The first MG cars using these codenames were revealed to the public as X10, X20 and X30 in January 2001, and it was only at the Geneva show that preceded the surreptitious visit to Modena that those same cars were identified as the MG ZT (with the 'X11' ZT-T 'tourer' version), ZS and ZR models.

Beyond the X10, X20 and X30 programmes (and their RD10, RD20 and RD30 Rover relatives) there would be other projects – many still on the 'secret' list at the time of writing – although X12 is the MG ZT-V8, X13 the MG ZT-T V8, and X40 the MG TF sports car; the details of X50, assuming it exists, have not yet been disclosed. RD-X60 is a project for an all-new mid-sized car intended in due course to succeed the Rover 45/MG ZS models. Rumours also abounded in the press of a new mid-sized sports car, tentatively referred to as 'X70', but altogether this meant that the next available project number in the portfolio was X80. According to Peter Stevens, there was also another potential meaning for X80: it could have signified the annual

An early Peter Stevens sketch dated 28 March 2001, but revealed as part of the publicity handout at the Frankfurt show six months later. (MG Rover)

The Qvale Modena premises looked more like a stylish corporate headquarters than a factory. (Qvale Automotive Group)

volume for the very low-volume supercar concept he had considered. For the time being, however, MG Rover's aspirations were much more ambitious.

The beautiful Qvale Modena factory had not been included in the assets that MG Rover acquired – although as it remained largely empty, MG Rover would be able to rent some of the space within the building – so one of the early decisions that had to be made was where the MG X80 should be built. Although the chassis manufacture could be retained, at least for the medium term, at Vaccari & Bosi, the fact that the body and trim were going to be substantially different meant that the possibilities for final assembly were much more flexible. Logic dictated that the most obvious home for the X80 could – and perhaps should – be at Longbridge, the site on to which MG Rover Group was increasingly consolidating all other aspects of its business.

According to Hudson, it would normally be the case within MG Rover that the person charged with overseeing a new car would be a 'project director' – invariably a product development engineer reporting to Rob Oldaker. In the case of X80, however, the project was arguably much wider in focus as it involved

assimilating as well as developing a completely new category of vehicle, quite different from the mainstream range. As a consequence, Hudson became a 'programme director', reporting straight to the top man at MG Rover: Kevin Howe. 'Kevin's view in particular was that this should be a programme role, as so much needed to be done across all of the functions, and therefore that I should effectively report to him, and try and pull together all of the functions that we needed to deliver the project, and that I should have the authority to do that.'

Having been tasked to take charge of the X80 project, Hudson wasted no time and pulled together a core team. Key to that team was the man who had previously lived and breathed the Qvale Mangusta: Giordano Casarini. As Hudson observed:

> Giordano obviously had a rich history in the Italian supercar and automotive low-volume industry; he'd been chief engineer working with and for Bruce as we moved on to the scene, he was effectively 'Mister Mangusta', and he had taken a very holistic view of the project, as you need to in those environments – he wasn't just doing the engineering, but had run the design of the package through to the design of the manufacturing system, the sourcing, logistics – the whole shebang; he had a finger in all those pies.

Hudson and Casarini soon developed a great mutual respect, even though their backgrounds were clearly quite different. 'I got on well with him from the word

Kevin Howe, chief executive of MG Rover Group. (MG Rover)

go,' Hudson says. 'Right from the start we thought we needed him in order to make the transition, to get his experience on the Mangusta: that was invaluable to us with regard to the move we wanted to make through to an MG product. And his technical skills and knowledge of the supply industry and so on were very useful.' In addition to Casarini, Hudson also approached a friend of his, David Linley who was at Lotus, and recruited him as the chief engineer for the new project. The team was therefore led by Hudson, with David Linley as chief engineer and Giordano Casarini effectively as senior consultant. Another key member of the team was the finance manager, Keith Twigg (who remained with the project through to the final production car), along with a project manager, making a 'core' team of five people.

In parallel with defining things such as the new styling and fundamental choices concerning body and trim, MG Rover also needed to fully understand what they had bought; a marvellous way to help with this was the opportunity to continue build, for a short run, of the existing Mangusta. Hudson admitted:

> Styling was certainly on the critical list, but obviously we had to conclude an in-depth understanding of the Mangusta's engineering, we also had to get the concept engineering of the new product underway quickly, and we had various commercial and manufacturing decisions that were concerning us at the time, such as how we should manage the factory in Modena: we had employment concerns – for example training issues, skill issues, and all sorts of things happening there.

Hudson's solution was to install a team of people in Modena 'to build Mangusta so they would acquire the learning effectively needed so that when we transferred the car we had that knowledge.'

Hudson installed a colleague, Gerry Larkin, to manage the Modena factory from June to September 2001, and he put in a team of about ten people more or less permanently from that time, to work alongside their new Italian colleagues, documenting the process

and doing the job of building the car. In the end, according to Hudson, MG Rover 'ended up with a complete "bible" of how the Mangusta was put together, from a parts, process and facility point of view – we experienced some very good project work at that point.' Hudson is fulsome in his praise for the local people who had transferred from Qvale:

> The Italians were a great bunch of guys and girls, whom we got on well with, from the shop floor up to the supervision side, particularly considering, as we know, that we were reviewing the manufacturing strategy at that point, and there was always an option for us to bring the whole thing back to the UK to build. Which would, of course, have resulted in all the Modena operations being wound down.

It seems that while the Qvales had a good stock of Mangustas to clear, they had enough orders in the pipeline to help with Hudson's plan: 'I can't remember the exact numbers now, but we were happy to help Bruce [Qvale] conclude the build of those vehicles. We built a number – I think it turned out to be around fifteen – of our own vehicles that we've since had dotted around in various places; they were used for a variety of chassis development work and some crash work – all sorts of things.'

Part of Hudson's remit was to assist some of the Qvale personnel to seek alternative employment wherever appropriate:

> It worked well, and I have to say that we worked effectively with the unions and the workforce representatives there. It was helped by the fact that we took a very proactive view to secure alternative employment, and the closure package was a good one. The Lamborghini and Maserati factories and various others were looking for skilled people, so we were able to liaise with those companies and make sure that everybody was gainfully re-employed – that worked out quite well.

An early sketch by Peter Stevens shows the original thinking for the MG X80. (MG Rover)

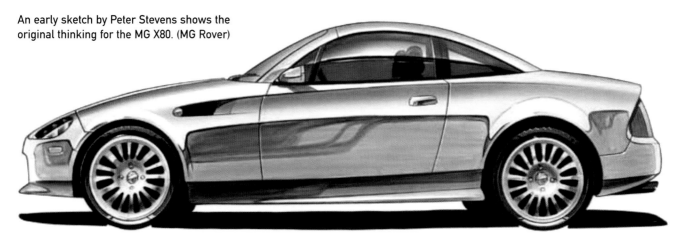

ABOVE AND BELOW: The clay model for the X80 takes place at Dove in the late spring of 2001; note the Ford Mondeo tail-lights and the prototype MG TF headlamps on this early iteration. (Harris Mann)

Having concluded the necessary studies and compiled the X80 'bible', Hudson and his team started to dismantle the facility at Qvale Modena and prepared to package it up, with the view of possibly returning it all to the UK. By this time, it was September 2001, and MG Rover was about to stage a public display of what the MG X80 might be like...

BOLD PLANS – THE ALUMINIUM MG X80

Hardly had the ink dried on the June 2001 MG Rover-Qvale deal than plans were being fleshed out for what exactly should be done with the project. We have already seen how, following the due diligence process, Steve Hudson and his colleagues had begun the task of researching the existing product, learning how it was built, and looking into the possibility of bringing the whole project into Longbridge. At the same time, the form that the new car would take was being refined.

Peter Stevens had already formulated a design 'path' for MG, and so some parameters for a new MG based on the Mangusta were already clear. We saw earlier how Qvale broke the news; at the same time Peter Stevens and his team had produced a series of sketches, one of which was issued along with MG Rover's press release of 19 June 2001; this proclaimed that:

> The MG X80 will be launched in 2002, giving the MG brand a world-class product in the high performance, luxury sports-car sector. Both coupé and roadster versions are planned, with manual and automatic transmissions. The new car will be positioned above the existing MGF roadster, and the new MG sports saloons and sports-wagon that will be launched this summer. [According to Kevin Howe] ...the MG X80 will be an excellent fit at the top of our family of MG cars. It also provides an opportunity to look at markets where we are not currently represented, in particular the USA market, the world's largest sports-car market, where we can now seriously evaluate the full potential for the MG brand.

Whereas the Qvale Mangusta had been aimed at around 500–1,000 cars per annum, MG Rover had more ambitious plans for the MG X80: according to Hudson, 'we were talking about a 5–10,000 lifetime proposition, for a car with a retail price tag of about £40–£50k, and we were thinking of 320HP and 385HP V8 powertrains.' In order to achieve the right balance of costs and expectations, the technology choices were very important, 'which is why we had the team spending a lot of time looking at the right structures and the right skills and experience to help us deliver that.'

The MG Rover team also proposed dispensing with the composite body panel option and, eschewing the massive costs associated with steel bodywork, decided on an aluminium alloy body. Modern developments in this field mean that aluminium bodywork is no longer the exclusive preserve of the hand-built craftsman – MG Rover proposed to use state-of-the-art 'superformed aluminium' technology for the body, married to the Vaccari & Bosi chassis. According to Hudson: 'We did quite a lot of work with Corus and Vaccari & Bosi looking at the value-engineering improvements that we could make to the chassis, which were numerous – we believed there were some good opportunities there.' At the same time, although the coupé had been the initial focus, there were plans to follow it with an open-top version within a year or so – and although relatively little work was done in engineering terms, there were tentative thoughts of seeking to use the roof 'cassette' from the Maserati 3200 Spyder.

For the interior design – another area where as many traces as possible of the Mangusta were to be erased – MG Rover worked with 'MG4'. As Hudson points out, the 'MG' part of that company's name is coincidental: 'It stands for "Mark Griggs", who runs the company. His specialist team had a lot of experience in plastics processes and technologies where they could help us with the interior package.' MG4 had emerged in February 2001 from

In June 2001, MG Rover unveiled a so-called 'Extreme' concept based on the MGF, with a mid-mounted 500 horsepower AER Le Mans engine. The headlamps were destined to appear later on both the original X80 and the MG TF of the following spring. (MG Rover)

This sketch of the MG X80 was released by the company in June 2001, when the existence of the project was formally announced to the public. (MG Rover)

the basis of GE Plastics' UK-based design company GE Polymer Design Associates as a result of a management buyout by Griggs and his colleagues.

As the team began to work together, it is fair to say that there were what might be termed mild clashes of culture: the philosophies of mass production and low-volume assembly have fundamental differences, even if many of the key goals, such as quality and production milestones, are common. It stands to reason that what is necessary or indeed normal practice for developing a car to be built in the hundreds of thousands, may be inappropriate for a car that will be built in mere hundreds or thousands; and so the members of the X80 team, coming as they did from different sides of that divide, often had to learn to understand and appreciate the other point of view.

Although he got on famously with his new colleagues, and infected them with his enthusiasm, Giordano Casarini found this process fascinating but frequently frustrating:

I remember that I said to Steve after I had been there just one day: 'Steve – this is against nature!' He said, 'What do you mean?' and so I said, 'Here are people who have been brought up, money has been spent on them, to make them think this way – quality, precision – everything has to go together in a certain way – specifications – everything carefully set out.' For example, to validate a fuel tank will cost £150,000 for testing – and they asked me one day 'how did you validate the tank for the Mangusta?' and I said, 'I never validated it – I used a Ford Mustang tank.' But they said, 'Are you sure that when you park the car at 15° inclination and then it is there in cold and then hot conditions, and then you start the engine…'

Superform Aluminium

When the MG X80 project was being programmed for bringing in house, there was talk of annual production volumes of around 5,000, somewhat larger than had been achieved with the Mangusta. Production at that level is in something of a hinterland – neither truly low volume nor mass production – and the economies of scale and practical production methods fall awkwardly between the two very different categories. One technology that certainly appealed was to use aluminium panels for some, or all of the bodywork, as these can be produced economically at output levels that would be too high for regular composite bodies, but too small to justify the major expense of tooling for steel bodywork. A leading proponent of the latest aluminium alloy body technology is UK Worcester-based Superform Aluminium, part of the £200 million Luxfer Group that also includes a sister company, Superform USA. Superform takes its name from a special process known as superforming – a hot forming process in which a sheet of aluminium is heated to 450--500°C and then forced on to or into a single surface tool to create a complex three-dimensional shape from a single sheet.

Customers for this process extend into the field of aircraft and include Boeing, Airbus Industries and British Aerospace; but within the automotive field, Superform has worked most notably with Aston Martin (on the Vanquish) and Morgan (Aero 8). In the USA, Superform is also contracted to supply the bodywork for the Ford GT supercar, being built as 4,500 cars from 2003 until 2005. Within the UK, Superform's Worcester headquarters, where the business began in 1975, deals mainly with customers in the UK and Europe. The company claims that 'the Superforming process is now the number one choice to supply complex three-dimensional formed aluminium body panels for the luxury and sports-car markets.'

ABOVE: The MG X80 as unveiled in September 2001 was a fixed-head coupé, and dramatically different to the original Qvale Mangusta upon which it was based. (MG Rover)

BELOW: From the rear, the MG X80 concept showed a distinctive array of small round tail-lamps – a pragmatic but elegant answer to the alternative of using expensive bespoke units or ones from a mainstream car. (MG Rover)

Casarini could see that such thought processes – entirely correct, proper and valid for higher volumes – could threaten to overwhelm the much smaller-scale X80 project: 'These guys are paid to think like this, and so I began to wonder if we could fairly expect people who were now working on our project to change their minds.' Casarini thought that a sensible option would be to move the project team away from the 'big company' influences of Longbridge, to force the team to fend for itself: 'From the beginning we asked them to move us out, and I said "anywhere – send us to Modena!". So then they accused me of wanting perhaps to go back to Italy – but I don't want to go back there!'

FRANKFURT: THE MG LUXURY HIGH PERFORMANCE SPORTS CAR

Tuesday 11 September 2001 in Frankfurt, Germany, started off like any other day. The massive Frankfurt Motor Show, dominated as usual by the local manufacturers who were allocated whole halls to exhibit their wares, was ready to open for the hordes of international journalists who had travelled from all corners of the globe to see what the last major European show of the year could offer. Frankfurt alternates with the Paris Salon, and as some national pride is at stake, each successive show strives to get brighter and more dazzling.

For MG Rover Group, the decision had been taken during the summer to use the Frankfurt show to 'test the water' with a full-size model of the MG X80, or at least one of the favoured styles for the project, fairly closely based on the sketch that had been released on 19 June as a 'teaser'. The X80 model was machined from plastic by TWR and finished to a very high standard in one of the new 'Monogram' personalized colours, and alongside it MG Rover prepared to show an early prototype of the proposed 'X12' V8-powered derivative of the MG ZT.

Preparations for the show had suffered from some of those eleventh-hour white-knuckle near-disasters: the display model was machined from a block of assembled pieces of special polyurethane foam, which had then been skinned and painted to show standards, the windows painted in black to give the illusion of transparency; but prior to being exhibited, the model suffered from differential expansion and contraction because it had not been allowed to settle in a cool environment for a long enough period, and this caused a noticeable crack to appear in the front end. On the stand, careful posing of the 'XPower Girls' who formed part of the launch ceremony ensured that the cracks went largely unnoticed. What did not go unnoticed, however, was the rather unflattering way that the car was posed and lit on the stand, and the people from TWR had some less-than-charitable words to say when they found that the temperature problems were being exacerbated by the proximity of a bank of extremely hot spotlights placed immediately alongside the car.

Seen outside the Frankfurt IAA buildings just prior to the show. (Kevin Jones)

LEFT: Kevin Howe performed the official unveiling of the MG X80 at Frankfurt. (MG Rover Deutschland)

ABOVE: The MG X80 was unveiled with the assistance of the 'XPower Girls'. (MG Rover Deutschland)

BELOW: The MG X80 was the star of the MG Rover stand. (MG Rover Deutschland)

ABOVE: Alongside the MG X80, MG Rover also unveiled this concept for a rear-wheel drive MG ZT V8 – dubbed the ZT XPower 385 on account of its proposed horsepower. (MG Rover)

RIGHT: One of the unusual bits of what Peter Stevens referred to as 'jewellery' – an air vent modelled loosely on that of the MGA of 1955. (Kevin Jones)

At the appointed hour, soon after lunch, MG Rover chairman Kevin Howe went through the speech and unveiling routine, starting with the almost inevitable corny joke alluding to England's recent victory against Germany in the Soccer World Cup. Then, after revealing the MG XPower 385 (the ZT V8), Howe moved across to another sleeker shape underneath a Union Jack sheet. He proclaimed to his audience:

> We believe sports roadsters and coupés are at the heart of any great sporting brand, and the MGF remains the epitome of the accessible sports car. But we have always felt that to be a global sporting brand MG should also have an icon product at the top of the family tree. [Referring to the purchase of Qvale's Italian subsidiary of Qvale, and the work that had gone on since then:] ...We have been able to use the excellent chassis and powertrain of [Qvale's] sports-car project in our MG X80. Peter Stevens, our design director, and his team have been working flat out on this project since June, and today I am delighted to reveal for the first time anywhere in the world the MG X80 2+2 Coupé. [Referring to the programme:] ...The car will be on sale next summer, and will be joined by a roadster in 2003. We will offer a variety of power outputs from 260 to 385Ps produced from 4.6ltr V8 engines. ...Indicative UK prices start from under £50,000.

The official press release varied little from the information set out in June: it stated that the MG X80 would feature a range of power outputs, from 260 to 385 bhp (SAE) produced from 4.6ltr V8 engines: 'The MG X80 2+2-seater Coupé will be launched in summer 2002, giving the MG brand a world-class product in the high performance, luxury sports-car sector. It will be joined by a roadster version in 2003, both available with manual or automatic transmissions.' Potential features listed included electronic traction control, limited slip differential, ABS braking, 18in alloy wheels, air conditioning, and a six-speaker in-car entertainment system with radio/cassette and CD auto-changer. Electrically powered items would include windows, door mirrors, driver's seat adjustment and a luxurious leather interior – all clearly competing, in MG Rover's own words, 'with established sports cars such as the Porsche 911, Maserati 3200GT and Jaguar XK8.'

At the arranged cue, the sheet was pulled off the car, and the MG X80 was revealed to a phalanx of flashguns and reasonably enthusiastic applause. Simultaneously, the X80 launch coverage went worldwide through the MSN Carview web sites, creating a 360-degree 'virtual tour' of the MG Rover stand; according to the site logs, there were 2.5 million page views on the Frankfurt MG pages, and as a direct result of this 11,000 people clicked over to MG Rover's own web site. It would be fair to say, however, that the X80 did not receive the rapturous reception that its creators probably craved, but this was because of unprecedented events happening simultaneously on the world scene: setting aside the merits or otherwise of the design as it stood, only a few hours before the covers were whipped off the metallic red model, terrorists had forced two aeroplanes to crash into the famous World Trade Centre 'twin towers' in New York, and suddenly public interest in any new motor car – never mind a critically important one in image terms for MG – completely evaporated.

The atmosphere at the Frankfurt show, as elsewhere, became tense and depressed, as the shock of what had happened in New York took hold. On a practical level, many of the journalists began to wonder how their journeys home would be affected; Steve Hudson was there, and commented 'We were wondering if we'd be able to get back or not!'. It was not an auspicious start to the public face of X80.

AFTER 9/11

The New York disaster has since become known simply as '9/11', and its tragic effects were far-reaching and dramatic. Beyond the obvious intensely personal and

The headlamps of the MG X80 were all-new, but would soon become familiar when they appeared as part of the facelift of the MGF that generated the MG TF. (Author photo)

Although the model displayed at Frankfurt had been solid, this sketch shows the elegant interior conceived for the X80. (MG Rover)

public emotions associated with the aftermath of the actual event, there were financial and commercial implications that affected the whole world scene. As far as MG Rover was concerned, not least was the effect that these financial uncertainties had upon sales prospects and business forecasts: to many people, it suddenly did not seem the best of times to be thinking of sending a new luxury sports car into the North American market. It should also be noted that there is another side to this view, and one or two commentators have put forward the alternative observation that, tragic though the events in New York undoubtedly were, they also became a convenient excuse for inaction.

Whatever the interpretation of events, there was no doubt that the reaction to the MG X80 show car had been mixed, and this seemed to give cause for concerns back at base in Longbridge. Questions began

to be asked of a programme that hitherto had been busking merrily along, gradually consuming funds that it has to be said were not unreasonable, given the levels of sales originally in the business plan. But because the cold wind of possible recession seemed to be whipping round the finance world, coupled with the continuing failure to find a partner with whom MG Rover could link up to develop a new mid-range car, all projects began to receive regular scrutiny – and X80 was no exception.

For the time being, however, plans were being put in place for the production facility. On Sunday 30 September 2001, under the headline 'Lira We Go! – Italy Snub as Longbridge gets £100 Million-a-year Supercar', Birmingham's *Sunday Mercury* newspaper first broke the news that MG Rover had decided to shift the entire X80 production in-house to Longbridge; the Qvale Modena factory would no longer be available, and at projected production figures of 2,000 per annum, there was certainly an argument in favour of consolidating production on MG Rover's main site – just as other outlying functions such as sales and

In the wake of the Frankfurt Motor Show, MG Rover continued exploring different options for the MG X80 – including these variants using headlamps adapted from the MG ZT. (MG Rover)

BELOW: One of several variations on the Frankfurt MG X80 theme, this version marries the same grille shape with cleverly modified MG ZT headlamps. (MG Rover)

ABOVE: A simpler, less ornate grille shape was considered. (MG Rover)

BELOW: In this version, the lower air intake has been made bolder. (MG Rover)

marketing were being brought on to the Longbridge complex. The news was welcomed by unions and local business leaders alike; the *Sunday Mercury* quoted the Birmingham Chamber of Commerce spokesman, John Lamb, as saying: 'Clearly the decision is of enormous importance and benefit not only to the Midlands' motor industry and supply chain, but also to the general economy.'

Picking up on the *Sunday Mercury* story, the BBC

The Involuntary Crash Test

Everyone knew that the Qvale Mangusta was a strong car – it had been subjected to the punishment of US crash-certification testing – but one day in November 2001 Steve Hudson proved it the hard way. In his own words:

We had done a bit of work down in the Cotswolds and I was driving back with the chief engineer, and I had my one and only serious accident. It just proves that you need to give these cars a little respect as well as enjoying what they can do! I was chasing a 'beemer' – I think it was a BMW 330 – and was coming out of a corner and was just about to overtake him. It was a day when we hadn't had a lot of rain for a while, but all of a sudden it had rained, and the road had got quite slippery. I suppose I must've put the rear wheels over the white line at more or less the same time, and the car broke away from the back end and got its wheels into the ditch, and we went down a drainage ditch and rolled over against a brick wall at the end of it. So we were sat there upside down in the Mangusta, and I remember asking my colleague if he was okay, and just seeing his backside as he got out through the window!

We were very pleased with the results – which is why I've kept the pictures – because you can see that the car was really in quite an incident and yet it remained in good shape, considering. The best crash test we did!

Naturally there was some consternation – and later amusement – back at base:

They thought we'd killed ourselves; we'd been doing some work with TWR down at their design studios at Leafield – Peter had got some of the design studio working with us on the product – and the accident was between TWR and Longbridge. And I think the head of engineering at TWR had gone past us while we were upside down in the ditch with an ambulance next to us, and he'd recognized that the car was a Mangusta; so he'd telephoned Leafield and asked who'd been down there that day, to be told that it was the programme director and the chief engineer! So they'd phoned back up to Rob [Oldaker] at Longbridge, and he rang up security on the gate, who began to think that perhaps we'd done ourselves in on the Fosse Way! So it all got a bit fraught. Kevin Howe still likes to remind me of it on a regular basis!

spoke to Longbridge trade union convener Adrian Ross, who said: 'It's excellent news that will give confidence to the West Midlands' economy. It is very specialized work, and employees will have to go through intensive training, but we have had people out in Italy over the past few months gaining expertise.' Speaking for the company, Gordon Poynter said that the fact that it was possible to accommodate production of the X80 under one roof at Longbridge was a prime factor in the decision to move it from Italy. However, he was keen to scotch any suggestion that the switch would generate many new jobs: 'We are talking about a very low-line production. This is not a mass-produced car as it is mostly hand built. There may be some new supply-line jobs, but this is not really about jobs and I cannot say how many are likely to be on offer.'

He went on to hint that decisions on possible sales of X80 in the USA were still pending: 'The car is already designed to be sold in America, so this could be done'; but added that 'We intend to begin selling a coupé model next summer, and a roadster version in 2003.' Bruce Qvale told the *Sunday Mercury*:

ARIA Group looked at a variation of the MG X80 concept and chose these sketches to be developed for their final proposal. (ARIA)

ABOVE: Aria Group went to the considerable trouble and expense of machining and finishing a quarter-scale model, using digital information. The company intended the roof to be unpainted aluminium. (ARIA)

RIGHT: Aria Group envisaged a clamshell arrangement for the bonnet, their argument being that this not only increased the 'exoticness' but reduced costs through deleting the front wing upper surfaces. (ARIA)

BELOW: The clamshell bonnet with its broad, sculpted shape helped 'highlight the powerful US engine underneath' in Aria's view. (ARIA)

ABOVE: **Inspiration drawn upon by Aria Group was supposedly from the MGA – in terms of grille and 'fender' (wing) shapes. (ARIA)**

BELOW: **The Aria Group's MG certainly had a mean and menacing front aspect, with the slanting 'eyebrows' over the headlamps lifted from the Rover 75/MG ZT design theme. (ARIA)**

RIGHT: **A sketch showing Aria Group's conception of a racing version of their MG. (ARIA)**

This is a reproduction of a full-sized computer-generated side view that ARIA produced as part of their impressive presentation to the MG Rover Board. (ARIA)

From the images I have seen of the X80, it looks like MG Rover has done a great job. The prototype has retained the Mangusta looks from a side and height perspective, and MG Rover has done some great things with the rear end. It's beautiful, and it's going to do very well. We are still doing market research with MG Rover for its potential return to the US market with the MG-X80 and possibly other cars.

Meanwhile, the mixed reception at Frankfurt had got the sales and marketing people at MG Rover worried, and on the company's web site they published a questionnaire that sought the opinion of enthusiasts: 'Your views are always important to us,' the introduction said; 'so help us to design and build more cars you'll love to drive in the future, by completing this questionnaire.' The survey asked participants to rank the Frankfurt MG X80 concept according to various word associations such as 'dynamic', 'aggressive', 'muscular', and then went on to ask the key question 'how important to you is it, that an MG-branded sports car reflects the heritage of the marque?' A number of 'competitors' were then listed for comparison purposes: the Jaguar XK8, Porsche 911, TVR Tuscan, Honda NSX, Mercedes SL, Maserati 3200 GT and the Chrysler Viper. Finally, the question was asked: 'Do you believe the X80 characterizes MG as a forward-thinking and innovative company?' It was a clear indication that the company had doubts.

The MG Rover Board decided to develop further possible designs for the X80, and they looked at styles that were, if anything, less radical than the Frankfurt X80; many adopted headlamps similar to, or adapted from, those of the Rover 75 with grille apertures, which in some cases were redolent of the MG RV8 or MGF (see pages 64–65). Clay modelling was carried out at the TWR studios near Witney, and it appears that the MG Rover Board began to take more than their usual personal interest in the detail of the design.

There is perhaps a risk that in such cases 'too many cooks spoil the broth', although my personal – though admittedly non-professional – view from having seen some of these designs is that they could have worked quite well. In addition, a Californian design consultancy, ARIA, became involved, largely, it seems, on a speculative basis as a potential springboard from other work they had been contracted to do for MG Rover – and they went as far as machining a quarter-scale model and producing full-size, two-dimensional renderings of their proposals. Peter Stevens recalls that, prior to these proposals, ARIA had also become involved in the packaging, and at the same time the MG Rover Board had been working directly with TWR: 'They'd been trying to decide how it should be – a case of "Why don't we try this, why don't we do that?" – and the ARIA folk were picking up on this and doing some schemes independently over in California, in all good faith, although speculative in nature.'

For the time being, therefore, the programme continued, passing Christmas 2001 and into the early part of 2002. However, there would soon be some major changes on the way.

chapter six

A Major Change of Direction

CRISIS POINT: THE PROJECT REVIEW OF FEBRUARY 2002

In late 2001 an announcement was made that seemed to offer great prospects for MG Rover: at last in China Brilliance Holdings it seemed that the Longbridge manufacturer had set up a promising financial and engineering partnership that could help secure the longer-term viability of the business.

Just five days before Christmas 2001 we were told that the two companies were 'in discussions relating to the formation of a wide-ranging strategic alliance and co-operation agreement'. Kevin Howe told me in January 2002 that the China Brilliance deal was:

Pop singer Sophie Ellis-Bextor was on hand to unveil the new MG TF at the Brussels Motor Show in January 2002. (MG Rover)

**Actress Tracy Shaw with the MG TF. This was Peter Stevens'
overhaul of the seven-year-old MGF; as well as styling
differences, there were fundamental engineering changes
under the surface. (MG Rover)**

...potentially a very far-reaching agreement – it cuts
through the areas and lines of new model development,
vehicle manufacture, engine strategies, the establishment of a common component supplier base, and the
establishment of a joint Research and Development
Centre. The situation is that we've not set a timescale
for the decisions to be made, but I can assure you that
the discussions are continuing in a very positive manner
at present.

In the background, MG Rover was also putting the
finishing touches to a significantly upgraded version of
its six-year-old MGF sports car – the result, with Peter
Stevens' styling changes and Rob Oldaker's
engineering changes (in particular to the all-new steel-
sprung suspension) – even warranted a change of
name to MG TF. Mid-January saw the MG TF unveiled at
the Brussels Motor Show, while at the tail end of that
month journalists were royally fêted at a well-run press
launch in Portugal. At that event, I asked Kevin Howe
about the US market, and he replied:

I get lots of e-mails from people who potentially want to
help us sell the car in the USA, or who simply want to be
able to buy it there. The demand is great, and as you know
we tested out the interest in MG at the SAE Engineering

Show in Detroit on the Chapman-Arup stand: the MG
being there on that stand drew so much attention that it
made *USA Today*; so the level of interest is genuinely high.
However, the whole question of entry into the USA is a
big decision for us. We will go back if we believe we've got
the right product to offer, and if we think we can do it
without it being a distraction to the main business.

However, Howe confirmed that the new MG TF had not
been engineered with the USA in mind, adding: 'We
don't believe that the changes that would be necessary
to homologate the car are justifiable.'

At the same session, Howe updated us on X80,
referring to the Frankfurt Motor Show:

At the time, I advised you that the evaluation of demand
was taking place, and particularly evaluation of
potential demand in the USA, and that European
availability was likely to be some twelve months later.
But with the number of different business opportunities
that are now available to us, we on the board have had
to update our business plan. We also received many
positive, and a few critical comments at Frankfurt, and
we've been busy addressing these in the development
programme. Consequently with these two live issues
we decided to delay production for a little later than we
had originally envisaged.

This was the first public admission that the
programme for MG X80 had slipped. Set against this

backdrop, however, there were other burning issues concerning the MG Rover Group. In mid-February the story broke that MG Rover was in talks with Indian company TELCO, to export the latter's Tata Indica hatchback; there was some irony in that the Indian press reported MG Rover as a BMW subsidiary. MG Rover was not prepared to confirm or deny the story at this stage; if anything, their attention was concentrated locally on the first bout of industrial upset that they had experienced since taking over the business twenty-two months earlier. In a no-nonsense approach to setting out their views, MG Rover told their workforce that there would need to be some 'refocusing' of staff, and there were plans for an on-site 'job shop' aimed at helping anyone not '100 per cent committed to MG Rover' to find alternative employment. It was a fairly blunt, uncompromising message, and not surprisingly it raised a few hackles. Within days, MG Rover appeared to be on the brink of possible strike action, potentially disastrous to the business plan, and there was a great deal of behind-the-scenes activity to avert disaster.

In the midst of this, there was a high-level review of the MG X80 project on 12 February 2002. According to Hudson, MG Rover had already decided that it was necessary to review all non-crucial programmes, and the X80 project, for which costs had been building without any indication of an early return, was a prime candidate for scrutiny. On the radar, too, was the Rover TCV concept – the first public showing of the style being developed for the new mid-range 'RD60' Rover car, seen as crucial to MG Rover's long-term survival. In Hudson's view:

We had a lot going on within the business plan – a lot competing for attention, leading to questions of 'Can we do this for less money?' That was number one. In addition, we were looking at the segment and the volume, because the segment was getting more and more competitive. A lot of products were competing in that sector and it was very crowded: without going into all the marketing analysis we did at the time, you'd got a new Maserati coming out at one end, you'd got TVR doing their stuff, a very credible product from Porsche, Jaguar, Morgan, and so on. We were looking at a proposition that was somewhere in the middle of this lot in volume, price and specification terms.

And the market opportunities were changing, too: 'A large part of the volume we'd considered had been potentially in the States, and with September 11 just behind us, that put a different perspective on things.'

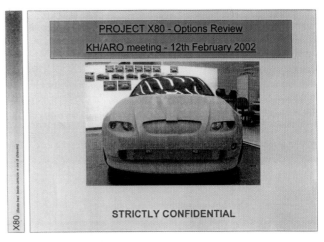

PROJECT X80 - Options Review
KH/ARO meeting - 12th February 2002

STRICTLY CONFIDENTIAL

X80 (Basta baci, basta carezze, e ora di chiavare)

ABOVE AND LEFT: **Revealed for the first time, these pages are taken from the crucial MG X80 project review of 12 February 2002.** (Nick Stephenson)

Design update:

X80 (Basta baci, basta carezze, e ora di chiavare)

The New MG Grille Shape

A feature common to all current MG models, and first seen prominently with X80, is the modern interpretation of the MG grille shape. Whereas the initial MG 'Z' cars – the ZR, ZS and ZT of 2001 – featured grilles that recognizably took their cues from traditional MG grille shapes, the newer generation of grille has a less complex grille badge plinth (the badge now sits simply in the centre of a broad, square-shouldered vertical rib) and also features a prominent horizontal bar, intercepting the central vertical bar. According to Peter Stevens, this stemmed from his work on the MG Lola Le Mans car, which features a small but still functional grille aperture: 'I was involved in the design of that car, and we wanted to make the grille tunable – something that came from my experience of racing and aerodynamics – and so that original inspiration was transferred on to the X80, the TF and now the other MG models.'

The new generation of MG grille shape, seen here on the 2002 MG XPower SV show car during finishing at QCR Motors. (Julian Mackie)

As we saw earlier, Hudson and his colleagues had been reviewing the 'style' of the X80 in the wake of its reception at Frankfurt: 'We were considering how we'd want to modify the style. I think that probably the over-riding factor was that, from a brand point of view, we'd also got to thinking that maybe we needed something different to make the car more of what we had had in mind originally – in other words, more of a pure sports car.'

As MG was concurrently setting out its store as a maker of 'extreme' sports cars, there was a school of thought that the X80 should no longer be aimed at being a sporting but smooth luxury cruiser:

In other words, we were thinking of a rawer car, more of a racer, more of a performance proposition. We had done some work to look at various options that the company had go-t along those lines, and one of those was to look at a much lower volume performance car. That sort of fitted

the bill better, sorted out some of our investment targets and was a very much more credible MG X80 from that point of view. This also allowed us to do something with the style, and to make the car a bit more outrageous, which Peter was keen to pick up on. So we went back to the board and recommended that if we went that way, we should take a different approach to the project delivery because it was moving away to something that required a less mainstream delivery model.

Peter Stevens could see the cost problems looming, and believes that a key reason for the critical review was the fact that much of the cost had been determined by the fact that engineering had decided – for reasonable reasons – to make the body in vacuum-formed super-alloy; but that when the volume forecasts fell, it was not possible to trim the required levels of investment to match. As Stevens explains:

ARIA had some experience of the alloy bodywork, as they'd worked with Don Panoz on his Panoz roadster. I suppose that the irony is that perhaps their experience ought to have told them not to do it! In the end, it just didn't suit our numbers at all, I think. So the project ended up needing ten or fifteen thousand cars to work as a business plan, and eventually it was consuming money at such a rate that the board called a halt – presumably because somebody went to the board and said 'Look, we've spent £17 million, and for another ten you could get it into production...' So the board stopped it and spoke to me and said, 'Go away for a week and think what we might do with what we've got.'

One possibility at this point was that the X80 project could have been killed off altogether, and all the investment written off and more or less forgotten. But that would've been a shame, and it would have been negative, having shown the car. So I went away, and then came back with three possible solutions. One was that we'd build something really outrageous just as a 'one-off', as a kind of technology demonstrator, and then we'd put it away, but having shown what we were capable of. The second possibility was that we'd pick a number like eighty – because the project was called 'X80' – and we'd build eighty cars, and they would be pretty expensive. The third option was that we'd do a limited production run of about 130 cars per year for four or five years. That [last one] actually looked the best business plan.

It was clear that if X80 was going to be drastically scaled back, it would no longer be directly related to the bottom line for MG Rover's balance sheet:

What I was asked to do was not to turn it into a project that made a large profit, because in industry terms it never would; even if it made £2–3 million a year in the

ABOVE: Although the MG ZT 385 concept had been unveiled at Frankfurt alongside the MG X80, the production MG ZT V8 – the 260 – did not arrive until two years later. (MG Rover)

BELOW: In due course, the MG ZT260 – in common with the rest of the ZT range – was given a facelift that brought its grille style closer to that first seen on the MG XPower SV. (MG Rover)

big scheme of things, that's nothing. But the instruction was that it absolutely wasn't to lose the company money. We would use it as a kind of benchmark of how good MG Rover could be at a high point, so it had to be fairly spectacular and work as well.

That meeting of mid-February 2002 saw an end to Steve Hudson's direct involvement with the X80 project, although he has had input since on specific issues. He looks back on his time on X80 with fond memories, but when I asked him if he felt frustrated at losing the opportunity to finish what he had started, he was pragmatic:

Yes, and no. I thought that it was a cracking project to work on, to be honest, and I'd thoroughly enjoyed what must have been the eight to ten months that I'd been involved in it. We'd been doing all sorts of good things, and obviously we'd been working extremely hard: we were a small team trying to pull resource from right across the whole of the organization, and were having to burn the midnight oil on a regular basis, but it was worth it. The upsides were, I remember, sitting in a car with Giordano racing Ferraris round the hills of Tuscany, and we were talking to Rousch and Ford, and banging around in supercharged Mustangs in the hills of California – those sorts of things were just fabulous!

From a business point of view, I know it sounds clichéd but I think that at the end of the day, we very much wanted to make the best decision for the business at that point; so we were recommending as a project team that we should take a different tack, effectively a new business plan. And from a product and styling point of view, that required a change of direction. I quite honestly didn't think that we were the right team; we were too mainstream at that point – both myself and some of the other people that we'd got involved. The project needed different personnel, people whom Peter Stevens knew from his network, otherwise it would've taken three years, and it would have cost about the same amount as 5–10,000 volume would have done, except that we'd have been doing hundreds.

What was needed was effectively a different culture: a team of people who could go and sit in an office on their own, off-site, on-site, wherever was most suitable, with no impediments from mainstream MG Rover – to get on with delivering the project, to sort of 'think outside the box', and to behave in a very much lower volume project-orientated manner, and to focus on the technologies and the processes that supported that. So it was not without some sadness that I moved away from the project and took on my new role. But I think that from a project point of view it was the right decision.

The raft of experience gained with the initial X80 concept was not all to no avail: there was useful input

to other projects, most notably the other Ford V8-powered project, the MG ZT 'V8'. MG Rover's director of sports cars, Graham Fairhead, went on to become the project director for the X12/X13. Hudson points out that this had obvious benefits:

Graham had got knowledge of the due diligence activities and the engineering plans that we'd drawn together for X80. We did get some synergies and realized some opportunities there, particularly with the mechanical configuration. So for example, we took a joint approach to the work, as we did with Ford from a powertrain specification point of view, which was very similar. We looked at brake specifications at the time, which allowed us to reduce investment and to realize costs opportunities by carrying across brakes. So, yes, there was a little bit of interchange there – though I wouldn't say a great deal because the cars were fundamentally different volume propositions.

It was inevitable that some of the backwash from the project review would leak outside the company, although it is perhaps to the credit of all involved that the full details have never emerged until now. The influential and ever-watchful *Automotive News* picked up some of the vibes at the end of February 2002, and spoke to John Parkinson at MG Rover, who told them that the company had delayed the launch of X80 by one year. *Automotive News* went on to report that 'sales of the X80 coupé were due to begin this summer, with a roadster version following in 2003'. But MG Rover officials said the coupé would not be launched until summer 2003, nor did they give a date for the launch of the roadster. John Parkinson was quoted as stating 'the X80's launch was re-evaluated after the September US terrorist attacks, and the resulting slowdown in the high-end sports-car market.'

A NEW DIRECTION FOR X80 – THE COMPOSITE SPORTS CAR

Having been given the green light to take over control of the X80 project, in addition to his other duties as design director, Peter Stevens reviewed what had gone before and made some fundamental changes.

The idea was that I would be left alone, and would live or die on the way that the project went. That was a pretty good expression of faith by the company, and the way it worked was that, being director of product design I would have to divide my week, with half of it being SV, and half of it mainstream MG Rover. That is perhaps not particularly clever because in the corporate turnover sense, I should've devoted something like two hours a week to SV, and the other fifty or so to the rest!

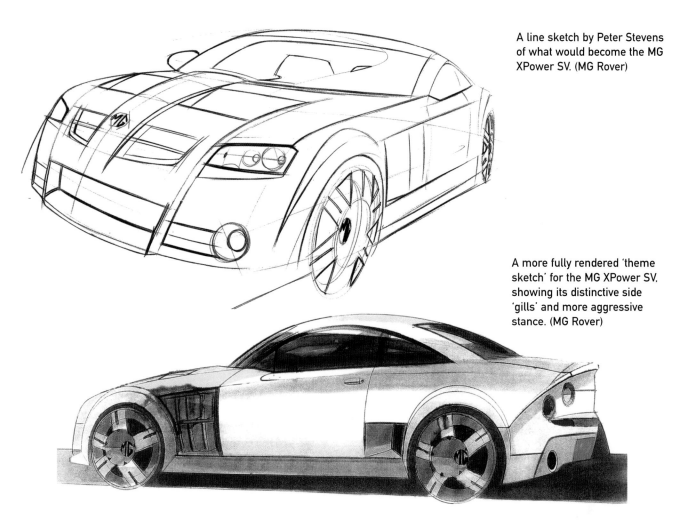

A line sketch by Peter Stevens of what would become the MG XPower SV. (MG Rover)

A more fully rendered 'theme sketch' for the MG XPower SV, showing its distinctive side 'gills' and more aggressive stance. (MG Rover)

When it came to the 'style' of the car, naturally Stevens was assisted by someone who was able to keep focused on X80 when he had to be elsewhere. He says that the main MG Rover studio was content with his involvement with X80:

> They were probably pleased because I wasn't in the studio every hour. What I then did was work with a young designer [Rakesh Chavra] on the MG Rover team, because the quick sketching and ideas stuff we can do quite speedily, but if you're doing more finished drawings it is actually quite time-consuming. So although it might seem patronizing to have someone drawing for you at that stage, it is a better use of time; so when we had sketches of details that we wanted modellers to follow, we'd use him to help.

Stevens is full of praise for Chavra: 'He is a good, talented young lad – a good, speedy drawer, and he worked well with me. He had to work direct, and he had to be there all the time with the modellers, so that if they came across an unresolved bit, he was there -- so just because I wasn't there, the job didn't have to wait.' At first the clay-modelling work had been carried out at Dove, but then premises in Leamington became

available that were owned by Arup and which had once been the base for the Austin-Rover Advanced Design Studio set up by Roy Axe around ten years earlier; now, as part of the giant Arup organization, known as 'Design Research Arup', or 'DRA' for short.

'There were no windows and no sun in there,' Casarini jokes, 'and it was great – we could get going and we did not have to use anyone else's procedures – the equivalent book inside MG Rover would not fit in a large bookcase!' Stevens agrees that the move to Leamington proved to be a good decision from a logistical point of view: 'it was about twenty minutes from the main studio, so my time could be more usefully spent!'

As well as the appearance of the car, an obvious area for review was the alloy body, for although this solution had some attractions for higher volumes, for the much lower numbers that Stevens was now contemplating, the finances for an alloy body were untenable. However, there was an interesting solution with an attractive 'high-tech' image that swiftly presented itself, as Stevens explains: 'Through this thought process I was convinced that we should do the body in carbon-fibre – the technology is better suited to small volumes, and also there is PR value in it, too.'

This rear three-quarter theme sketch for the SV shows an interesting layout of tail lamps and lower valance. (MG Rover)

Much closer to the definitive article, this theme sketch clearly shows the bold grille and side treatments for the MG XPower SV. (MG Rover)

BELOW: The MG XPower SV in clay form, seen in the definitive form as digitized for production. (Author photos)

ABOVE: **The MG XPower SV clay at the DRA studio. The castor arrangement under the front wheels allows the extremely heavy clay to be moved around the surface table. (Author)**

However, Stevens adds that with this new technology, there are pitfalls for the unwary: 'Carbon fibre is presented as a wonder material. Samples we are shown look great, but in practice panels don't work out. We took various sample panels and put them through the paint processes, and some didn't make it through.'

But on the positive side, Stevens could see fringe benefits for MG Rover as a whole:

It is interesting technology for the company to learn about, because in parallel we were looking at panels for the ZT385, and there was a lot of speculation, gossip and rumour about how you make low-volume but cost-effective panels. And a lot of inexperienced people were coming up with wild ideas and wild quotes, and so I thought that here was a chance on this project to learn exactly what it costs and what you can get.

[As an example, Stevens and his colleagues had been considering a carbon-fibre bonnet for the ZT385…] …and people had been coming up with ludicrous prices. And then there was the issue of painting – people saying you'd have to use a totally different paint process for the carbon-fibre panels. So this was a nice learning opportunity, too.

I also thought it was a good kind of high-profile thing for a company that constantly needs to reassert that it is alive, and that it is reasonably ingenious and creative – and that sort of project can do that. But that wasn't to be put on the balance sheet, because although it is a positive in marketing terms, we couldn't say 'we can afford to lose money because it's getting us a million quid in publicity'. Which I think was reasonable – I was happy with that.

Stevens knew that he would have to pick the right people for the project – for as Steve Hudson pointed out earlier, the way that the X80 would be taken forward from now on would be fairly alien to mainstream production. Stevens therefore pencilled in what he saw as the best candidates:

I said that I wanted to have a small team with Giordano to lead it – I'd seen what a remarkable fellow he is – and I wanted to take Ian Moreton from Prodrive because he has the experience of low-volume, high-quality, speedily delivered projects: he just gets on with the job and doesn't understand not hitting the date, because in motorsport they don't hold up the event for you. Also I wanted one financial bloke who would look after our finances so that I didn't have to do that, which is why we kept Keith Twigg on board – who, considering he came out of 'mainstream' MG Rover finance traditions, fully appreciated and understood our point of view: he's a very clever bloke and has an ability to present a simple and clear business plan.

At DRA, as the clay took shape, Alistair Herschell looked after the engineering of the body, and also – in due course – the interior. In his own words:

The car ended up more like the original proposal in terms of how the shapes were divided up, and panel split lines would be made; so it all settled down fairly quickly. We started working with OPAC quite early on – we had the panel split and the structure agreed, as well as the manner of fixing on to the tub – and that shortened the development cycle. We did an initial rough scan of the clay to get an approximate idea of the car in order to get the panel split right, while the engineering was being done in parallel.

The slim and elegant headlamps used for the MG XPower SV are based on those from the 2002 Fiat Punto. (Julian Mackie)

At the rear of the SV, Peter Stevens adapted more Fiat units, but they have been cleverly enhanced by the use of machined alloy bezels. (Julian Mackie)

The scanned data from the clay was passed to the surfacing specialists (CARAN) and once the surfaces and panel splits were resolved, the data for the tooling could be passed to the body tooling contractor. According to Herschell, there were a number of testing challenges during the course of this process: 'In the case of the front clam we had to look at how it would be fixed to the chassis and the inner panels – all the

packaging was needed to know what angle the bonnet would go through when opening and closing, and that would determine the operation of the latching and hinges.' Some aspects of the new car were supposed to remain, as they had on the Mangusta, but fundamental changes – such as the decision to go for a fixed roof – led to necessary compromises. 'For example, we tried to keep the glasshouse similar to that of the Mangusta – but we still had to develop the fixed rear quarter glass and rear screen [the Mangusta had neither],' Herschell explains. 'We wanted to carry over the window mechanism, but in the end we still ended up with new parts anyway! We tried to carry over as many parts as possible, but often you end up making so many changes, sometimes you might as well have started from scratch!'

The decision to drop plans for an open version did have other benefits, however: 'It was a carry-over chassis – but as soon as we went to a coupé body, the back end was different to the open car and so we were able to simplify that part of the Mangusta chassis.' Nevertheless, the chassis still posed other challenges for Herschell and his colleagues: 'One big challenge for us was dropping the body over an existing chassis and getting a sealed tub – not an easy task.'

Herschell is justifiably proud of his part in the project, and he is keen to stress that one of the particularly rewarding aspects for him personally was in helping to move forward the technology of the carbon-fibre car: 'While carbon-fibre technology is normal for a race car, to actually get all our panels to have the right level of surface finish and rigidity was quite a challenge – and there isn't any ready, off-the-shelf advice for this. We were certainly pushing the boundaries forward with our work – we were driving the technology.' Herschell adds that it is not just the comparatively low price of the carbon-fibre shell that makes the SV so special, there is also the fact that it has a full FIA roll cage: 'The roll cage serves a structural purpose in the car – it is a key part of the structure: and that is quite something, in my opinion.'

In addition to changes of style and structure, several other pragmatic actions were needed to cater for the change of plan, including abandoning the idea of bringing the X80 into Longbridge. Even before he started formally in May 2002, Ian Moreton could see some of the magnitude of the task ahead of the X80 team: 'At the first meeting I had with Peter and Giordano and a couple of others, including Keith Twigg, it was clear they had a huge task. Later the same week they were going out to Italy – and in fact when they arrived the lorries were already there to take the stuff back. They actually stopped the lorries and got on the phone to some people that Giordano knew, and they took everything around and put it in a warehouse locally in Modena.' Giordano Casarini confirms this:

Ian Moreton

From almost the moment that the X80 project changed direction, it was clear that it needed to be driven by a small team that was used to the special ways unique to very low volume production. It did not take Peter Stevens long to seek out the service of Ian Moreton, with whom he had worked on several previous occasions. Born in Nuneaton, Warwickshire, on 2 February 1958, Ian Moreton grew up with cars in his blood, and started his career with an apprenticeship at his local Ford main dealer. His interest in motorsport, and his practical aptitude, led him to move in September 1979 to Roger Clarke Cars of Leicestershire, a Porsche, Lotus, Alfa Romeo and Ford dealership.

Just a few months later, in February 1980, Moreton joined a manufacturer's motorsports team, the Peugeot Talbot competitions department. Here, as part of the rally team, he helped Peugeot Talbot achieve a number of national and international wins, including the 1981 World Rally Championship. When the Talbot marque was discontinued and the British competition efforts dropped, Moreton moved over from January 1984 to join the Prodrive rally team on the outskirts of Banbury, Oxfordshire: 'I was one of the original employees under the guise of the Rothmans' rally team, preparing cars for European, Middle East and World Championship rallies, and I attended events as the "Number One" technician on the car.'

After just over six years, Moreton took up the role of 'test and development manager' for the UK arm of the Subaru motorsports programme. This meant managing a team of twenty people and co-ordinating the mammoth logistical exercises involved, while at the same time overseeing arduous testing programmes all over the world, not to mention working alongside the engineers and technicians at Pirelli in Italy. Subaru subsequently became a household name through successes at the World Rally Championship.

From April 1997, Moreton assumed the role of project manager at Prodrive, responsible for managing a variety of disparate tasks. One project was a complete 'design and build' programme for the Proton rally team: 'We had ten months to take a two-door road car and turn it into a world rally car.' No mean feat, except that the end product never emerged on the world rally stage – though through no fault of Moreton or his colleagues. Next was an F1-style hospitality unit: 'We did this for David Richards, at a time when rallying was still in little motorhomes and lots of different service parks. David wanted to have a centralized motorhome for servicing and corporate entertaining, like circuit racing – and Peter Stevens did the theme for it.'

In the midst of this, Moreton became involved in the first of a number of road car projects:

Ian Moreton, production manager MG X80. (Ian Moreton)

The Subaru P1 [a limited edition of 1,000 cars] was one of those projects that needed to be done to support the rally programme, and we were told by Subaru's Japanese parent company that it wasn't possible to bring the car into the UK and sell it. David Richards [Prodrive] said that he knew a couple of people who could probably make it happen – which was Peter and I. And Peter had worked with Subaru already on the rally cars, so we went over there, and to cut a long story short, five A4 folders of faxes later, we ended up with 1,000 cars on the dock!

[By the time that Moreton got a call from Peter Stevens about the MG X80 project, he was deeply involved through Prodrive in international rallying; but the chance to work on an MG project intrigued him, and so he went along to find out more:]

When I first came and sat down at the table with Peter, I found that I had worked with a number of the people before – it was Peter's trusted colleagues! This was at the end of March 2002: I had a think about it and gave in my notice at Prodrive where I'd worked for some nineteen-plus years, and joined MG-X80 on 1 May 2002. I had to do a few days for Prodrive on the Argentina rally, but Prodrive generously allowed me do a few days in April to get up to speed with what was happening.

[At MG X80, Moreton's job title was production manager:] I might describe it actually as keeping the wheel on sometimes! My job involves supporting other members of the team when they're up against it. The job also involved working with some of the suppliers that Giordano knew, some of whom I also knew. Some things had already kicked off when I arrived; I went to Italy and had a look at what they were doing there, and there were people there who had been with Giordano on many projects – and I thought to myself that as I'd also built up a reasonable phone book, between us we could probably get this done.

By the spring of 2004, with SV production gradually moving under the wing of Longbridge, Moreton was looking for a fresh challenge, and he found it at Aquada as project manager for the new 'HSA2' high-speed amphibious vehicle. So 16 July 2004 was a poignant day for Moreton and his colleagues, as, for the time being, he left MG; but it saw the completion of two of the most intense years of his life – two years that nevertheless saw a project successfully delivered. On the same day, the fifty-first SV was completed: car 151 had been built for Phoenix chairman John Towers.

Alistair Herschell

Behind the front line in any enterprise there is usually a small core of key people who oil the wheels and keep the machinery working, but rarely share much of the limelight. The MG X80 project is no exception to that rule.

Alistair Herschell started work at Nissan straight from college, and remained there for nine years, after which he went to work at Jaguar on the X400, which became the 'X-type'. After that, Herschell moved to Lotus where he met David Linley. 'At Lotus I mainly worked on client projects, such as some for Proton, but then I became involved in the M250 project for a new Lotus intended to replace the Esprit.' The M250 project was later dropped, and Herschell spent a brief interlude at Bentley before returning to Lotus to work on the second series of Elise and the Vauxhall VX220.

'While I was there, Dave Linley gave me a call and encouraged me to come across to work with MG on the X80 project – that was right at the early stage of the project.' The team looked at various technologies to do the car, but when they eventually settled on the idea of 'superformed' alloy for the skin, they had a look at the Panoz Esperante sports car in the USA. Herschell believes that in the circumstances, it was a relief to eventually pull away from that technology: 'There were lots of technical problems [...] – aspects such as the fixing methods – and it remained a very low-volume technology.'

Herschell is convinced that the move to a moulded body was a good one. At the 'superform' stage, the X80 project team had a fairly complete design:

> We were certainly at about the stage where we were ready to commit to tooling, but there was a holding period that in the end allowed us to stop. That was in effect the Frankfurt show car. I have to say in retrospect that nobody had much love for that design. The styling story is that that was the sort of style they wanted for the volume and market sector in which they were looking at selling. There was probably a longer time taken over that design than the later one – in the latter case, Peter Stevens knew what he wanted to do, and it was a quicker process...'

Alistair Herschell

Longbridge was ready to bring everything back there – all the assembly line from Modena so that they could build the car in Longbridge. But instead when Peter was reassigned the work we asked ourselves why we should do this – the logic no longer applied. We had to face a big problem, in that the chassis of the car is a very important piece with 800 welds and made of steel, and it is an important thing, too, as it has forty-eight jigs to be put together by Vaccari & Bosi. Vaccari & Bosi has a series of beautiful factories – they have been building chassis for Ferrari since 1956, and historically, every steel chassis on a Ferrari had been made by Vaccari & Bosi.

As the X80 was now going to be made in much smaller quantities, there seemed to be no sense in the major upheaval involved. For Casarini, however, this meant that a big issue was how to deal with Vaccari & Bosi, who had been gearing up for the higher-volume version of X80:

> We had this guy whom we had originally told we would take 10,000 chassis – 'don't throw them away – keep everything! We'll make 10,000 in five years!' But then the project with those quantities was cancelled, and we had to decide who was going to tell him! At first, this seemed an unenviable task: he is a big guy – do you know, when he is bored, he takes his Caterpillar and creates the side of a mountain! You go into his factory and he has 300 workers, and you have to look among the workers to find him – he is there making stuff and welding – so I thought to myself 'he is going to destroy me!'
>
> A possible solution was that we would go and would tell him that the project was being 're-dimensioned', meaning that we would now be making a few hundred cars rather than several thousand; and that in order to compensate him for that, we proposed to him that he should assemble the rolling chassis.

The assembly process of the Qvale Mangusta, which naturally still formed the basis of the process proposed for the MG X80, included a discreet stage where the chassis – kitted out with suspension, powertrain and 'NVH' (soundproofing) – could be started up and moved under its own steam before the bodywork jigging started:

> So we proposed to Mr Bosi that we would transfer the section as far as the rolling chassis into one of his buildings – he had other buildings nearby in Modena – and he would make the rolling chassis instead of just making the chassis itself: in other words, he would become a sub-assembler. Now, I knew that his dream was to become an assembler. Ferrari and Maserati now give out sub-assemblies like corners and rear sub-frames – parts of cars, in other words – and so I knew this proposal would appeal to him.

David Price Racing (DPR)

David Price has been active in motorsports for three decades, and was involved in first bringing the big Rover 'SD1' saloon to British touring car racing. He started out as a Ford apprentice, but began his motorsport involvement by working in the evenings on race cars for friends and his own customers. As those cars proved successful for their owners, Price's reputation spread, and he never looked back. By 1977, Price had established a training school for F3 drivers, and many who would go on to become household names in the F1 field owe Price a debt of gratitude for helping them on their way – drivers such as Nigel Mansell, Martin Brundle, Mike Thackwell and Johnny Dumfries.

In 1987, Price branched out into the emergent field of composite manufacture, and established 'DPS Composites' in partnership with Phil Sharp; the latter had been at McLaren at the time that John Barnard had created the world's first carbon-fibre race-car chassis, the Grand Prix-winning McLaren MP4. Meanwhile at DPR in 1989, Price ran a test programme for Johnny Herbert for the Benetton F1 team; after this he was appointed race team director for the Brabham F1 team. He also became involved with Richard Lloyd Racing, where he helped with their Porsche racing efforts – and met Peter Stevens, also working on the project.

Price then moved to a position at Mercedes as technical team manager for their World Championship sports-car team. During his sojourn there the team won many races, including both the World Sports-car Championship title and the Le Mans 24-Hours race. Next it was the Japanese marque Nissan that secured Price's services, ostensibly for their assault on Le Mans with Martin Blundell in the hot seat.

In 1995 David Price Racing (DPR) managed a pair of McLaren F1 GTR teams, sponsored by West and Harrods. This was a great year for DPR, as the McLarens succeeded in grasping the 1995 European and World GT Championships. DPR next ran two factory Panoz race cars in the 1997 Le Mans race, and five cars for the 2000 event, while he also linked up with Williams Grand Prix Engineering for the development of the BMW V12 LM for the 1999 Le Mans. While the racing team management is undoubtedly where David Price enjoys himself most, he is equally dedicated to the composites side of the business, managed ably by Peter McKenzie, who has

Dave Price of DPR took a close personal interest in the development of the new generation of the X80 programme. (Ted Higgins)

been with the company since 1990.

DPS Composites manages everything, from the production of complete car assemblies, including monocoque chassis, to body panels, engine components and suspension systems. The commission from MG Rover to produce the master body tooling and many of the production panels was a major scoop for the company, as it allowed them to bridge the gap between race cars and road cars – helping MG and its various partners move forward the technology of carbon-fibre bodywork. Peter McKenzie was in overall charge of the MG X80 commission, in which DPS took the raw model data from the 'surfacing' specialists CARAN (see pages 90–91), and used it firstly to design every single panel (as well as individual drawings for each of the approximately 3,200 cut pieces of carbon fibre), and then to produce the master tooling. Having done that, DPS took on the manufacture of complete sets of panels for the first fifteen cars, before handing series production to Belco Avia.

According to Casarini, another factor was the trend in Modena for various companies such as SAIMA-Avandero to take on board not only the management of service parts and 'just-in-time' storage, and but also to carry out part of the assembly processes for some of the parts themselves:

What they do is, they take over your purchase office function for you – you give them the list of materials, and they would supply the parts to your assembly line, and they store the parts in their buildings. Every morning they have lorries that go out to the assembly lines of Ferrari, Maserati and so on, and as a result these car companies have no need of storage and they don't have to worry about missing parts – they have suppliers working specifically on this. This all started with Ducati – Ducati said to a supplier, 'Why don't you assemble parts for us, rather than bringing just the parts to us?' and so these storage companies started putting together sub-assemblies.

According to Casarini, Mr Bosi could readily see that with his ISO9002 certification, he could follow a similar line.

Also, thinking of the future of Ferrari and Lamborghini, it is hard to imagine that in four to five years' time they will still be making cars with steel chassis; everybody is going to aluminium or carbon, and Bosi is the 'king' of steel, and so probably he has thought to himself that if he doesn't diversify, his business will fall. So, being a company that already makes many different things – in another of his factories they have traditionally made all the suspension bits of Ferraris – maybe putting the things together makes sense.

Vaccari & Bosi already had a network of small factories in and around Modena, including one that makes wishbones for Ferrari, and it was apparent that he had some spare capacity, as Casarini was well aware:

Our opportunity for him was great – we knew that – so we went over there, and instead of him becoming mad because an order for 10,000 chassis was being reduced, he was happy – very happy! We started over there, and we have a big operation going, and so we just transferred the assembly line that was going to come to Longbridge. We physically stopped the lorries in Modena, diverted them to these buildings, and unloaded everything there; we have reassembled the assembly line in there, we made a parts storage facility, and we have retained a few people that are key to the operation.

MG X80 Italy was established in July 2001 under the guise of the original version of X80, but as part of the new Stevens/Casarini/Moreton programme, the focus shifted from a simple information gathering and 'winding-up' exercise to one of establishing the new facility managed by Vaccari & Bosi, as well as working with the other Italian suppliers. With the development of the new 'low-volume' strategy, the local knowledge of the MG X80 Italy staff became invaluable. The office at via Dalton, Modena, was split into two departments: 'technical', comprising two key people (Vittorio Filippini, manager and Stefano Garuti, methods) and 'purchasing', also with two people (Antonio Ara, manager with twenty years' experience at Maserati; and Meris Bertocchi). Overall financial management was under Biagio Maltese, while Paolo Corradini was responsible for the local aspects of 'body and trim', and their ability to work within the Italian business network proved essential to keeping the project running.

A BIT OF THEATRE: THE FIRST ACT

Peter Stevens knows from long experience that not everybody is necessarily on board with a project, and that key decision-making moments can be readily influenced one way or the other by subtleties not always easy to foresee. Sometimes the only way to

precipitate a reaction with the required outcome is to provide a careful nudge – and often the best way to achieve that is to stage-manage a bit of theatre – not to deceive, but to prove a point. As Stevens points out:

There were still people inside the company who thought we should have just scrapped the whole thing, and who didn't see any of the emotional side – which is fair enough, because their job in the company was to remove the emotion and turn it into a business. So as far as those board members were concerned, I respected their views, but I knew consequently that we constantly had to win over the board to support us – because there was no doubt that X80 was an indulgence.

Stevens had been given the brief by Nick Stephenson to go away and develop the X80 as the low-volume car he had originally foreseen, and he was as good as his word, keeping the actual development of the car a closely guarded secret, even from the MG Rover directors. 'I deliberately kept the board away from looking at the car, and they didn't see the clay model until we had already started some work on XP1.'

Before long, the time came when the board needed to see and understand how the project was taking shape, so Stevens arranged for them to visit and review progress:

I brought them along to show them the sketch progression and how we had designed the interior and how the exterior would end up, and then we showed them the full-sized clay almost exactly as you see the car now. We had orchestrated that XP1, with its noisy exhaust, and it would be started up out in the yard – it had just come back from DPS [Composites] who had built it.

In the run-up to this, Ted Higgins of David Price Racing (DPR) got a call from his boss, David Price himself: 'Dave said to me I would have to take it up to MG Rover – that Peter was going to do a surprise showing of the car to Kevin Howe and the board.' There was some nervousness on Higgins's part: 'It had literally driven ten yards at this point; Peter thought that we'd driven it somewhere, but in fact we hadn't!' So Higgins took XP1 to the Leamington Spa studio in a covered trailer, from which the prototype was carefully decanted and wheeled into position. 'I had to push it round to the back door, and wait for somebody to come out and tell me to fire it up!' Higgins remembers.

With the XP1 exhaust pointing into the building, and the thumbs up given, Higgins fired the engine. Meanwhile, Peter Stevens had timed everything to the minute:

Just as we'd looked at the sketches and we looked at the clay, there was this V8 firing up, and everyone else was looking around as I just carried on with my talking. Eventually, Kevin Howe said 'What's that outside?' So I said 'Oh, bother! They're not supposed to be back until later, making a noise like that: I'll go and tell them to be quiet!' But he insisted 'What is out there?' and I said, 'Oh – just a prototype…' and so we opened up the doors, and of course there was this matt-black car.

Thanks to Colin Jones at Dove, who had already taken some plasters off the clay to get the prototype going, XP1 looked to all intents and purposes just like the clay inside the studio. At this point, Giordano Casarini – in on the act and supposedly supervising XP1 – began apologising profusely 'Oh – now it interrupts! But do you want to go for a ride, Kevin?' Howe readily agreed, strapped himself in, and off they went. Casarini took Howe round the block in it, while Ted Higgins crossed his fingers: 'It hadn't been shaken down or anything at that stage – and the catalytic converters were dragging on the floor and glowing red hot – but Giordano roared all round the estate in it.' According to Stevens, 'When they came back, there was Kevin Howe getting out of the car with this big grin on his face! So then we could say: "This is the finished clay – and this is how it'll be on the road!" And they said it was fine!'

THE XP PROTOTYPES

The MG X80 project has involved the creation of a small number of prototypes, codenamed XP1 to XP4 inclusive. As Peter Stevens explains:

All these are effectively off the moulds that Colin [Jones] took off the clay [at Dove], so they're all derived from that tooling rather than the production tooling. Also they are all built on modified Mangusta chassis, whereas when we got to the production specification cars – 101, 102 etc – those were on pukka SV chassis and proper tooled carbon panels, which is where we get a different dynamic because they [101, 102] are much lighter.

As originally conceived, XP3 and XP4 were intended for launch exhibition purposes only, but as there are understandably never many SVs sitting around surplus to requirements, these two cars have been used for exhibition purposes. According to Stevens, 'What has happened is that these two [XP3 and XP4] are being constantly called upon, every hour of the day, because people realize the SV is a good thing!'

The four XP prototypes are as follows:

The XP1

The XP1 was a high-speed cooling and stability test car that was used extensively for development work. This matt black car ran at over 200mph (320km/h) at the high-speed test track at Nardó (see below). It was subsequently fitted with a 510Ps engine and was used for calibration and engine integration work. The paintwork on XP1 was done personally by David Price of DPR: Ted Higgins recalls that, 'Dave wanted it painted matt black so that it looked like a "stealth car", so we went out to B&Q and found some blackboard paint, and Dave painted it himself on a Saturday morning. He came in here with some rollers and a hand brush – being matt, the paint quickly goes off flat – and he finished painting it inside an hour.'

XP1 was an important development mule, according to Peter Stevens: 'This was the car that we built running the 465 horsepower engine, and it was the one where we looked at the basic systems such as the brakes to make sure that they were adequate. We also tested the gearbox, especially the six-speed one that we were trying, and used it to do some initial high-speed stability testing, which is when we went down to Nardó.' XP1 was also used for some of the interior development work.

XP1. (Author)

ABOVE AND BELOW: XP2 at Dove in September 2002 when it was finished in grey primer. Later refinished in black, it was used for chassis testing at Nürburgring and Bruntingthorpe (see pages 116–117 and 120). (Author)

The XP2

This was the aero development car, at one point fitted with a 325Ps engine. It was originally finished in grey, but latterly was refinished in matt black to be consistent with XP1. XP2 has also been used for exhaust and chassis development work, including testing in and around the Nürburgring in Germany.

The XP3

The XPower grey car: it was first shown at the Birmingham Motor Show in October 2002; since then it has been exhibited at various shows including Barcelona, Bologna and Amsterdam. XP3 has also been used for chassis development work, using some of Ferrari's favourite test roads, south of Modena in Italy. It was displayed in Cannes for the 2003 Film Festival. In the spring of 2004, XP3 was refitted with a production-type interior to allow it to continue to fulfil a useful display demonstrator role.

The XP4

The first automatic transmission development car, finished in 'Monogram Sunspot Yellow'. The introduction of the automatic version was planned to follow the main manual derivatives.

ABOVE: **XP3. (MG Rover)**

BELOW: **XP4. (MG Rover)**

MG RETURNS TO LE MANS

On 15–16 June 2002 MG returned to Le Mans for the second year running; hopes were still high, and they were buoyed up by the fact that alongside the factory entries there was a single 'privateer' entry, by US-based Knighthawk Racing. This time the two factory MG Lolas made a fair showing, but both eventually succumbed to transmission woes, though one kept going until half-way; the Knighthawk car meanwhile expired in flames. It was extremely frustrating for the MG Rover team, who did their best to hide their disappointment. On Sunday 16 June the Le Mans survivors kept circling the track while MG fans sought to drown their sorrows. Up on the MG hospitality platform, with a grandstand view of the track, Nick Stephenson stood silently watching the pair of GT-class Corvettes going round as a pair, keeping in

DPR undertook extensive testing of the XP1 prototype, seen here on a rolling road. (Ted Higgins)

The substantial cooling fan seen here was necessary to avoid heat-soak during the intensive rolling-road sessions undertaken by DPR. (Ted Higgins)

formation to the end of the race at four o'clock. The appeal of a car more closely based on an identifiable road-car was obvious, although getting there might be another thing.

'ACO', the Le Mans organizing body, announced rule changes for the Le Mans 24 Hours race from 2004 onwards, with an increased opportunity for participation by cars racing in the 'GT' closed production-coupé category, at that point dominated by the Porsche 911 GT3. There was certainly a possibility that, funds and resources permitting, an FIA GT contender might be wrought from the basis of the X80 project.

As these thoughts circulated, news broke that the task of developing and building the first running MG X80 prototypes had been given to David Price Racing and his associated company, DPS Composites. A news item in *Autosport* suggested that DPS was already building the first working prototypes of the X80, and 'could have a race car up and running as early as November'. Peter Stevens was quoted in the magazine as saying 'the idea is to give a club racer the chance to move up to the international level arena with a car that is cheap to buy and run. From the initial evaluation, the car appears to have a promising future. The plan is to do something in GT, but until we make the first one, nothing is definite.'

Testing at Nardo

Achieving test speeds in the order of 200mph (320km/h) requires test circuits that can safely and effectively accommodate such high velocities. The optimum test set-up would include a suitable straight section of road – but such lengths where you can accelerate from zero, up to 200mph, and then drop safely back to zero again, simply do not exist in Europe; even the longest runway in the United Kingdom, at RAF Fairford, is not long enough. This is, of course, why record-breaking endeavours have so often taken place in out-of-this-world settings such as the Utah Salt Lakes. The alternative approach is to use circular test circuits set in a 'bowl' formation, but even here there can be practical limits – the maximum speed that many can stretch to is 150mph (260km/h).

For the X80 test programme, therefore, it was necessary to look overseas, and the only practical candidate was the 8-mile (12.6km), circular banked test circuit outside the town of Nardó in Lecce, southern Italy, not far from the city of Bari. Here, the crème de la crème of the motor industry test their supercars – and so the X80 would be in exalted company. Under the direction of David Price Racing, the first X80 prototype, XP1 – a hybrid of Mangusta and X80 bits – was readied for shipping to Italy, setting off on 19 June 2002. Although the front end of XP1 sported the more or less definitive 'SV' nose, the parts for the rear bumpers and doors had not been finalized at the time of the Nardó test, and so from the rear, XP1 looked like a mongrel cross between old and new.

For the actual testing, the X80 team recruited the services of Danish-born former Le Mans and Daytona winner John Nielsen. Peter Stevens was most impressed: 'He was great! Giordano was very taken with him because he gives great feedback; he is also enormously hard-working, as brave as a lion, and a thoroughly good man. And for the first high-speed test session of a car like this you do need someone who knows what they're doing!' Strangely enough, it seems that 200mph (320km/h) was first achieved right at the outset, but when Ted Higgins and his colleagues from DPS set out to repeat the trick, they found their efforts hampered by high winds at the Nardó oval. However, the objective of testing was successful – XP1 was run in both its normal format with the wing and a second diffuser under the front – and Stevens and his colleagues were ecstatic with breaching the 200mph so easily: it was a good omen.

XP1 emerges from the DPR workshops in preparation for its journey to southern Italy in July 2002. (Ted Higgins)

The XP1 prototype shortly after loading into the trailer for shipment to Nardó. Note the fact that at this stage, the rear of the car still resembles the Qvale Mangusta upon which it was based. (Ted Higgins)

At the time David Price confirmed to me: 'We've undertaken to build five prototype road cars, ranging from a fully equipped European "GT", to a very high performance lightweight "club-sport" type car, with a few other iterations in between.' The original plan, according to Ian Moreton, had been to what he called 'knife and fork' the five cars to give the Consortium something to see in each of the combinations: RHD, LHD, club-sport and various road configurations. The five prototypes were scheduled for delivery and final assessment in November 2002. In fact the first running prototype was already built, and would soon be subjected to shakedown testing. That car, of course, was 'XP1', which, as we have seen, used a Mangusta chassis and glass-reinforced plastic body, the latter made by Dove using the styling clay as the basis of a buck. Although XP1 would be followed by XP2, the plan for five different running prototypes by DPS, envisaged in June, would be dropped within a month. It was about time for another crisis…

CARAN Design

Headquartered in Sweden, CARAN was formed in Gothenburg in 1984 to provide consultancy services to the Volvo Car Corporation, starting with accessory work such as on roof boxes, and ski and bike holders for Volvo cars, and then growing to become the largest preferred supplier to Volvo cars. According to Richard Springall, CARAN's UK technical manager, based in Rickmansworth, the original focus of CARAN UK remained Swedish work, but this focus has since shifted:

I was a contractor who had joined in 1994, but I later went away to work on other Volvo projects; I eventually came back about 3½ years ago to this office to build up this part of the operation. Our focus now is not just to do Swedish work here – we now do UK and international business work from these offices. CARAN UK has, at any one time, up to around 100 people working for it, with a core team of personnel including myself, and from here we manage people out at various sites as well as those working here in this office.

CARAN's services include the provision of design personnel, styling design or studio engineers, surfacing people or CATIA/CAD technicians and process engineers – all the way through the design process. For the X80 project, CARAN was ultimately responsible for manipulating the body-surface data derived originally from the styling clay, refining that data both in terms of making it relate to practical buildable body components, and in terms of ensuring that the outer body surface in particular – the so-called 'Class A Surfaces' – were of the highest visual production-feasible quality.

The process – resulting in assets of mathematical data suitable for pattern and tool production – involved the use of two proprietary software packages, manipulated by a total of eight skilled technicians based at CARAN's UK subsidiary to the north-west of London. The first part of the process involves the use of 'CATIA' software to model the surfaces of

As well as the false-colour images, ICEMSurf is also used to produce conventional 3D images that allow the finished model to be viewed using a variety of virtual light sources. (CARAN)

the car, inside and out. CATIA data is the mathematical information that is shared with other suppliers to allow the simultaneous production of everything from components to jigs; so other partners, including OPAC and Anderson & Ryan – not to mention MG Rover themselves – were critically dependent upon CARAN's 'master data set'.

For the external surfaces, a particularly high quality of visual finish is obviously critical, and for this another piece of software, ICEMSurf, comes into play. According to Springall, ICEMSurf is an industry-standard system for so-called 'A-Class' surfacing:

We're the largest independent user of ICEMSurf in the UK; we have seventeen licences for this software. We take a laser scan of the complete clay surface, which can comprise many millions of points with their x, y, z co-ordinates; that then forms the basis of the data we work with. Our task is to place that data in a CAD format that can then be used by the rest of the engineering part of the project. I've used ICEMSurf on many vehicles, including MG Rover vehicles, for a number of years, and it has established itself as the market leader; it is the industry-standard surfacing tool, and it gives very good results, and

As well as the so-called 'Class A' exterior surfaces, a great deal of work went into developing the equally crucial engineering surfaces – the hidden 'skeleton' of the body structure, seen here in an impressive 3D rendering. (CARAN)

An ICEMSurf rendered image of the SV. (CARAN)

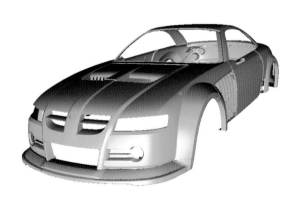

CARAN Design

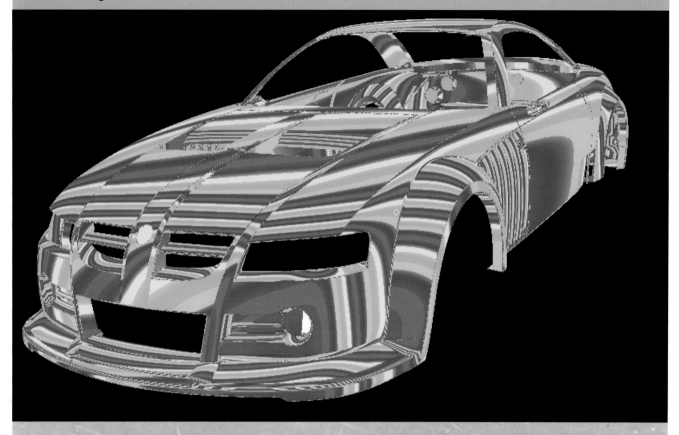

In order to help visualize otherwise almost invisible surface defects – awkward changes of curvature or errors in surface detail – CARAN produces a false-colour image using a software tool called 'ICEMSurf'. (CARAN)

has very good analysing features, which give you good feedback that the shape you are creating is smooth and of the right character. Our role on surfacing is not only to capture the shape of the clay model but also to ensure that the shapes are possible to manufacture – so we have, for example, enough 'draft angle' for a given tool direction so that we can actually make the components.

The multi-coloured rendering illustrated here (above) is a screen-shot of a tool within ICEMSurf, which provides an analysis tool for interrogating the surface of a digital model. Springall explains:

The colours join up areas of equal curvature, rather like 'isobars' on a weather chart. So if you had a panel with a constant radius of, say, 3000, then that would appear as one colour. Where the colours merge gives an indication of where the highlights will run. In a studio, with a real model, there will be a line of straight fluorescent strip lights which give a similar effect; as you move the position of your eye, the lines reflected on the model will play over the surface indicating where highlights fall. In ICEMSurf, you move a virtual light source and the colour bands will appear to ripple over the surface. A trained operator can use this to pick up any oddities in the surface.

CRISIS II: TEETERING ON THE EDGE OF OBLIVION

In the spring of 2002 there had been new-found optimism at MG Rover: the relationship with China Brilliance looked promising, and funds were trickling in from MG Rover's Chinese partner, while a small batch of re-badged Rover 75 saloons was shipped eastwards. At the same time, the other relationship – with Indian conglomerate TELCO – was promising to provide a spiritual successor to the Mini Metro, and thereby help generate much-needed extra sales for MG Rover dealers.

However, two events in June – quite apart from the disappointment at the distraction that was Le Mans – conspired to unsettle the people at Longbridge, and threatened to undermine a whole range of peripheral activities such as X80. MG Rover had been moving from a long-standing parts-distribution relationship with Unipart – like Longbridge, formerly part of British Leyland – to a new arrangement with Caterpillar Logistics. The new set-up, brokered when BMW still owned MG, Mini, Land Rover and Rover, was supposed to promote new efficiencies through the adoption of new technology. In practice, however, the roll-out of the new systems was not without teething problems, and the result was nearly catastrophic, with a major backlog in parts delivery to MG Rover dealers that threatened to undermine their workshops and parts sales. The problem became so acute that during June 2002, MG Rover took the drastic step of stopping car production for a week to divert all the parts to support the service side.

As if this problem was not bad enough, the deal with China Brilliance suddenly started to unravel. The first signs that all was not well came on 4 June, when the *Financial Times* ran a story that China Brilliance's chairman Yang Rong was being investigated by the Chinese government for financial irregularities; these charges were vigorously denied by the company, although nobody seemed to know the whereabouts of the unfortunately named Mr Rong. The story refused to die, and then, sixteen days later, came the news that Yang Rong had been replaced by Wu Xiaoan, formerly vice chairman. There was an ominous silence about the MG Rover deal from the Chinese end – in sharp contrast to the great pains that were taken to talk up the future of an entirely separate deal between China Brilliance and BMW. MG Rover claimed that it was 'business as usual'; but to observers, this seemed very much a case of putting on a brave face.

The combined effect of these problems, that were hardly helped by a disastrous fire at an important supplier of seat foams, meant that the MG Rover Board had to quickly review their various programmes yet again, and consider terminating anything that was not important to the core of the business plan. Ian Moreton remembers how this new tide of crisis threatened to sweep over X80 once more:

> I'd just gone in somewhere without my phone, and when I came back to my car I got a very strange [voicemail] message from Giordano: 'Come back to the office now – Peter needs to tell us something.' I was only five minutes away from the office and so I came whizzing back – and could immediately see some very long faces, and Peter finding it very difficult to tell us that the project might have to stop.

There was some debate on the reasons for this – it was chiefly seen as the China Brilliance situation – but the X80 team was still shocked: 'We all went home feeling gutted because everyone had been running at 100mph.'

That night was difficult, as the team found themselves looking at an uncertain future. 'I'm sure that nobody slept very well,' Moreton remembers, 'but we came back to work the next day and began to think

what we could get to in terms of a sensible place so as not to waste what we had already done – for the project had effectively wasted a good deal of money in the past before we inherited it, and we didn't want to go down that path again.' Moreton and his colleagues picked on, as an example, the surfacing of the car, where they had already spent 94 per cent of the budget and another 6 per cent would have seen it finished. 'We went through the main eight to ten items to establish where would be a sensible point to get to.' Soon a picture emerged of how close the project was to delivery.

> We sat down and made a chart with several columns. There were the main eight suppliers we were working with, plus another line for all the small contractors we were using, such as people moving the cars around for us, and doing things like testing paint samples; and we drew a line to show where we needed to get to in order to get to a sensible point where we wouldn't lose everything we'd spent.

Moreton also knew that if the people left the project – in particular those at CARAN – the team would never get them back:

> ...so we'd effectively lose all the surfacing information on the car. So we started a column for how much we were actually exposed to up to date with order cover; and then there was another column, which was how much we had verbally exposed ourselves to through our enthusiasm, and through other people wanting to get involved; then there was a third column, which was to cover all the people who had done work and whose services would still be needed to come to a sensible stop; and then there was how much it would cost to tick over; and finally how much to finish it.

Overall, Moreton estimated that the project was about 70 per cent there; 'probably another 5–10 per cent was needed to get to a sensible stop, and then you only needed another 18–20 per cent to get to production.' Moreton laughs that '...we laid it all out on a piece of paper because the accountant usually works the numbers so that nobody can actually understand them – he is a master at that, and in fact in the factory he has a reputation for his numbers, such that nobody dares to ask how he got them because nobody is brave enough to ask what they mean!' The simple table made it clear that it would have been a tragic waste not to finish when the project had come so far. 'At that time, people were looking at lots of accounts sheets, and so our simple sheet with its clear bottom line was an obvious benefit to us.'

A particular concern at the time was that some third parties were doing work as or through friends:

We were going at breakneck speed, and not everybody had order cover in place. That is obviously frowned upon at MG Rover as elsewhere, but people were getting involved in the programme from the infectious enthusiasm of all the people involved – and of course that can be quite dangerous, but was what had happened. So we started feeling really conscious that this would have been bad for the people who didn't have order cover, and you find that you're a very small cog in the works when you've got no order cover. There were people whom we'd gone to, and upon whom we had depended – and there were our own reputations to consider at the end of the day. We had a week or two where we – Peter, Giordano and me – thought that there was a possibility that our reputations could be ruined by this, and of course it had taken us a long time to build those reputations up – and usually whenever we are involved in a project, it flies…

The timing of such crises is never convenient, but this one came just as the school summer holidays were underway: 'none of us had particularly good holidays,' Moreton says; 'I went to Disneyland in America – which of course is a licence to print money – and I was there wondering if I would have a job to go back to! But with a lot of work, Peter managed to get orders and with myself and Giordano going up to the Consortium offices with the orders, getting them signed, taken straight round to purchasing and sent out, at least people we had dragged in were covered for the work they had done!'

In the midst of this chasing around, the MG X80 team heard that the Phoenix Consortium Board members were going to be having a meeting at Longbridge to discuss which projects were going to be cancelled and which would survive. 'We got a tip-off from the inside that this was going to take place at four o'clock, and so Giordano and I shot up and collected XP2 – which by now was serving as our development car for exhaust systems – and we came roaring back down the motorway at 200 km/hr to the factory'. On the way, there had been heavy rain, and as a consequence of less-than-perfect water-proofing, Moreton and Casarini found themselves sitting in wet seats. 'The water was running in, as we had kept the old "A" posts on to which had been fixed the glass-fibre roof – and Giordano didn't like the look of the M-6 sized bolts that were holding the roof up, to the extent that he was sitting there holding the roof on, while I was undertaking in the pouring rain with no wipers on the M42!'

XP1 – still under the care of DPR at this stage – moved gradually closer towards the definitive shape of the SV, although at this point the roof is still only an aerodynamic approximation with a small rectangular rear window. In the background is Mike Coyte, who worked on fitting the XP1 GRP body to the Mangusta chassis. (Ted Higgins)

**XP1 parked outside David Price Racing HQ in Surrey.
(Ted Higgins)**

In the best traditions of such seat-of-the-pants exercises, Peter Stevens was outside pacing up and down: 'We'd had a few hold-ups,' Moreton recalls, 'but we got into the factory, pulled up outside where the meeting was going on, and the Consortium came outside to have a look.' 'Oh yes!' remembers Peter Stevens, 'it turned up at Longbridge and blasted around the block outside the boardroom, and they all came out, and Kevin Howe said, laughing: "How the hell can we make a rational decision about this car when you buggers turn up with it?" And I said 'Oh yes, it's maddening – they were supposed to take it to the engineering shop, and they just brought it here instead!"' Moreton remembers that Kevin Howe and John Edwards came over to see the car: 'I was standing there with soaking wet trousers, and I cannot think what Kevin Howe thought of me!'

There then followed a tense period of waiting for the X80 team, during which time Moreton says that it was difficult to get any feedback:

Then, after a few weeks, the consortium said we needed to make sure that the 'bill of materials' stacked up to a figure that we'll call 'X' – which happened to be the same as the old Mangusta programme had been. So we set to with a sharp pencil to establish how we could produce a car for that amount. We had to get around the fact that we were all purists, and the idea

that we could, for example, be producing the car using GRP, and perhaps not the best style wheels and seats, was actually quite difficult for us; but once we'd got it into our heads that all we had to do was to get a bill of materials that answered the question and the accountant was happy with it, we were okay. In reality, people aren't going to have that base specification – they'll dress the car up – so we managed to get the figures to add up to meet the objective.

Then we found ourselves in what was termed 'tickover plus' – although we weren't sure if that meant ticking over at F1 speed, or like an old diesel engine. We assumed it to be ticking over like an F1 engine and so carried on – a little bit naughty perhaps, but we believed that the consortium, and in particular Nick Stephenson, really wanted to see this car happen.

This 'tickover' period led to an eight-week slippage, and according to Moreton, because of this slippage, it was decided that there was no point in building another show car because the team were unlikely to learn anything more from it. This led indirectly to a scaling back of the programme planned for David Price Racing.

In the midst of this period of uncertainty, a fairly accurate artist's impression of the current iteration of X80 appeared on the front cover of the 4 September 2002 issue of *Autocar* magazine. The picture was a computer rendering based on a photograph sent in by a reader, who had spotted one of the test mules by the side of the road and snapped off a shot. A cynic might

ABOVE: Ted Higgins and his colleagues took XP1 – minus its detachable roof – to a nearby park in Great Bookham for these photographs of a hypothetical open version. (Ted Higgins)

BELOW: The roof-less version of XP1 makes rather a fetching open top race-car. (Ted Higgins)

DPR to the rescue: an observant reader of *Autocar* magazine snaps the stricken XP1 outside his home in Surrey. (*Autocar*)

Here, Ted Higgins holds the door of XP1 while a resident of East Clandon snaps a photo that would later appear in *Autocar* magazine. (*Autocar*)

Using the reader's 'scoop' shots as a basis, *Autocar*'s in-house artists produced this fairly accurate impression of the new version of X80. About the only thing they got wrong was to assume the use of Audi rather than Fiat Punto headlamps. (*Autocar*)

RIGHT: The revised X80 made
the front cover of *Autocar* of
4 September 2002. (*Autocar*)

BELOW: Just how close the *Autocar*
artist's impression was can be
gauged by comparison with this
photo of an actual SV on the road.
(Julian Mackie)

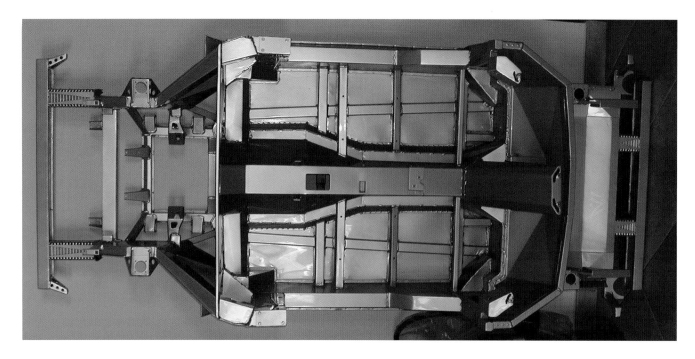

ABOVE: **This bare chassis was used for reference by DPR, and was at one stage to have been used to build a racing version of the X80. (Ted Higgins)**

LEFT: **The Mangusta chassis is cleverly constructed from laser cut flat steel sections – not overly pretty, but functional and strong. (Ted Higgins)**

suggest that Peter Stevens had engineered this, but Stevens insists that while the mischievous thought might have occurred, it was not the case this time. Ted Higgins of DPR confirms this:

> It was on its way back from Farnham – we'd taken it round Farnham town centre for a road test, come back up the A3, and then it broke down at East Clandon. A lad then walked out of his garage – we were parked opposite, up on the grass verge – and he started taking pictures, because he thought he was taking pictures of the new McLaren. And then two weeks later it appeared in *Autocar* and they thought we'd staged it – but we hadn't; it had genuinely broken down!

Naturally a tow rope was needed to recover XP1, with the aid of a car 'borrowed' from the DPR car park, but quick thinking ensured that embarrassment was avoided. According to Stevens: 'Luckily they realized in time, for if the photographer had seen the tow rope they'd have thought the car was broken, and that could have been potentially very negative for us...' The problem was swiftly traced to the fuel pump, as a consequence of which, according to Higgins, 'we modified the pump and it was no problem after that.'

An unfortunate casualty of the summer 2002 crisis was the abandonment, for the time being at least, of plans to take the GT racing version of X80 to extend MG's exciting Le Mans adventure. DPS had already built XP1 and was halfway through doing a second one. As Ted Higgins confirms:

The Theatre Impresario

As we have seen, from time to time various bits of what may loosely be termed 'theatre' took place. Peter Stevens makes no apologies for the need for the occasional touch of smoke-and-mirrors when the fate of the X80 project was in the balance. Stevens recognizes that the break from BMW had been a real shock to the people inside Rover Group: 'Folk realized that they could easily have ended up without a job, and so a culture that probably grew in the BMW time – where there was the temptation to think that all the difficult stuff would simply be done by BMW because they had loads of money – had gone away, to be replaced by dedicated groups of people working very hard and objectively on the "Z" cars.' But then, after the initial shock had faded, to be replaced by a new spirit of optimism, some people began to think the problems were all in the past: 'They kind of came up to the surface, discovered they were still alive, and went back to working as a big company would do if it were extraordinarily well-funded.' Clearly this was not sustainable, and as costs were seen to be rising in the second year, there came a period of looking very carefully at the contributory value of each project.

'And each project was to be considered, not emotionally, but from a straight accountancy point of view,' Stevens stresses. 'So of course, the result of that was that everybody had to make a good picture of their particular project but naturally, with a project like X80, even if one sold every car with all the extras, the actual financial contribution to the company bottom line would be tiny compared to a lot of other things.' As a result, Stevens felt compelled to continuously re-sell X80 on an emotional basis; in his view, 'that was the only way to escape from purely rational thinking into emotional thinking.'

Another thought was that perhaps X80 was soaking up the services of people who could have been involved in other things, which in Stevens' view missed the point that maybe if they were doing less exciting things, 'perhaps some of them might want to move on and out of the company to something else – so the presumption was unfounded.' X80 teetered near the brink more than once, and so 'when it came up in rational examination of the project, it was necessary for us to remind the board of the idea that this was emotional, and it was high profile – because there is no doubt that there were some people solely basing their opinion on financial gauges – who would say we should stop it. And there were folks who thought it was barmy – there were probably some who thought that it was a bit of an indulgence of the board – because it kind of looked like fun, and they had seen that aspect of it…'

Away from the corporate heart of the company, Stevens strongly believes that the X80 also served another important but financially intangible purpose. 'I felt – and I still do – that having the SV make unexpected guest appearances around the factory was exceptionally good for morale generally, because it was a really loud, strong, noisy indication that things were going on. Because normally, with similar projects that can take four years, the guys in the factory don't get to see anything until it is about three-quarters of the way through the project, and normally they don't even know it's been going on because of the security aspects; and so here was something that they could see was going on, and which we certainly didn't mind them seeing or hearing…'

Then we were supposed to build two left-hand-drive ones and two automatics; but they said 'No – it's going straight into production – you're not doing this', and they sort of wound the race-car project down. We were looking at going to the 2003 Le Mans and then the 2004 Le Mans, or certainly going to Sebring in 2003 and making an evaluation from there – it would have been lovely – or even then doing 'Petit Le Mans', which was in September 2003; but instead it all wound down until Dave [Price] told us it had stopped.

However, the appearance of X80 splashed across the cover of *Autocar* put a fresh complexion on things, according to Moreton:

That made it more difficult for the consortium not to allow it to go to the Motorshow! They didn't particularly want it to go there, as they weren't sure whether they were going to build it! But then Marketing thought it was going to the Motorshow, and actually what happened was that Peter fed it in as 'Oh, it is going to the Motorshow', and the next thing was that it became fact that the car was going to the Motorshow…

By the time this photograph was taken by the author in September 2002, XP1 was much closer to the definitive SV shape. (Author)

chapter seven

Destination Motorshow

ALL SET FOR BIRMINGHAM: BUILDING THE SHOW CAR

Having made the decision to exhibit the MG XPower SV at the Birmingham Motor Show in October 2002, all the stops were pulled out to complete a show-quality prototype. At this stage, the production tooling was still some way from completion, and so the services of Dove were called upon once more to build a complete, fully functional bodyshell on to one of the Qvale Mangusta chassis. This was a considerable task, for it involved working closely with the design team – principally Peter Stevens himself – with many detailed decisions having to be developed on the fly. This was intended to represent, as far as was possible, the appearance and functional capability of the definitive SV, although for the show car, Stevens decided to produce a 'Club Sport' version with a special motorsports-oriented interior and a magnificent 'technical'-looking, adjustable rear spoiler.

The photographs shown here of the bare, unfinished shell of XP3 were taken at Dove on 9 September 2002, a few days before it was due to be shipped down to its next port of call – QCR Motors of Nuneaton – for final painting, trimming and preparation to show standard. On that day, Peter Stevens was on hand to explain his philosophy for XP3:

I wanted to find some description for this particular car so that every time we did something else we could test that against our efforts here; and so we have imagined that with this one, a couple of wealthy enthusiasts want to do the Motor Tour de France, where you go to all the race-circuits and hillclimbs in France and you have to drive between them.

[In order to meet the dual criteria of road car and race car, XP3 took on a sort of Jekyll and Hyde character, as Stevens goes on to describe:] ...If we look, for example, at how we fit the bonnet, it has bonnet pins on it and they're fancy ones – but bonnet pins nevertheless, because that is what you'd expect on a racing car. There is a visible roll-cage inside the car, and there are two areas where you can put crash helmets just behind the seats. There is also a little bit of luggage, which Colin is doing right now: namely two bags for racing overalls, which slot into the spare wheel that sits in a recess just behind your shoulders, as you would expect for a Tour de France car – so each of the occupants would have a bag with their racing gear in it as well. So the car is truly race ready, and the idea is that if a customer wanted one of those, he could have exactly that model of car. If you want something even more extreme – it is always Nick's idea to be more exciting – then we could do it.

Although the overall appearance of the 'SV' was quite different to that of the Frankfurt car, the roof architecture was very similar. In the preparation of XP3, the car intended for the Birmingham Motor Show, the old TWR model was cannibalized for its expensive hand-made windows. (Author)

Seen here under construction at Dove is 'XP3' – destined to become the show car for the public debut of the MG XPower SV. (Author)

The building of XP3 at Dove allowed Stevens to resolve one or two details, in particular some aspects of the body shape (mostly the kind of details that only someone with an expert eye such as Stevens' would spot), and some practical considerations – for instance, having an opening boot at the rear of the car, and not a full opening tailgate, which only added weight and complication on a car with motorsport aspirations). The end result of Dove's hard work was a finished, structurally functional GRP body shell and key fixtures built over a Mangusta chassis: all that had to be done now was to turn this into a gleaming, eye-watering show car.

By 27 September 2002, when the next photographs were taken, XP3 was being painted and fully fitted out as a running prototype at QCR Motors. Much burning of the midnight oil took place while Frank Hook's skilled team provided a paint finish that shone like liquid glass, and a busy group of contractors buzzed like insects around the car, fitting trim, mechanical components and electrics.

On 2 and 3 October 2002 the finished XP3 was the subject of a static photoshoot for the first official press photos; this took place inside the 'Dimlock Building', a disused factory in west London, the moody industrial atmosphere of the interior of the building giving just the sense of menace that the sales and marketing team – led by former McLaren and Lamborghini PR man Nigel Gordon-Stewart – wanted to generate in relation to their new car. Four days later, XP3 was transported to a disused power station in Kent for the production of a promotional video; this would also form a backdrop to the motor show launch.

Speaking to me between the two sessions referred to above, Ian Moreton pointed out that although XP3 might appear finished to me, Peter Stevens was already looking at further small refinements for production: 'Between today's photo shoot and the Motorshow [22 October] we've got two days set aside for the video [7 and 8 October], and then there are a couple of things that Peter wants to change now that he has seen the car all together – minor grille details, mainly – so we'll look at these next Wednesday [9 October], and then when they're done we'll go for a final polish and examination of the paintwork, and the car will go to the Motorshow…'

Although a high-level delegation had called to see work-in-progress on XP3 when it was still at QCR Motors, the whole MG Rover board only saw the finished car on Monday 21 October 2002, the day before it was due to appear for the first time in the public glare at the NEC. Peter Stevens was adamant that this was what he deliberately intended: 'I wanted them to see the car only at the end; Kevin Howe told me he thought it was like the Dance of the Seven Veils, but that was one of the things that kept the interest going – another of the crucially important bits of theatre.'

LEFT: The nose section of XP3 being finished at Dove. (Author)

BELOW: Behind the nose-cone for XP3 can be seen the fully-functional Mangusta chassis to which prototype MG XPower SV parts are being fitted. (Author)

ABOVE: Like most creative people, Peter Stevens uses his notebook to crisply and clearly illustrate the changes he requires – all who have worked with him on similar projects speak highly of his ability to swifly communicate ideas. (Author)

BELOW: Shortly after arrival at QCR Motors from Dove, XP3 is about to undergo preparation for painting and trimming. (Harris Mann)

ABOVE: In an age of high-technology computer-aided equipment, it is refreshing to see new techniques being carefully married to traditional craftsmanship. (Author)

ABOVE: The combination of bright lights and wet floor provide an atmospheric setting for the photo shoot. (Author)

LEFT: From the outside, the Dimlock building is unprepossessing. (Author)

BELOW: Setting up for the photo shoot. (Author)

RIGHT: The outcome of a full day of shooting at the Dimlock building in West London was the moody but effective set of official launch images for the MG XPower SV. (MG Rover)

LEFT: The MG XPower SV has a brutal presence, shown to good effect in this low-level shot. (MG Rover)

LEFT: One of the unsung heroes of the X80 project is Steve Black – with the project since spring 2002 – who is seen here assisting with the video shoot for the SV launch. (Nik Moore)

QCR Motors

Hidden away on a quiet industrial estate in Nuneaton, Warwickshire, is a small but busy enterprise known as QCR Motors. Overseen by the larger-than-life Frank Hook, QCR goes about its business of finishing both parts and cars for a range of big-name industry clients, Jaguar and Land Rover amongst them. Frank Hook and his business partner Charles Crees founded QCR Motors in 1975, and as they built up their reputation, so their order book grew. Nowadays QCR combines specialist sub-contract painting of parts with body-shop contracts for a number of local prestige dealers, as well as the finishing of racing and show cars. During the 1980s, QCR worked with TWR Racing to refinish their Group A racing cars in their distinctive livery. This involvement continued into Group C racing, and the equally distinctive 'Silk Cut' cars. In 1992 JaguarSport contracted QCR to custom finish their Jaguar XJ220s, and this led indirectly to a similar arrangement with McLaren Cars, in which QCR refinished the McLaren F1 to the individual buyer's colour requirements.

ABOVE: The nose section of XP3 during the final stages of painting at QCR Motors. (Author)

BELOW: In order to achieve a glass-smooth paint finish for the show car, a great deal of careful hand-flatting and polishing was required. (Author)

ABOVE: Each body-coloured part of the XP3 show car had to be treated with the same level of care. (Author)

LEFT: As well as painting, trimming of XP3 was undertaken on site at QCR Motors. (Author)

For the video shoot, MG Rover took XP3 to a disused power station building in Kent, ensuring an atmosphere that matched the static images. (Nik Moore)

In order to get a smooth tracking shot, a substantial arm was used to mount the camera. (Nik Moore)

THE UNVEILING AT BIRMINGHAM

At Britain's National Exhibition Centre, on the outskirts of Birmingham, the biennial motor show is usually an opportunity for the indigenous motor industry to stage a special demonstration of its wares. The show in October 2002 was no exception, and with a number of debuts expected – including the proposed rebirth of the classic Invicta marque – media interest was high. As a matter of fact interest was whipped up even more than usual when Patricia Hewitt, MP – the government's Trade and Industry Secretary – made some caustic critical comments about what she considered to be sexist publicity posters advertising the show – and of course the old maxim always holds true that there is no publicity like 'bad' publicity.

All this political intrigue was a sideshow as far as MG Rover was concerned, for the main event on their stand was to be the public unveiling of the MG XPower SV. As the appointed hour approached, one or two senior figures from other companies could be seen among the crowd, among them Andrea Zagato, personal friend of Giordano Casarini and son of the founder of Zagato. Zagato has been revitalized under Andrea's stewardship and has been involved in the production of some stunning limited production Aston Martins.

The main speech at the NEC was by Kevin Howe, but he graciously saved the highlight of the show for Peter Stevens, who joked that Howe had been his warm-up man – although he hastened to add that 'no one could ask for a more supportive or enthusiastic warm-up man'. Stevens then went on to explain to his audience the change of philosophy from the Frankfurt concept, saying that 'the X80 as you saw it was going to be a fine motor car. But at board level we realized that it did not push forward the boundaries of what we feel MG stands for. All MGs should have independence of spirit, a sense of risk and excitement, value for money in our chosen markets, and extreme driving pleasure. What we are now going to show you is my vision of what an extreme MG should be.'

He continued: 'It is just the first of a series of cars from MG Sport & Racing's XPower brand,' and explained that the role of XPower was as representative of 'the ultimate in sporting vehicles from MG'. Horsepower, we were told, would start at 326, 'but customers will be able to specify the amount of power they want – although we may limit that to around 965bhp!' Summing up, Stevens said that the SV would, like all other current MG models, 'extend [the] expected performance envelope and break the established rules. But it will also have impeccable road manners. As our chief engineer, Giordano Casarini would say: "The car will aggress you!"'

Early arrivals at the MG Rover stand on the morning of Press Day were greeted with this sight. (Author)

At the appointed hour, the SV unveiling ceremony took place, assisted by a suitably 'menacing' actor and a pair of MG XPower girls, to the accompaniment of dry-ice smoke and a thumping base-line. (MG Rover)

British TV actress Tracey Shaw poses with XP3 on the MG Rover stand at the NEC. (MG Rover)

The Unexpected Exploits of XP3

The following is one of those unscripted events that abound in the stories of many projects – the sort that no one can quite believe really happened. In the tradition of the great mystery stories, the 'names have been concealed to protect the innocent'. Not surprisingly there was a heavy demand for exhibition appearances by the MG XPower SV, but in the early days there were simply no production cars to spare, and so the redoubtable show car, XP3, was called into service. Demand was not confined to the UK, however, and so XP3 became something of a well travelled motorcar – although not always under its own steam, as it was not built to production specification. One such excursion abroad meant that XP3 had to be accommodated overnight at the premises of a friendly local dealer in the neighbourhood. At first, everything went well – cordial relations were established with the proprietor of the establishment, the car was left locked in its trailer, and the delivery driver retired to a local hostelry for a good night's rest.

But imagine the driver's surprise when he returned first thing the next morning to find the locks removed from the trailer, the doors wide open – and no car inside. Walking around the nearly deserted premises, the driver found the workshop where he detected fervent activity – and came across XP3, surrounded by men trying to fit the front splitter back on to a damaged front end. Even now, the exact circumstances remain confused, but it seems that a customer had expressed interest in the SV, and the car had been 'freed' from the trailer to allow the car out – and it was damaged while being manoeuvred. No one back at MG Rover could imagine anyone thinking that such an idea was sensible – and afterwards the dealer seemed to lose much of his formerly excellent command of English and went off on holiday. And what of the XP3 display? In the end some small potted plants had to be arranged in front to hide the repairs…

All that was needed then was the customary backdrop of dry ice and loud music, at which point a trio of models – a pair of skimpily clad MG XPower girls and a token 'heavy' – paraded around XP3 to a phalanx of flashbulbs. Afterwards, Stevens cheekily started the engine of XP3 to briefly show off its lusty V8 growl, and claimed that 'this is a focused, high-performance sports car for drivers who think TVRs are for wimps'.

Meanwhile, away from the spotlights, Kevin Howe admitted that MG Rover was evaluating its joint venture with China Brilliance, and that there was a question mark over the collaboration. Howe told reporters that he had met Yang Rong, the former chairman of China Brilliance, at the beginning of October 2002; this was while Rong was still embroiled in legal action in an attempt to regain the assets of the company he had founded in 1990, and which had now been confiscated by the Chinese government. Howe maintained that the deal was still alive, but that he and

Gordon Stewart was the recipient of a deposit cheque that was thrust into his hand, and within days MG Rover was delightedly reporting substantial interest and orders for the car. By 4 November 2002, as the NEC show closed its doors, MG Rover reported as follows:

> Huge levels of interest have been shown in our car ranges, and at the final count in excess of 1,000 orders were taken, representing over £12m at showroom prices. Interest in the new MG XPower SV has been especially high. Customers have shown a keenness to be the first to enjoy the thrills of this exciting new car, and the first three months' production has already been sold.

By the time the doors closed at the NEC, twenty-nine SV orders had been taken. It was a fantastic welcome for the SV; all that Peter Stevens, Giordano Casarini and Ian Moreton had to do now was to build the cars...

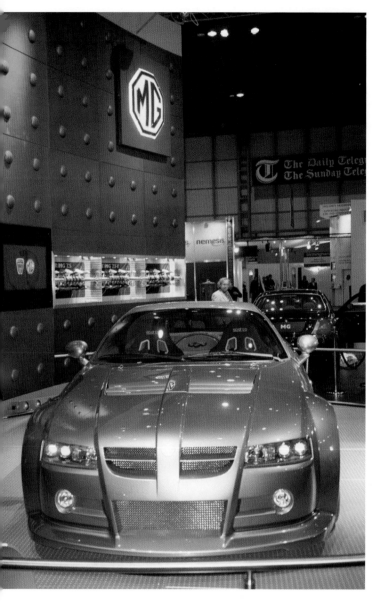

The MG XPower SV formed the centrepiece of the MG Rover stand. (Author)

A consistent (and popular) theme of the 'XPower' brand has been the use of a dedicated promotional team of 'XPower Girls'. (Author)

his colleagues were taking stock of the situation. 'When MG Rover was started, China was never on its radar screen,' he told the *Birmingham Post*. 'We are evaluating whether Mr Rong will be able to see his side of the deal through. We are keeping an eye on that – there is a new power base in China, and we are now dealing with those people.' Within a fortnight, however, an unnamed China Brilliance source told *Automotive News* that the deal was effectively dead: 'We are contacting MG Rover, and want to talk with them on a high level about the future of the two companies. We have not had a chance to meet with them yet.'

Following XP3's welcome on Press Day, it continued to be the central attraction on MG Rover's stand for the duration of the show, and visitors were packed five deep at most times during the busier periods. Nigel

chapter eight

Making It Real

ONWARDS TO PRODUCTION

Even though the XP3 shown at Birmingham was a runner – as it would demonstrate on a number of subsequent occasions – it was not a 'true' SV in as much as it utilized a hand-laid GRP body and a Qvale Mangusta chassis. Moreover, the interior of XP3 was a one-off intended to represent a 'club sport' specification, with racing-style instrumentation and a hand-built cabin that used hardly any production parts. The fact was, the definitive SV interior was still in the final stages of being developed, some of the design work being carried out to Peter Stevens' direction by Harris Mann, better known for his role in the distant past as the Longbridge senior designer responsible for the Austin Allegro, Leyland Princess and Triumph TR7. Working with Mann was Nick Gwinnutt: as well as ensuring that the interior married up to the exterior panels being detailed by CARAN, Gwinnutt was the liaison man with trim specialist Anderson & Ryan.

An interesting aspect of the SV project was the fact that while the chassis is immensely strong and efficient in terms of weight, it does not have the aesthetic grace of, say, a tubular structure. What this means in practice is that the chassis is not something of which to make a visual feature, and so the interior of the car in particular had to conceal the chassis from view. This posed something of a problem, as Alistair

ABOVE: The carbon-fibre body structure is clearly visible in this view of the first production-specification car. (Author)

LEFT: The first car with genuine carbon-fibre bodywork takes shape at Design Research Arup (DRA). (Author)

RIGHT: This view of the partially-built pre-production prototype shows how remarkably compact the MG XPower SV actually is. (Author)

BELOW: As the exterior was finalized, work continued on the interior – seen here in clay form. (Nick Gwinnutt)

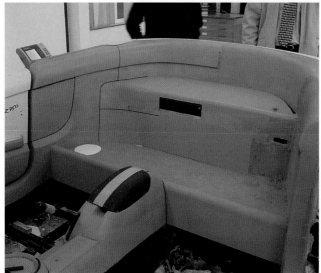

Herschell explains: 'In an Elise, for example, you can leave some of the chassis elegantly exposed, but we could not do that with the SV – and of course to mask it without adding unnecessary weight was quite a challenge!'

Meanwhile, in the same way that MG X80's UK operation worked with local suppliers such as Anderson & Ryan, XK Engineering and others, so MG X80's Italian offshoot was similarly engaged in liaison and associated work within Italy. As an example of the complexity of the arrangements, MG X80 Italy deals effectively and efficiently with about 400 suppliers, 150 of whom are in the Modena area. Dealing with small producers and handling such small quantities is a relatively unknown concept at Longbridge, where the systems and processes, both technical and financial, are geared to rather larger-scale operations – and so this was an obvious area in which MG X80 Italy could excel.

In the midst of all this work there was another piece of what might be categorized as 'Peter Stevens theatre', when Peter Robinson, European correspondent of *Autocar* magazine, published an account of riding shotgun with Giordano Casarini. Casarini had taken 'XP3' down to Modena, as much to show the car off to the MG X80 Italy staff and the sports car community of Modena as to exhibit it at the

Autocar's European correspondent Peter Robinson rode shotgun alongside Giordano Casarini on a memorable trip that saw XP3 visit Ferrari and arrive for display at the Bologna motor show. (*Autocar*)

ABOVE: En route to a rendezvous at Maranello, this is XP3 at a fuel stop. (Peter Stevens)

BELOW: The Ferrari workforce express curious interest in the interloper parked outside Ferrari's famous 'Cavallino' restaurant, next to the factory at Maranello. (Peter Stevens)

The end of an exciting day in the Italian Alps for XP3. (*Autocar*)

Bologna Motor Show. In the article, Robinson wrote of an enjoyable day spent with the mischievous Stevens and Casarini, who in between driving XP3 at ten-tenths round the hill surrounding Maranello, lunched with Robinson at 'Cavallino' – the Ferrari restaurant – with XP3 parked provocatively outside. It was supremely clever product placement, both in the magazine and on the streets of Maranello.

In addition to local supply liaison, a number of other issues had to be dealt with by the Italian office, a consequence of components being used in new ways, or in a market context not originally anticipated by their originating supplier. An example of this was the use of lead-based materials in the clutch linings of the Ford powertrain, a practice that is permitted for cars manufactured and sold in the United States, but not for those within the EEC. Various other issues have also transpired to make the role of MG X80's Modena office vital – such as the need for the (British) Department for Transport's 'Vehicle Certification Agency' (VCA) to inspect and check the various facilities, a process for which they allocated eight days – two days each in Modena and Torino, and four back in the UK.

HANDLING AND PERFORMANCE DEVELOPMENT

Some of the development work on the MG XPower SV was carried out by Steve Randle and his team at Randle Engineering Solutions, a sub-contractor Ian Moreton had used before on the Subaru P1, and whose impressive curriculum vitae also lists the McLaren F1. Steve Randle and his team use their own specially developed software to simulate the way a car will behave, and their work proved invaluable in helping to refine many of the basic parameters of the SV suspension system. In later stages, much of the work was continued by MG Rover's in-house chassis development team, but further aspects as yet unexplored of Randle's work will still prove useful as the motor sports' version of the SV comes to fruition.

Like a number of those at MG Rover involved with X80, chassis engineer Wayne Nation was involved with the first generation of the project before moving on to other things; but then he came full circle back to the definitive MG XPower SV at a later stage. The photos show a metallic blue Qvale Mangusta that is more special than its exterior might lead us to believe; this car was the culmination of the earlier work by Nation and his colleagues, led by Andy Kitson. As Nation explains:

Anderson & Ryan

Canley-based Anderson & Ryan is a specialist supplier of high-quality interior trim – both low-volume and entirely bespoke – and the company is proud to acknowledge some international celebrity and royal customers amongst its clientèle. Dave Anderson and Kevin Ryan, both former Jaguar apprentices, left the firm in 1982 and set up their own company. According to Anderson:

We realized we had gone as high as we could within Jaguar, as it then was. We bought a second-hand sewing machine for £200, and set ourselves up in business. We wanted to work on fresh cars and not just classic restorations, but we had to work our way into this sector without the benefit of having anything to show. Then we got lucky and got some truck work – and we've never looked back after that!

The company has certainly gone from strength to strength: for instance, the number of staff has recently doubled in the space of five years, and now there are forty employees working mainly in its design and manufacturing facility on Coventry Business Park. As well as the one-off commissions, Anderson & Ryan has a healthy business supplying luxury car manufacturers – their old employer Jaguar, for example, taking Jaguar XK8, X-type R seat covers.

Keith Collins of Anderson & Ryan, working on parts for the MG XPower SV. Here, Keith is primarily doing 'pre-trim' work, gluing on the foam to prepare for the leather, and trimming it to the correct shape. (Craig Anderson)

Roy Marston finishing off the leather trim. (Craig Anderson)

We started working on the Mangusta, and this car [the blue Mangusta] represents the developments that we came up with whilst progressing the project towards the older X80 concept – a GT car, if you like. Since then, of course, the targets for the project have changed considerably, and the car became much more 'extreme' than was originally planned.

At the time I spoke to Nation he was deeply involved in the final proving stages of the SV, and was using the much-used XP2 prototype with the blue Mangusta as a yardstick while various suspension and aerodynamic tweaks were being explored. For the test session at Bruntingthorpe, Leicestershire, I witnessed that the rear tyre size had been changed on XP2; the tyre profile was greater, and therefore gave the tyre a larger overall diameter. As he explained:

The rear rim width has also been increased, because when you have a bigger side wall, you need to give it greater stability, and the way to do that is to widen the rim to increase the stiffness [of the tyre]. It has led to some changes in the handling balance of the car, so neither the Mangusta nor the XP2 handle the snow the same now – as a matter of fact, XP2 now has rather more grip. The project team wants to try it, so we're working with it, but we must adjust the car accordingly so that it works properly with that tyre size. We can get the handling balance at low speeds: say, if you drive it around at 50–60mph [80–100km/h], the car will handle nicely.

Higher speeds pose their own issues, of course, because aerodynamic forces become more obvious. With the current aerodynamic set-up on the car, at higher speeds it is more critical and less forgiving, let's say. We can improve that with adjustments to the aerodynamics, which we're reasonably comfortable we can do, but if we can't do it with the aerodynamics alone, we will maybe have to make adjustments to the chassis; but what that tends to do is to make the car less 'involving' to drive – it's a bit of a trade-off, one way or the other. The right answer is to get the aerodynamics correct and the chassis set up right so that they work properly together – and so that's what we've been trying to do.

One of Nation's colleagues is Alun Isaac, who on the SV was engaged at looking at the operation of the power-steering system. Whereas at one time the idea of power steering in a sports car might have been frowned upon, nowadays it is essential when cars have to be versatile enough to be driven by many types of driver, of varying strength and competence, and in particular when such large tyre contact patches are involved. 'A lot of Alun's work is trying to assess the "catch-up" performance – whether the tug from the power assistance in the hydraulic system will actually

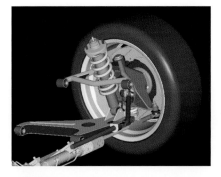

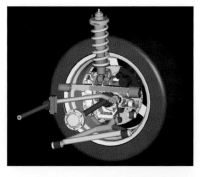

FAR LEFT: Randle Engineering Solutions produced this false coloured image showing the proposed front suspension. (Randle Engineering Solutions)

LEFT: This is the equivalent rear suspension. (Randle Engineering Solutions)

BELOW: Wayne Nation is one of the small MG Rover chassis team who were tasked with developing the SV chassis. (Author)

assist you at very high steering angle velocities, because having a big capacity tug costs you a lot in terms of power and fuel consumption,' Nation explains.

The testing carried out at Bruntingthorpe tied into wind-tunnel testing at the MIRA facility, and feedback from Nation and his colleagues was used by Peter Stevens, Giordano Casarini and Nation's colleague Andy Kitson to model various configurations in the wind tunnel. For both the wind tunnel and the circuit, some of the aerodynamic modifications could be trialled by the time-honoured method of lumps of foam and gaffer tape, the crude spoiler seen in some of the photos being dubbed a 'toblerone' by the MG team for obvious reasons. 'All it has to do is to give the car the aerodynamic values that we're looking for. It doesn't have to be styled at this stage,' Nation explains. 'But what we can do is to take the car into the wind tunnel, measure it and take off all the horrible bits of plastic, and then Peter Stevens can use the information to help develop a really nice wing or spoiler.'

One of the options that Nation looked at during the Bruntingthorpe session was the effect of a much larger rear spoiler, for as he explains:

We had a condition where the back of the car was lifting through aerodynamic lift – in other words, you go faster, and the car starts to rise and loses grip. And of course if you ask the car to generate side-force, that side-force doesn't diminish just because there is aerodynamic lift – you've still got your 400kg on the rear axle, and you've got to generate that side-force even though the aerodynamics have taken some of the contact pressure away! So we had to contend with this, and the options are usually very limited, really – it's rather like putting the back wheels of the car on a less sticky surface. [The basic MG XPower SV does not have a rear spoiler as standard, but as Nation points out, it is highly likely that many customers will want one:] If the SV-R version has this great big wing like XP3, even if we developed it with a less extreme wing, you can well imagine that the customer will go into the showroom and say, 'I want the big wing on the back!' I'm sure a lot of customers will do that!

Alongside the 'XP2' prototype, Andy Kitson's team – including Wayne Nation and his colleagues – also had the use of this blue Qvale Mangusta that had previously been used within the original X80 programme. (Author)

LEFT: Wayne Nation (centre) supervises the temporary attachment of a foam 'spoiler' to allow on-track testing of its aerodynamic impact on handling. (Author)

BELOW: The matt grey finish of XP2 lends the car a certain 'stealth' look. (Author)

BELOW: MG Rover chassis fitter Ramin Tolouie changes the dampers on XP2 during a test session at Bruntingthorpe. (Author)

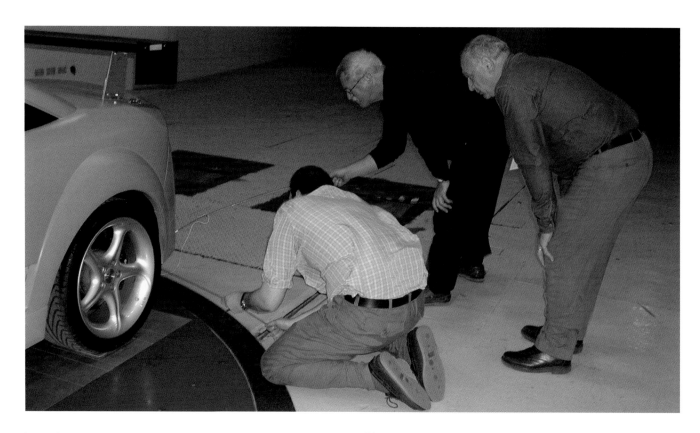

Peter Stevens (centre) and Giordano Casarini (right) in the wind-tunnel at MIRA with XP1. (Ted Higgins)

Wool tufts on slim metal poles allow the air flow to be examined inside the windtunnel at MIRA. (Ted Higgins)

Nation and his colleagues are experts at getting the right compromise for the type of car they are dealing with – and as he explains, one day this could be the SV, and the next it might be a small Rover. Some things are common to all these exercises, however, and that is safe handling:

> Imagine that you're going down a high-speed road and do nothing with regard to steering input – with your hands off the steering wheel – and the car goes along smoothly. But we then look at what happens to the car if you make a small steering input – does the car respond very quickly or is it rather slow? And what's more, is it something the driver is comfortable with – and also is the response that you get from the car delivered in a linear fashion or not? If you put a small input to the steering you should get a small reaction from the car that's nice – and that's okay – but if you put a bit more in, you want a bit more response, but that needs to be a consistent and linear response so that as a driver you can understand the car – so that all the time, the driver doesn't have to 'think' – the reaction should be linear and even throughout the range, but it must also be even from straight ahead to an angle.

Achieving this needs balance, not only in the obvious place, at the front of the car, but also at the rear:

> What is commonly misunderstood is that people think that the steering of the car is only an issue affected by the front of the car. But that's far from the truth. In

reality, the way that the car responds to steering input is massively influenced by what's happening at the back of the car – by which I mean the compliance in the bushes.

[Nation makes his point by comparing two broadly similar cars, the Rover 75 and MG ZT:] ...We did the suspension set-ups on all those variants. The Rover 75 has a sub-frame that is rubber-mounted to the body, and the lateral stiffness of the bushes is such that the back of the body can move laterally. These bushes are very stiff but nevertheless there is some movement – you wouldn't see more than 1.5mm of lateral displacement. When the customer drives the car, he is unlikely to be able to detect this movement. On the MG [ZT] however, we took out the rubber bushes and put aluminium spacers in there instead, and the result was a massive difference to the steering precision. If you drive an MG ZT alongside a Rover 75 you can certainly notice the difference. The whole thing – and it isn't just about this car – is to get a compromise between a whole host of details that affect the way the car rides and drives. It is just a case of getting the compromise of these things right. And of course, what would be an appropriate compromise for the SV is different to, say, that for the MG ZT. We have to try to determine what the customer would want.

All in all, Nation has been an enthusiastic supporter of the MG SV; he believes that as a halo car it is a great ambassador for MG Rover: 'There's a tremendous sense of optimism in the company, and I think that the people who surround these projects help that.'

Testing culminated with a five-day session in Germany during May 2003, during which the team, led by Andy Kitson, were able to measure their car against a Boxster 'S' generously loaned for the purpose by Porsche. Kitson told me that on the second day, the team moved to a track near Stuttgart: 'It had a massive 300m steering pad – much bigger than anything available in the UK. That allowed us, for example, to enter the pad at 120mph [200km/h] and carry out turn in, lift off, throttle on, gentle braking, firm braking and emergency braking, confident that there was plenty of safety margin!'

Kitson and his colleagues wanted to check the high speed braking and handling balance, and there was obviously rather more room for this than at Bruntingthorpe. 'There was also a very flat and even surface – in other words a homogeneous surface to allow consistent testing -- and this allowed us, for example, to be sure that the vehicle response to an ABS event was OK. It is obviously useful to be able to test the car on less-than-perfect surfaces too – such as at Bruntingthorpe – but a smooth surface is better for calibration.'

The Porsche Boxster 'S' that Kitson used as a reference car had a switchable dynamic control system,

Peter Stevens looks thoughtful, while behind him Andy Kitson looks on, during a testing session at MIRA. (Michael Whitestone)

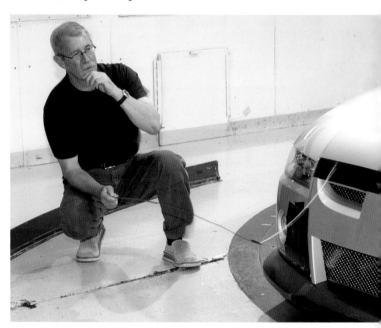

Peter Stevens examines the air flow around the nose of the first production specification MG XPower SV at MIRA. (Michael Whitestone)

something the SV does not boast (although it does have a traction aid system), so Kitson maintains that the German car was an excellent comparison tool. 'We found that on flat surfaces you have to be very aggressive with the SV to get oversteer – there was a very high level of grip from the rear.' The next couple of days were spent up at the Nürburgring and the local autobahns. 'With the changes we'd made, we found that the car was very stable up to the maximum speed that we were able to test – 160mph [250km/h]. The car was very constant in terms of handling behaviour throughout the whole speed range, and we're extremely pleased with it. We checked lane change manoeuvres, the effects of crosswinds and road irregularities, and we found the car really stable.'

ABOVE: Here XP2 emerges from the garage at the hotel near the Nürburgring. (Andy Kitson)

BELOW: A travel-worn XP2 after a session at the Nürburgring. (Andy Kitson)

Kitson and his team spent a couple of enjoyable evenings at the Nürburgring – the circuit is only open to 'the public' in the evenings, as a few weeks of the year are allocated to the 'Industry Pool', a group of motor manufacturers. Rover Group used to be part of this with BMW, but MG Rover has not continued the arrangement. In Kitson's words: 'Fundamentally we found that the X80 [SV] has a better elasto-kinematic performance than the Porsche – the "kinematics" describing the geometry adopted by the wheels as they move through the range of suspension travel, whilst the "elasto" adds the effects of compliance from pivot bushes and mounting stiffnesses.'

In the case of the mid-/rear-engined Boxster 'S', Porsche has necessarily engineered the car to deal with the weight distribution, whereas on the front-/mid-engined Mangusta, and of course the SV, the basic kinematic performance is good. 'At any speed, we found that yaw was constant, and the car needed few adjustments through bends – we felt we could carry more speed into a bend than in the Porsche.'

Kitson reports that they developed enormous respect for the Porsche, but in certain circumstances, and especially on damp roads and at sustained high speeds in excess of 150mph (240km/h), the SV often proved the better drive:

> The SV was very constant in terms of handling behaviour throughout the whole speed range, and we're extremely pleased with it. We checked lane-change manoeuvres, the effects of crosswinds and road irregularities, and we found the car really stable. Braking at 150mph [240km/h] on the Autobahn in the X80 was confidence-inspiring with a good pedal feel, especially when check-braking to brush off speed, and that was better than the Porsche.

In fact, Kitson said that it was the first time that he or his co-driver could recall being able to discuss the performance of the car while driving it at 160mph (260km/h): 'Usually you have to concentrate too hard on other things to allow that, and this was a good measure of the confidence we had in the car.' Though even Kitson, loyal man that he is, had to concede that the Porsche had some plus points: 'It has a nicer gear change and clutch – but we were not disappointed with our car!'

During the various circuit and autobahn road tests, a number of aerodynamic 'tweaks' had been tried, the engineers reporting back on the relative merits of different spoiler configurations, and the addition or subtraction of various aerodynamic aids. By early June, the MG X80 team were ready to take the car back to MIRA for what was intended to be the final session –

largely a case of validation, but an opportunity to make final minor adjustments to squeeze the absolute best out of the car. Peter Stevens announced after that session (where the wind-tunnel photos seen here were taken) that he was well pleased with the outcome: 'We think we have now got the balance about right,' he told me afterwards.

Andy Kitson, too, was well satisfied, and highlighted just one of the many minor things that perfectionism engenders: 'We found it necessary to blank off the top of the side ducts, and we also found there were some minor lift issues through the louvres in the top of the bonnet hatch; we found that a quite dense mesh had been used on the first production car, and this was proving a problem, so we've specified a more open mesh.' To give an indication of the degree of difference, the fine mesh in the bonnet louvres caused an increase in lift of 0.008. 'Admittedly this is small,' Kitson concedes, 'but attention to detail gives the best results.'

THE THOUSAND-MILE PRODUCTION LINE: BUILDING THE SV

The build process of the MG XPower SV begins – as it did with the Qvale Mangusta – with the production of the chassis structure at Vaccari & Bosi's Pievepelago factory, in the shadow of the Apennines. Here it is welded from sets of simple pressings and flat sheets of high-strength steel. It is then shipped 55 miles (90km) by road to a Vaccari & Bosi facility in Modena, where it is e-coated and painted by immersion to ensure it is fully protected against corrosion. Once this has been

The Hydratrack differential. (MG Rover)

ABOVE: One of the jigs used to assist with the fabrication of the SV Chassis at Vaccari & Bosi's Pievepelago factory. (Dave Woods)

ABOVE: The 4.6ltr all-aluminium Ford four-valve per cylinder used for the MG XPower SV. (Author)

LEFT: The Vaccari & Bosi facility at Modena, with the first running chassis at the end of the line. (Peter Stevens)

RIGHT: The rolling chassis built at Modena is capable of running under its own power. (Author)

BELOW: Overhead view of the Vaccari & Bosi unit that assembles bare chassis – delivered from the company's separate chassis facility – into running chassis before shipping to OPAC for body assembly. (Peter Stevens)

completed, the painted chassis is moved a short distance across Modena to another of the versatile Mr Bosi's units.

This facility combines a series of storage isles with four assembly 'stations', at each of which the SV moves one step closer to life. At Station One the bare chassis is kitted out with key items that will be concealed when other parts are mounted over them, obvious examples being the custom-made wiring loom and 'NVH' acoustic sound fabric. At the next station, the Sean Hyland-supplied Ford V8 unit, complete with transmission, is fitted into the chassis; also the suspension – using wishbones fabricated in a facility next door, which also makes suspension parts for Ferrari and Maserati – is installed at the front and rear. At Station Three the exhaust manifold and system are married up to the engine; and at Station Four, the radiator and associated plumbing are installed, and the various systems vacuum-purged before being carefully filled with precisely metered amounts of their requisite fluids.

By this stage, the running chassis can be started and moved under its own power; however, the penultimate stage before final inspection and despatch is to check and set the wheel alignment. Once everything has been checked and deemed satisfactory, the SV rolling chassis are shipped to Torino (Turin), the next call on their journey.

The Carbon-Fibre Process for the SV

SP Carbon Fibre

SP is one of the world's leading specialists in carbon-fibre materials and composite technology; its presence just off the south coast of England, in the Isle of Wight, comes from the boating connection, because one of the early drivers for light weight and great strength has been the top end of the racing boat construction business. Another growth area demanding both strength and low inertia, is the wind-energy business, and here SP has developed its expertise in the specialized field of wind-turbine blade technology.

Until now, automotive applications for carbon fibre have tended to be confined to the top end of motorsport, or for high-priced exotics such as the McLaren F1. The trouble is that not only is the material expensive to produce, store and handle, it requires time-consuming and consequently expensive hand-laying and baking in special pressurized ovens known

One of the early production cars poses outside the impressive SP headquarters on the Isle of Wight. (SP)

SP made its name in the high-tech marine sports and wind-turbine business. (SP)

as autoclaves, which not only 'bake' the resin but also ensure that trapped air is expelled. Carbon fibre has become gradually less exotic, however, but it is still unusual for it to be used anywhere other than in extremely low-volume applications; steel, aluminium and other less exotic composites remain the normal material of choice for production of anything more than a handful of cars. As Martin Starkey, automotive projects manager at SP told *The Engineer* magazine: 'For mass-producing 20,000 cars, using metals such as steel and aluminium is still likely to be the cheapest option; but if you are producing from five up to around 2,000, carbon fibre could be the answer.'

Starkey claims to have dramatically cut the cost of a carbon body shell from £40,000 to around £10,000, a remarkable reduction of 75 per cent. Clearly thinking of the MG XPower SV, which demonstrates his point, Starkey is keen to stress that £75,000 carbon-fibre cars are now realistic. The secret ingredient in SP's formula is the new type of material they have developed. The composite material typically used by luxury car makers is so-called 'pre-preg', which as the name implies, comprises separate layers of pre-impregnated carbon fibre and glue film surrounding a honeycomb core. Traditional pre-preg has the desired properties of strength and light weight – but it remains extremely costly. In order to tackle the costs issue – and significantly to expand sales potential – SP has developed a dry, porous, 'breathable' material, in which the fibre is separate from the resin: 'You can extract the air very easily, and you no longer need expensive autoclaving, you can simply set out the layers and have a single cure at the end,' Starkey

explains. The resultant carbon-fibre component weighs 20 per cent that of a steel equivalent, and 35 per cent that of aluminium, for the equivalent stiffness.

A further problem with conventional carbon-fibre bodywork is the difficulty, and consequently the expense, of achieving a good paint finish. Not only is there the frequent problem of pinhole-size imperfections in the surface of the material – caused by air becoming trapped during the production process, leading to 'fish-eyes' in paintwork – but also movement can occur in the resin with respect to the extremely rigid carbon fibres, leading to what is called 'read-through' as the position of the fibres literally becomes visible. The previous approach to the problem for carbon-fibre road cars has been to apply thicker layers of paint to effectively conceal the problem, but SP has developed a special surface layer consisting of a fine fibre structure sandwiching a catalyzed resin film, which forms a uniform surface on curing, and can be lightly treated prior to relatively conventional painting processes.

Belco Avia

In a side road in the small sleepy town of San Pietro Mosezzo, situated in the Piemontese Province of Novara, just off the A4 Autostrada and roughly halfway from Milano to Torino, is a small, relatively unprepossessing factory that is home to a remarkably high-tech production facility. This is the home of 'Belco Avia', expert fabricators of composite carbon-fibre structures for everything from top-class racing boats to Ferrari F1 race cars. The facility is presided over by the very elegant Dr Aaron Colombo – handsome and impeccably tailored in an aristocratically Italian way, his sunglasses carefully arranged Alice-band fashion

Dr Aaron Colombo (left) discusses one of the master moulds (for the boot box) with Giordano Casarini. (Author)

On the left is the master 'female' mould, and to the right the panel cast against it. (Author)

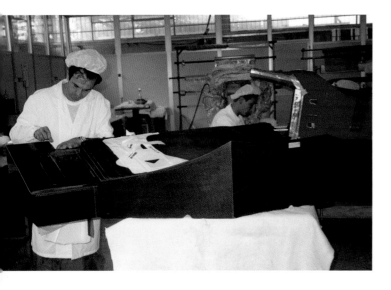

ABOVE: All the panels are 'cooked' in special autoclaves like this one at Belco Avia. (Author)

ABOVE: MG X80 production manager Ian Moreton (left) discusses the lay-up instructions for the louvred side panels with chief engineer Giordano Casarini. (Author)

LEFT: All the laying-up of the carbon-fibre panels at Belco Avia – using pre-cut kits of carbon fabric supplied in cardboard 'pizza boxes' – is carried out in a clean room with carefully regulated temperature. (Author)

in his neatly coiffed greying hair. sitting on the desk of Dr Colombo's simply furnished office is a striking lifesize carbon-fibre female bust, its seductive shape remarkably similar to the figure of his pretty secretary: Dr Colombo could only be an Italian.

Belco Avia was founded in 1994 by Colombo to produce limited production runs of specialist composite parts for racing boats and automotive prototypes; on Colombo's CV are projects such as Guigaro's 'Nazca' concept car. Inside the buildings at San Pietro Mosezzo there are clinically clean NASA-style temperature-controlled areas, maintained at 22°C, where skilled operatives under the watchful eye of checker Filippo Spalla assemble the various parts for the MG XPower SV, using the 'pizza boxes' of carbon fibre shipped in from SP Systems. Freezers keep the material at −18°C until it is ready for use. Two large autoclaves are used to 'bake' the carbon-fibre components at 120°C under pressure. Experience by Dr Colombo has shown that the pressure he uses is just enough to 'squeeze' the material into the corners of the moulds, but at the same time not enough to cause pressure damage to the surface.

Belco Avia makes all the 'greenhouse' of the SV – the roof inner, roof outer, boot-box, side and front quarters – and the company has also made some of the moulds they use, also carbon-fibre, typical examples being the louvred front fender panels and the boot box. Once completed and trimmed, the finished panels are then ready for despatch to their next port of call – OPAC of Torino (Turin).

ABOVE: The staff of MG X80 flanking Giordano Casarini and Ian Moreton (third and fourth from left respectively). (Phil Barnes)

BELOW: MG X80 Italy is based in these impressive headquarters on the outskirts of Modena. (Author)

OPAC Torino

Founded in 1986, the OPAC Group – with facilities in Turin and Milan – caters for a diverse range of products in the automotive, rail and nautical sectors. The latter field includes the production of cost-is-no-obstacle tailor-made equipment for some of the world's most luxurious and exclusive (up to £12m) yachts: mechanical gang-planks, sliding cabin tops, automatic doors and stainless steel cranes for tenders are among the fabulous toys that Angello Sacco and his staff create on a regular basis.

Of more particular interest to us here, however, is the company's impressive track record in the field of low-volume car production: OPAC has built the bodies for many cars, including the Maserati Biturbo, Alfa Romeo SZ, Bentley Azure, Bentley Continental, Aston Martin, Zagato design, Lamborghini Gallardo and even the Ford StreetKa among them. In addition, Pininfarina subcontracts OPAC for the manufacture of roof structures for the MG TF.

OPAC is equipped to take on every stage from feasibility to series production, and while the traditional skills remain important, Sacco and his general manager Giancarlo Grinza are justifiably proud of their advanced design and CAD drawing facilities, their metal-forming shops with numeric control millers, and, most remarkable of all, the plasma and hydro-abrasive cutting equipment, the latter able to slice through steel more than 100mm thick using water at working pressures of 4,000 bar – and sophisticated mini-robots that can be seen applying beads of glue to panel seams with unnerving, lifelike precision.

When it came to the MG XPower SV, OPAC was contracted to build the body-in-white (or 'body-in-black' as carbon-fibre bodies tend to be known); but before that, they became involved with the design not only of the assembly jigs but also

L–R: Giordano Casarini, OPAC general manager Giancarlo Grinza, and OPAC managing director Angello Sacco discuss the fine points of the SV production facility at Torino (Turin). (Author)

A 'CAD' image showing the body, roof and 'boot-box' assemblies. (OPAC)

This computer-generated image shows the integral FIA standard roll cage fitted over the inner roof structure. (OPAC)

ABOVE: One of the early production specification MG XPower SV cars sits in one of the jigs at OPAC's factory in Turin. (Author)

RIGHT: Similar to the previous view, this one shows the roof outer skin installed. A series of images like this serve as a useful tool to aid in the design and control of production. (OPAC)

OPAC Torino

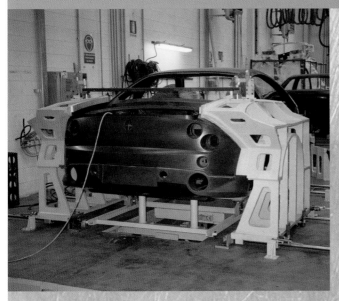

In this view, symmetrical specially cast and machined aluminium jigs hold the carbon-fibre panels with extreme precision during gluing. (Author)

ABOVE: The integral steel FIA specification roll cage is sandwiched between the inner roof skin (see in this shot) and the outer skin (which is to be added once the adhesives have set). (Author)

RIGHT: One of the OPAC technicians installs the hinges to allow the separately built doors to be assembled on to the bodywork. (Author)

The roof assembly has been married to the main tub as the bodywork takes shape at OPAC. (Author)

The SV bodyshell is nearing completion. (Author)

were able to advise on some aspects of the actual panel design work being carried out in the UK by CARAN Design. As Giordano Casarini explains, the kind of experience that OPAC has is invaluable:

Many changes have been introduced as a direct benefit of Angelo Sacco's expertise and experience – many fixing issues were not immediately apparent on the drawings at the design stage. For example, there was a potential problem with the boot outer skin distorting as the glue sets when it is bonded to the inner; from his experience, Mr Sacco suggested changes to the trimming process so that more material was left around part of the perimeter of the boot outer until assembly, after which it could be trimmed.

XK Engineering

Like several of the other Midlands-based specialists involved with the MG XPower SV, XK Engineering of Shilton, near Coventry, counts the Jaguar marque as high on its list of business importance. However, unlike most of the others, XK's interest in Jaguar affairs largely revolves around the classic Jaguar scene, stemming from the foundation of the company in 1981 expressly for the purpose of specializing in top-grade Jaguar restoration work. That business expanded to take in the production and worldwide sales of parts for classic Jaguars, which remains an important outlet, but at the same time XK Engineering's workshops and skilled staff have expanded into the area of prototype building and low-volume specialist vehicle finishing – in particular some highly specialized paint spraying – having, in their words, 'painted some of the most challenging substrates known...'.

ABOVE: *The third production-specification car (car #103) – finished in XPower Grey – is readied at XK Engineering for its debut outing to the Goodwood Festival of Speed. (Author)*

BELOW: *The smart 'Bloomberry' interior of the third SV at XK Engineering. (Author)*

To OPAC in Torino

The rolling chassis produced at Vaccari & Bosi's Modena facility is an impressive thing to see, but the MG XPower SV is still only a fraction of the way through its journey. From Modena, the rolling chassis are taken by lorry, by logistics company SAIMA-Avandero, down the Autostrada to Torino where they are received by OPAC. Here they are brought into a compact dedicated facility, specially set aside for MG XPower SV production. The facility is split into five production areas, and also has a testing rig with a measuring plate and five-axis automated test-machine, which measures some 600 reference points on each body/chassis assembly prior to shipment. The OPAC facility sees the various carbon-fibre components – sourced variously from Belco Avia or DPS Composites – sequentially fitted on to the rolling chassis, using specially engineered jigs that have been precisely machined using the CATIA data supplied by CARAN Design. Because of the precise nature of the CATIA data, and the equal precision of carbon fibre as a material, it was possible for OPAC to machine these jigs accurately even before the first body panel tooling was ready.

In front of the main facility is an area where sub-assemblies such as the doors, boot-lid and bonnet are prepared. On the opposite corner of the unit, 'Station One' sees the chassis fitted into its jig while the roof structure is installed in three basic operations. The roof inner skin is clamped in place, then the FIA specification roll-cage is glued within it and the adhesive allowed to set for about four hours. Then the roof outer is glued and clamped over while it cures. An overhead chain then transfers the whole roof structure to the second station, to be mated with the chassis structure. At this stage, the carbon-fibre boot box is also added. The chassis with roof and boot-box installed is then moved to the next station where the wings and door hinges are added, while the final stage sees the doors, rear bumper and remaining components installed. The whole process typically takes eight hours per car – much of that time taken up by the various inter-process curing periods.

Finishing and Trimming

For customer production cars, the MG XPower SV is finished within the dedicated MG 'Sport & Racing' facility at Longbridge, but as this new unit was being established, MG Rover worked with more specialist outside suppliers who were experienced in the special finishing and trimming work associated with low-volume cars – in particular the specialized process of painting carbon fibre. Ian Moreton reserved the special show-car work for QCR Motors, who had done such a superb job on XP3, but for the first 'production specification' cars – using carbon-fibre panels and built on the line at Vaccari & Bosi and OPAC – he chose XK Engineering of Shilton, near Coventry.

Dave Woods and his team at XK are used to working on low-volume commissions as well as one-offs, and with their experience in the peccadilloes of composite car bodywork, they were ideally suited to tackle painting of the early production-proving cars.

XP3 parked outside the X80 Italy offices. (Peter Stevens)

chapter nine

Into Production

THE FIRST PRODUCTION SPECIFICATION CAR

Although XP3 – and, in due course, XP4 – were both used as demonstration vehicles, neither was truly representative of the SV in dynamic terms. The next step in the evolution of the SV was therefore the production of the first true pre-production prototypes, using as many 'off-tools' parts as possible, not only to 'prove' the production process, but to facilitate the final stages of testing using genuine SV cars with the correct chassis and carbon-fibre bodywork. In many ways this was a much more difficult process than the creation of the earlier 'XP' cars, for it necessitated not only the completion of several aspects of the design (including the interior trim), but also the proper co-ordination of supply routes and material specifications between the many sub-contractors.

When XP3 appeared at the NEC in October 2002, Peter Stevens had promised that car number one would be ready by the first day of May the following year – and he was determined to hold to that date

because it was important not only to show that the small team he headed could deliver, but also to provide some positive news for MG Rover as a whole, since the euphoria that had surrounded the launch of the Rover-derived MG saloons was beginning to fade. By early 2003, Ian Moreton and Giordano Casarini were both in the midst of a whirlwind of commuting back and forth across Europe, with occasional forays to North America to see Sean Hyland or Rousch; at one point the two were almost running a relay race, passing the metaphorical baton to one another at Stanstead airport as each travelled in opposite directions to or from Italy.

In the middle of March the first production specification SV running chassis emerged from Vaccari & Bosi's Modena factory, before it was shipped to OPAC to have some of the DPS carbon-fibre panels fitted. Problems with a mould that had been damaged by the vacuum suction caused by releasing the first panel meant that there had to be repairs before more panels could be produced; but fortunately this did not hold up the crucial first car, dubbed '101'. Just before

The first two production specification cars – chassis numbers '101' and '102' – and both finished in Starlight Silver – were finished to perfection by XK Engineering. They are seen here in April 2002, days before '101' was driven to Longbridge on 1 May. (Author)

ABOVE: XK Engineering is used to high-quality low-volume work, as well as one-off prototypes and classic restoration works. (Author)

BELOW: The cockpit of car '101' in the process of being fitted out at XK Engineering. (Author)

specimen was delayed slightly to allow it to be exhibited in a partially painted state on the SP Systems stand at the important 'JE' show in Paris during April 2003. Although they were known as '101' and '102', these cars were in fact chassis 006 and 007: 'previous numbers have been used for post-tests and other purposes' Moreton explains; stressing, however, that car '101' is the definitive 'first production car'.

By the end of the first week of April, '101' was at XK Engineering, with Anderson & Ryan personnel on site to install the interior trim, while work continued on the second car and was due to start on the third; thus from a necessarily slow start, the pace was gradually building up: 'I had to get some of the people at our contractors back up to speed very rapidly – after all, they'd been almost dormant for quite some time. A few of the normally immaculate Italians had a few hairs out of place as a consequence!' Moreton laughs. Further fine-tuning at this stage saw minor changes to some of the bracketry, and a mission to OPAC to resolve a problem with the gluing process that had led to stretching of the skin – a problem soon solved with the expert advice of OPAC's Angelo Sacco.

In mid-April there were discussions with Belco Avia, who were at that point being tasked with taking on more of the carbon-fibre panel production; while back in the UK the team at XK Engineering was working hard to ensure that '101' would be ready for its 1 May date at Longbridge: trimmers, electricians and other technicians were busily fitting, fettling and feeding back into the design process as they went, while a small number of MG Rover personnel were also becoming involved as part of the planned 'technology transfer' intended to facilitate the eventual move to Longbridge. The last few days of April saw much burning of the proverbial midnight oil: on Wednesday 30 April the team at XK worked right round the clock into Thursday morning to make sure that everything was as near perfect as possible. Ian Moreton flew back from Italy on the Wednesday and went straight to XK's premises at Shilton where the final touches were being put to the first car; he was there until four in the morning before the car was considered ready to meet its critics and admirers. It was a very tired team that eventually loaded SV '101' into a covered trailer for transfer to a discreet corner of the car park at Hopwood Services just off the M42 at the crack of dawn…

Giordano Casarini and Ian Moreton brought '101' to Longbridge and met a very relieved Peter Stevens: the three men had delivered on their promise, and for Moreton it was a significant day for other reasons – it was exactly a year to the day since he had joined the project. Pulling up outside MG Rover's headquarters building, the team was met by Kevin Howe, Nick Stephenson and John Edwards, each of whom took turns in the car. Before long there was a crowd three

At this stage, only the roof panel of car '102' has been painted – note the carbon weave visible on the door shut and roof pillar. (Author)

the end of the month, '101' arrived at QCR Motors for painting in 'Starlight Silver' (a 'good engineering colour' claims Ian Moreton).

Moreton is full of praise for the team from the paint specialists, Dupont: 'They have been very good all the way through – they are very professional, and are top class on checking things such as the correct temperatures, and critical application criteria such as paint thicknesses.' By this point, Longbridge's own paint team were becoming involved, the intention being to learn the new processes in order to allow final assembly to move in due course to a new dedicated facility at Longbridge; for people used to dealing with steel bodywork and machine-sanding, the specialized and more labour-intensive processes peculiar to composite bodywork were a new experience.

As car '101' was being finished, a second silver car also began to take shape – although production of this

The XPower Grey car – chassis '103' – was used for some action photography at Silverstone. (MG Rover)

deep around '101', and the mood at Longbridge, on that morning at least, was one of heady optimism. When the car was signed off on 17 January 2003, Stevens and his team were asked when the board would see the first production car. 'I'd promised that we would have car number one on 1 May at 1pm – and we delivered,' Stevens told me shortly after the presentation took place, adding: 'Nick Stephenson also gave us his order – his car will be XPower Trophy Blue': this is the car that was specially photographed for this book on Salisbury Plain.

Moreton explains that the choice of colours for the first cars was a mix of good 'engineering' colours, in particular the first two in Starlight Silver, while the third was XPower Grey...

...Then there's a dark metallic red that we've provisionally called 'Razzy Red', as well as a 'Monogram', 'Sunspot Yellow', and there's one in British Racing Green, one in Pearl Black and three different blues – one like a royal blue. We can try different trim combinations with those. The black car will have a tan interior, the red ones the red interior. I feel the dark blue leather and the silver look nice together, in the same way that the dark blue roofs go well on the silver MG TFs. Of course, we can do whatever the customer wants in the end, but we've not chosen too outrageous combinations at the moment. The ivory interior even looks a little like a traditional Jaguar XK8 interior.

MOVING TOWARDS SERIES PRODUCTION

Successfully meeting the 1 May deadline was a magnificent achievement, but of course in context it was just another milestone on the project plan; neither Moreton nor Casarini could afford much time for pause, as the first production cars were beginning to follow along behind '101'. Car '102' was eventually finished following its visit to the show in Paris, while car '103' was made ready for display at the Goodwood Festival of Speed on 12 and 13 July 2003, immediately after which it would be air-freighted from Heathrow to Rousch in Michigan for emissions-testing and certification work.

ABOVE: The rear bootlid spoiler is standard to the SV-R, but optional on the SV seen here. (Julian Mackie)

LEFT: The side gills – which seem likely to become a new MG hallmark – are fully functional. (Julian Mackie)

ABOVE: The rear edge of the doors are neatly scalloped to feed air into a subtle vent to improve braking efficiency. (Julian Mackie)

RIGHT: The 4.6ltr Ford Mustang specification V8 of the MG XPower SV. (Julian Mackie)

BELOW: This particular MG XPower SV, photographed on the Salisbury Plain especially for this book, had only been delivered the previous day to its new owner, Phoenix Venture Holdings deputy chairman Nick Stephenson. (Julian Mackie)

ABOVE: On the move, the MG XPower SV has a really powerful presence. (Julian Mackie)

LEFT: The boot spoiler is fully functional and honed in the MIRA wind tunnel. (Julian Mackie)

BELOW: The exhaust-pipe tips poke neatly through the lower valance – a typically thoughtful piece of Peter Stevens' attention to detail. (Julian Mackie)

ABOVE: The bonnet surface also features practical 'gills'. (Julian Mackie)

BELOW: The SV is low, squat and ground-hugging. (Julian Mackie)

BELOW: Powerful Brembo brakes are used to haul the SV back from speed. (Julian Mackie)

Sean Hyland

A Canadian and former pro-rally and Firehawk protagonist, Sean Hyland began his highly regarded business building top-class performance engines in 1988, when he founded Sean Hyland Motorsport (SHM) at Langton, Ontario. SHM initially concentrated on race-car and street-car preparation and parts sales for a growing and loyal clientèle. In 1995, SHM launched their own line of components for the new Ford 4.6ltr aluminium V8 used in the Mustang GT and Cobra, and over the ensuing nine years have built up a leading position in the field of Ford 4.6, 5.4, and 6.8 modular performance parts.

Hyland explains: 'Development continues here every day as we push the envelope to ever higher levels of power and durability. Everything we sell is engineered and tested in house first.' By 1999, as the business grew, SHM was ready to move to larger 15,000sq ft (1,400sq m) premises at Woodstock, Ontario, where the company is now based. The Woodstock facility houses a full machine shop, fabrication department, 'Superflow' bench and engine dyno, as well as a 'Dynojet' chassis dyno. Hyland's experience in the Ford 'modular' engine must easily rival that of the Ford Motor Company itself – to the extent that Hyland has even written his own book on extracting the best performance from the engine range.

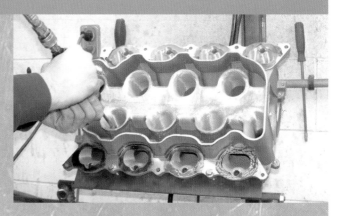

The intake manifold is ported by hand, and then 'TIG'-welded back together again. (Sean Hyland)

Sean Hyland himself concentrates on the readings of an SV engine on the dynamometer. (Sean Hyland)

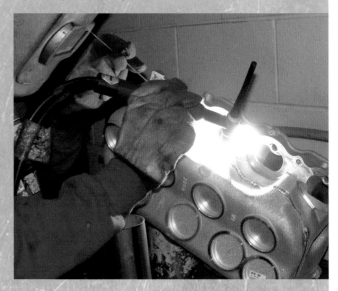

Careful 'TIG' welding to reassemble the intake manifold after porting by hand. (Sean Hyland)

Each valve seat is carefully machined. (Sean Hyland)

The head studs are being installed in this photo, which also shows the generous 94mm bore of the 4.6ltr unit. (Sean Hyland)

Each MG engine is run in on the dynamometer, tested for power and verified for cylinder leakage. (Sean Hyland)

Here, the forged steel crankshaft is being installed in the cylinder block. (Sean Hyland)

Precision timing of the camshafts is a vital aspect of the MG XPower SV-R engine. (Sean Hyland)

Meanwhile, there was some debate about the range of engine specifications that should be used – for in truth the Ford modular V8 is a versatile unit, and with the added bonus of working with a highly regarded engine builder such as Sean Hyland, MG could choose the best options dependent upon the best terms and availability. For a brief interlude, the idea of a supercharged Ford-sourced engine re-entered the fray an idea previously explored with the first-generation version of X80 – but in due course the choice settled on the 320 horsepower 4.6ltr unit for the MG XPower SV, and a 400-horsepower, 5.0ltr 'XPower' version of the all-aluminium, thirty-two-valve, four overhead camshaft V8 engine built by Sean Hyland for the MG XPower SV-R (the production version of the SV-R was formally unveiled at the 2004 Geneva Motor Show).

FIRST EXPOSURE: THE INITIAL PRESS REACTIONS

MG Rover knew that interest in the MG XPower SV was going to considerably outweigh both its direct financial importance to the company and the number of cars that would be available, but the fact that the car had been unveiled in its more or less definitive form at the 2002 NEC show meant that before long, onlookers would be expecting to hear more about the dynamics to see if they matched the looks. As we have seen, however, what the public saw – XP3 and, to some extent, XP4 – were not real MG XPower SVs. Nevertheless, as well as at the Goodwood Festival of Speed, an SV made guest appearances at the CSM/MG Owners' Club event at Brands Hatch and (slightly more obscurely) at the Max Power Show. However, what had still not happened by the end of 2003 was a proper independent assessment of the car by a motoring journalist – and, as the saying goes, the 'the natives were getting restless'.

Peter Stevens was acutely aware of this, but at the same time he and his colleagues wanted to be as sure as possible that any car they placed at the mercy of a motoring journalist was free of pre-production quirks and glitches. Whilst the SV was by now mechanically almost ready for the full production green light, some aspects – in particular the interior – were still a little way from completion. At the end of October 2003, MG Rover rather 'upped the ante' by announcing that the SV would be on sale from the beginning of November. In their press release, director of MG Sport & Racing Kim Johnson claimed: 'The MG XPower SV, which combines high reserves of power and motor-racing safety features, is a true race car that has been built for the road. It can either lead on the track, or cruise along the King's Road. It is the ultimate MG.' The price of the SV was given as £75,000, with availability 'through a network of specialist XPower

ABOVE: **The third production specification car was used for promotional photography. (MG Rover)**

dealerships, or directly from the MG Sport & Racing factory.'

To bolster the credentials of the car, MG Rover gave former F1 driver and MG Le Mans driver Mark Blundell a turn round the track in the car, and he offered his opinion: 'The MG XPower SV is aggressive and raw, and at the same time stylish and refined. I have driven many of the world's top sports cars, and this car is in the same league. From the unique sound of the exhaust to the precision steering, the MG XPower SV has all the qualities I look for in a sports car.' Everyone had a lot of respect for the view of Mark Blundell – as well as his former Le Mans team mate Anthony Reid – but in the cynical world of the journalist, the response was along the lines of 'they would say that, wouldn't they?' Around this time, Nick Stephenson was approached by Jeremy Clarkson and asked to provide an SV for Clarkson to drive around the dedicated circuit at Dunsfold used by the BBC *Top Gear* programme. The view was, that this

LEFT: **Mark Blundell has a long association with MG – he was involved in early testing of the MGF back in 1995 – and he also took part in MG's Le Mans entries in 2001 and 2002. Blundell's talents were also used to fine-tune the MG XPower SV. (MG Rover)**

LEFT: This blood-red interior trim is known as 'Bloomberry' on the options list. (MG Rover)

BELOW: Mark Blundell poses alongside MG XPower SV '003' at Silverstone. (MG Rover)

ABOVE: The interior of Nick Stephenson's MG XPower SV is bright, elegant and classy in an understated way. The light grey colour is known as 'Gunsmoke'. (Julian Mackie)

LEFT: More attention to detail, with the MG logo neatly etched into the door-tread strips. (Julian Mackie)

The SV has a five-speed gearbox as standard, but for the SV-R a six-speed is available. Automatic transmission is a third option. (Julian Mackie)

Nick Stephenson's SV has a Momo wheel. The clever seatbelt system obviates the need for a conventional steering column-mounted airbag. (Julian Mackie)

The SV dashboard successfully marries MG Rover, Ford and bespoke parts. Later cars have subtly different instruments to this early model. (Julian Mackie)

LEFT: The rear of the cockpit has been finished with the same impressive attention to detail as the rest of the interior. There are no rear seats, however: the space is intended for the occasional stowing of luggage. (Julian Mackie)

BELOW: The seat harnesses are effectively a cross between a full race harness and a conventional three-point belt. (Julian Mackie)

The Millbrook High Speed Bowl

Well before the press were jostling for their so-called 'exclusives', I was privileged to experience the production-specification MG XPower SV at first hand. The call came from Giordano Casarini, with an offer for me to ride shotgun in Kevin Howe's personal British Racing Green SV while it was subjected to some high-speed 'validation testing' by MG Rover vehicle test project engineer Paul Linnell at the high-security Millbrook facility near Bedford. The purpose of validation is to test the performance of the car in production specification, and to generate the data familiar as the 'manufacturer's figures' that line the back pages of car brochures, press material and magazine 'first impression' road tests. 'We're here to measure the maximum acceleration times – the 0–60mph and similar figures of the type that you will often see published in a magazine such as *Autocar*,' Linnell explains.

Linnell has been with the company since the early days of the MGF programme, and becomes involved in projects at various levels, and not just ones as near completion as the SV: 'In general it depends upon what stage the project is at,' he explains. 'If we're dealing with an early prototype, then obviously we help to develop the engine tune and sort the aerodynamic aids, and try to ascertain maximum speeds.' At

The MG XPower SV looks thoroughly at home at Millbrook. (Alisdair Cusick)

Kevin Howe's MG XPower SV at speed on the Millbrook Test circuit. (Alisdair Cusick)

the back of the car, Linnell fixes a lightweight (and expensive) high-tech piece of equipment that adheres to the glass-smooth paint of the SV boot with rubber-faced vacuum pads. This is a special measuring rig, similar to the type used by many of the leading car magazines. Linnell explains that the underside of the box-like section of the rig, which sits just inches above the ground, contains both a light source and a photocell: 'The beam shines down on to the tarmac and reflects back to be picked up by the sensor, and this data is used to calculate vehicle speed.' This is far more accurate and reliable than using other on-board means such as relying on the speedometer.

Linnell uses the rig for most situations, including standing starts, although it is less secure at the very high maximum speeds that can be attained on the high-speed bowl. The rig feeds through a slim cable into a lap-top computer that Linnell rests on the passenger seat, and this computer is equipped with a dedicated programme that carries out the calculations, using datastreams of speed versus time and

The Millbrook High Speed Bowl *continued*

distance. As soon as the car starts off from rest the computer starts recording, and can then monitor parameters for set pre-determined speeds to see how rapidly the car accelerates either from rest or through the gears.

Although the top speed of the SV is comfortably in excess of 160mph (260km/h), the curve and banking of the Millbrook bowl do have an effect on speeds at the upper limits. 'The neutral speed in lane 5, at the top of the Millbrook banking, is 100mph [160km], so by 150mph [240km] you're turning in quite a lot – it's a bit like turning a corner, basically,' Linnell explains. So the speed we see in the upper reaches of the SV's performance envelope will have to be 'corrected' to provide an equivalent straight-line value. Although never unrefined, this car is never quiet – that purposeful engine note is always there, reminding you of the power under the bonnet (not least that it also has plenty more to offer) – but then, that is just what you want: you would hardly expect such a potent supercar to behave like a demure princess.

Linnell eventually maxed Mr Howe's SV at 154mph (248km/h), but afterwards Giordano Casarini explained that the correction factor to be added to compensate for the cornering losses is 7mph (11km/h) – so what we have been privy to is an adjusted top speed of 161mph (259km/h). Comfortably the fastest production MG ever, then – at least for the time being.

MG XPower SV on the outer lane of Millbrook's ...wl. (Alisdair Cusick)

Although there were no official racing versions of the SV at first, the company did allow cars to be used for various Motorsport publicity purposes. (Dave Stokes)

would be a good outlet to expose the car, and it would be driven in a controlled environment, on a circuit, and so would be less likely to upset the journalists who would in due course subject production cars to the rigours of more conventional road tests.

By late November it had been decided that the car that Clarkson would be given to try would be an SV-R, with the more powerful engine, and the chosen specimen would be Peter Stevens' personal car – which was still being built. In what seemed to have become an MG X80 tradition, there was again much burning of the midnight oil, and the car was only considered ready for despatch for its appointment with *Top Gear* in the small hours of the very morning that it was due to be shipped off for still photography before the action sequences. There was some nervousness about the gearbox (well founded, as it transpired), but Peter Stevens would accompany the car on its trip for filming. Ian Moreton explains:

> The SV-R is normally supposed to be fitted with a six-speed gearbox, but they put a five-speed one in this car. The Longbridge Engineering team found that the six-speed needed a different extension, and so they had no alternative at such short notice but to fit a five-speed. They were up at XK Engineering until five in the morning fitting it [the gearbox]; I'd just come back from Italy, arriving at Birmingham at 11pm the previous evening, and then going straight there [to XK] until 3am! I was, as you can imagine, a bit worn out after that!

Top Gear magazine 'piggy backed' on the BBC TV test report by Jeremy Clarkson. Here, Clarkson speaks to camera during the circuit test of an SV-R. (*Top Gear*)

RIGHT: Clarkson sets off in the SV-R at BBC *Top Gear*'s Dunsfold test track. (*Top Gear*)

BELOW: The *Top Gear* track-testing inevitably takes its toll on the SV-R's tyres. (*Top Gear*)

ABOVE: Both Jeremy Clarkson and *Top Gear*'s resident track expert – known only as 'The Stig' – had great fun with the MG XPower SV-R at Dunsfold. (*Top Gear*)

ABOVE: Clarkson contemplates the driving position of the SV-R. (*Top Gear*)

RIGHT: Clarkson was quite a tight fit in the SV-R cockpit – in fact he bumped his head on the can't-rail during a particularly exuberant piece of cornering. (*Top Gear*)

LEFT: Jeremy Clarkson clearly enjoyed his session in the SV-R at the *Top Gear* test track. (*Top Gear*)

BELOW: Clarkson was disappointed with certain aspects of the SV-R – in particular the gear change quality – but some things, like the engine note, he thought were fantastic. (*Top Gear*)

ABOVE: The XPower Grey MG XPower SV-R as driven by Jeremy Clarkson, photographed in December 2003. (*Top Gear*)

LEFT: The striking blue cockpit of MG XPower SV-R '103', photographed for *Top Gear* magazine at the *Top Gear* test track at Dunsfold. (*Top Gear*)

LEFT: The distinctive bonnet louvres are not simply decorative: they serve to ventilate the engine bay without upsetting the car's aerodynamics. (*Top Gear*)

BELOW: Like those of the SV version, the headlamps on the MG XPower SV-R are basically the same as those from the 2002 Fiat Punto. (*Top Gear*)

BELOW: The Sean Hyland-built V8 engine in the MG XPower SV-R. (*Top Gear*)

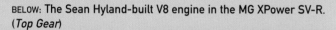

Sound Solution: HP Chemie Pelzer

When BBC TV's *Top Gear* presenter Jeremy Clarkson drove Peter Stevens' personal SV-R prototype around the Dunsfold circuit, he enthused about many aspects of the car – in particular the sound that it made. No small part of the credit for that success is due to automotive acoustic specialist 'Lab2000', a subsidiary of the German company HP Chemie Pelzer that works with supplier Automotive Installations; both operations are based at Rugby, not that far from MG Rover HQ. Rod Morris-Kirby is the acoustic development manager for Lab2000, and he and his colleagues were involved with the X80 programme from the beginning: 'In 2001, we benchmarked a Qvale Mangusta and in fact we wrote a fairly scathing report on it, together with a report on what we believed could be done. Then everything went quiet for a while…'

By the time the X80 project had been refocused as a carbon-fibre-bodied car, weight had become even more of a critical factor, and so in the summer of 2003, Morris-Kirby had a call from MG X80's Alistair Herschell, who wanted the work to be restarted – and urgently. By this time the Lab2000 team had already completed projects such as the Mercedes-McLaren SLR and HM Queen's special Bentley limousine, and

so in the case of the MG XPower SV they were able to apply the very latest technology – in Morris-Kirby's words, the SV is 'truly state-of-the-art'. Sports cars are a particular speciality of the Rugby office, and so it was ideally placed to help:

We were able to write a story of what we thought this car should sound like. The team involved had recently been involved in the acoustic development of HM Queen's Bentley state limousine, and we went down to XK Engineering to look over the prototype there. We were able to tell Giordano straightaway that we could produce an acoustic package weighing around 20kg –and that would be an instant saving of 25kg; Giordano was thrilled at that news!

[Morris-Kirby told the X80 team that the work involved would take ten weeks, starting with a detailed analysis of the car.] We use a term we have coined, which is 'Acoustic DNA', where DNA stands for 'diagnostic network algorithms'. We manipulate the character of a noise, which is why we use the term 'DNA', as we feel it is like the characteristics of life. Our aim is to bring forward the nice sounds and the important noises, but to cut back the

'Lab2002' – responsible for developing state-of-the-art sound reduction in the SV -- use the term 'Acoustic DNA', where DNA stands for 'Diagnostic Network Algorithms', to describe the noise patterns in a car. This is the MG XPower SV marked up with black tape lines to define 'noise areas' for acoustic measurement and analysis. (Rod Morris-Kirby)

This cone-shaped device is a very high-power tube noise source that was used to measure the echo time inside the cabin. (Rod Morris-Kirby)

In the midst of all this, there was more press speculation about the parent company, and the London broadsheet newspapers waded in with a story claiming that the Phoenix directors were 'feathering their own nests' and failing to act as the honest stewards of the business that they claimed to be. It was an awkward situation for some of the people involved with the MG SV, in as much as one external supplier wanted to know why it was that he had read in his local European newspaper a story that effectively suggested that the

Phoenix directors were standing at the door with suitcases full of money.

By the time that Peter Stevens and his SV-R made the journey to meet Clarkson, MG Rover was becoming uncomfortable again about certain quarters of the press. However, Clarkson at least was able to put Stevens at ease over the thrust of his piece: 'He said he was sure his audience would be far more interested in how well the SV performed than about the financial controversy in the newspapers.'

irritating and unnecessary. So, for example, we squash any gear whine, and too much noise from the rear tyres – but at the same time you do want to hear some sound from the front tyres – for example when you are cornering and the road surface slip characteristics change partway through a corner. We analyse sounds from sources such as the noise radiating from tyre treads, and follow the path those noises take through panels, and how they are in turn transmitted again from those surfaces.

The noises can also be broken down into different categories and paths. We do a sound scan of a car and we might find, for example, an imbalance between the two halves of a twin pipe exhaust system – and so the client may need to take this back to the exhaust supplier; this is an iterative process. So the objective is to end up with a good sound; we wanted to bring out the full flavour of the Mustang engine – part of our job is to maximize enjoyment.

Morris-Kirby is particularly complimentary about the way that the X80 team empowered his team in developing the optimum solution: 'The MG guys gave us a free rein to let us change things – and that was great because it really paid dividends.'

The SV marked up and ready for testing at Lab2000. The end result of the testing was to produce anti-noise material some 20kg (44lb) lighter than conventional felt. (Rod Morris-Kirby)

The programme was aired on Sunday 14 December 2003, and although Clarkson was disparaging about the gear change and some aspects of the interior, overall he liked the car – in particular the fantastic noise it made as he tore round the circuit in it. When it came to track times, the gear-change problem between second and third clearly hampered the programme's resident track expert, and the result was that the SV-R couldn't quite eclipse the Porsche GT3 that the show had tested. The disappointment of the *Top Gear* studio

audience was palpable, and flavoured Clarkson's concluding remarks about the car.

Stevens accepts many of the criticisms, but counters that MG Rover had submitted just one car (rather than two – one specially set up for the track driver and another for Clarkson, a common ploy with some manufacturers) but also the Porsche against which the SV-R was being judged was not exactly street-spec: 'The Porsche they had [on *Top Gear*] was not just like the one you can go and buy straight out of the showroom: it was specially set up – and it is so easy to get a more powerful engine – nobody seems to know this – they've got crates full of bits that they can use to make the car go quicker'.

In addition, Stevens had been at pains to point out before the test that the car was his own, and as he wanted to keep it as a pure performance car, with weight at a premium, he simply did not want 'fripperies' such as satellite navigation – the lack of which Clarkson later declared was a surprising omission in a £75,000 motor car. Another point that *Top Gear* seemed to gloss over was the fact that the SV offered something that no other car below £200,000 could boast: a full state-of-the-art carbon-fibre body.

Overall, Stevens concluded that the appearance on *Top Gear* was a good thing: 'I don't think it did us any harm. What we haven't had is any negative comment on the lateness of the project – the "it's late", "it's not appeared", "an MG that hasn't turned up when they said it would" sort of reaction. By actually letting *Top Gear* drive it, the world knows that it exists, it runs and so on – so there is a positive perception of it.' As is normal practice with Clarkson, the appearance on BBC TV *Top Gear* was followed up by articles in both the February 2004 issue of *Top Gear* magazine and in Clarkson's weekly column in *The Sunday Times*, Britain's best-selling large-format Sunday newspaper.

In his *Top Gear* magazine article, Clarkson enthused again about the sound that the SV-R engine made: 'I'm trying to find a way of conveying in words what the sound of the SV engine is like, but it's a struggle,' he began. 'I actually don't think I have got the writing skill to do it. Normal engine-type words – bellow, growl, roar – are hopeless … it's more than a sound, it's a moment.' Clarkson's report conveyed his genuine enthusiasm, as well as his disappointments – chiefly the price, which he thought at £75,000 put the SV in the heart of stiff competition. 'Fix the trim, fettle the suspension and make it good. Make it worth seventy-five grand. Inside the SV there's a great car waiting to get out.'

FINISHING AT LONGBRIDGE – THE MG SPORTS & RACING FACILITY

Geneva 2004 saw another outing for the SV – in fact it was the second time at the Swiss show for MG's supercar. However, whereas XP3 had represented the

ABOVE: For its second foray to Geneva in March 2004, MG sent along one of the new XPower SV-R models. (MG Rover)

ABOVE: The 2004 Geneva show MG XPower SV-R featured a distinctive all-blue interior. (Andrew Roberts)

RIGHT: The SV-R version is most easily recognized by its substantial rear wing. (Andrew Roberts)

ABOVE: The 'R' version of the MG XPower SV is even more purposeful and menacing, with silver side gills and a substantial boot-mounted rear wing. (MG Rover)

LEFT: This overhead view of the MG XPower SV-R shows the gills in the sides, bonnet and grille aperture, as well as the generous cockpit. (MG Rover)

BELOW: MG XPower SV-R at speed on a wet track. (MG Rover)

ABOVE: The MG XPower SV – and the R derivative, seen here – is surprisingly compact in side profile. (MG Rover)

BELOW: The 'MG XPower' badge is subtly different from the standard MG logo. (MG Rover)

BELOW: The side gills of the MG XPower SV and SV-R are functional as well as eye-catching – and as a feature are likely to be seen on several other future MG models. (MG Rover)

OMITEC

As a state-of-the-art, high-value sports car, the MG XPower SV was obviously a prime candidate for a high-tech vehicle management system. MG XPower dealers are also quite widely spread, and statistically, therefore, any vehicle problems are likely to occur some way from conventional diagnosis and resolution. For the SV, therefore, Giordano Casarini and his team worked with the Wiltshire-based office of Omitec Group, a leading company in the field of automotive diagnostics and information technology. The Omitec 'Remote Service Platform' (RSP) is integrated in the heart of the electrical system of each SV, and allows owners to immobilize their cars from afar, protecting them from theft even when the perpetrator has the keys.

As well as remote immobilization, the RSP platform allows drivers to make calls to emergency and assistance operators, intelligently routing calls to the most appropriate operator. The in-built satellite-tracking component allows assistance to be dispatched to the actual vehicle location even if the owner is lost, and tracks the movement of any stolen vehicles. In addition to the security features, the Omitec RSP monitors the vehicle condition, providing advance warnings of any fault conditions, possibly averting breakdowns. The fact that the RSP is also integrated with the SV's other systems has the added bonuses of improved reliability, and the simple fact that a would-be thief cannot 'unplug' the system without rendering the car unusable. Dan Poulson, managing director of Omitec Telematics claims: 'The Omitec RSP is a truly world-leading system, providing MG XPower and SV owners with unmatched security and service capabilities. We have spent three years researching and developing a product that improves the driver's experience, focusing on genuine benefits and avoiding novelties and gadgets.'

The system may be fundamentally gadget free, but there are some peripheral features that could be of interest to track-day enthusiasts: 'It is possible to monitor and record track times and associated performance for download on to the owner's lap-top computer' Poulson explains.

SV at the 2003 show, this time round it was a Titanium Silver left-hand-drive SV-R with a blue interior: car 109. Once more, the preparation of the show car meant much hard work up to the line; it was eventually finished at Longbridge after the remainder of the show cars had been despatched, and it was driven on a covered trailer through France and into Switzerland – but it made it in time. Pricing had been realigned slightly since the November 2003 announcement, with a new starting price of £65,570 for the most basic SV, rising to £82,950 for the SV-R. Amongst the distinctive features defining the SV-R were larger Brembo brakes and a standard boot-mounted spoiler.

At the Geneva show, MG Sport & Racing announced that the list of special 'XPower' dealers within the UK had grow to fourteen, and that their task was 'to ensure that owners receive the best possible support … to sell and service not only the MG XPower SV but also an expanding range of XPower performance cars, parts, accessories and merchandise.' We were told that 'numerous orders for the XPower SV and SV-R have now been received from overseas markets, and a full export programme to Europe and beyond will be underway by the end of 2004.' Meanwhile, just as the SV-R was wowing crowds at the Geneva Show, Frank Hook and his merry men were putting the finishing touches to another near-perfect show car (car 139 SV-R finished in Dusty Blue – a light silver blue – with blue interior) for the biennial 2004 NEC show, now brought forward to a new May slot instead of the traditional October date.

While MG Sport & Racing was concerning itself with the show cars, at Longbridge the main priority was the more important task of producing customer cars. The arrangements with XK Engineering and QCR were intended to be temporary, with the finishing work

MG Sport & Racing at Longbridge is the international headquarters for MG Rover's sporting activities. (Author)

One of the first MG XPower SV cars to be finished off at MG Sport & Racing during build in July 2004. (Author)

gradually transferring to Longbridge; while in the spring of 2004, studies were begun into the possibility of bringing the whole manufacturing process in house – shades of the earlier plan re-emerging, perhaps. The operation at MG Sport & Racing is a compact but bustling operation to the south of the main Longbridge plant, that brings together the final stages of preparing the SV and SV-R cars for their expectant new owners – who are welcome to come and inspect their purchases in the final stages before delivery.

The set-up at MG Sport & Racing is broadly modelled on that at OPAC, with four main bays available for work on cars, supported by bays set aside for headlamp and wheel alignment as well as quality inspection. MG XPower SV production is overseen by John Linforth, a Longbridge veteran of fifteen years who has worked on most of the company's products in that time, most recently – prior to MG Sport & Racing – on MG Rover quality. Linforth explains that the eventual objective will be to take in each SV and SV-R as a painted rolling shell: 'We'll trim it, fit the glass and set it properly for despatch.'

In March 2004 the first MG XPower SV was delivered to an external customer, the car in question being car number 112 (finished in Monogram 'Sunspot' Yellow). The first production 'customer' specification cars had already been delivered the previous autumn – but the customers in that case were in fact MG Rover and Phoenix board members, who had been used as expert critics to ensure that the cars subsequently delivered to outside 'real world' customers had been as thoroughly developed as possible. This had inevitably added delay to the project, but anything aimed at securing the best quality for customers should surely pay dividends, and is laudable as a consequence.

By the summer of 2004, the cars coming through the Longbridge facility had already moved ahead in quality terms, and MG Sport & Racing was successfully taking on board more of the actual assembly and finishing work. At the time of a visit I made in July 2004, a pair of MG XPower SVs were being scrutinized by MG Rover quality personnel – one car had been painted in Italy and the other by MG Rover's own in-house paint team. The long-term goal is to facilitate the technology transfer necessary for combining MG Rover's quality standards with the specialist processes involved in painting carbon-fibre bodywork – the chief beneficiary being the customer.

chapter ten

Onward to the Future

MORE PRESS EXPOSURE

It was not until June 2004 that the mainstream weekly motoring magazines had the chance to appraise the SV-R, and then both *Autocar* and *Auto Express* took it to task on road and track. What happened was that *Autocar* was given the chance to include the SV-R in a track-day session at Brands Hatch, but as is the way in the world of journalism, as soon as *Auto Express* looked certain to have the 'first exclusive', *Autocar* brought forward their coverage of the SV-R in the form of a mini-test, with the car also splashed across the cover.

Veteran MG over-watcher (and former Rover employee) Richard Bremner was lukewarm about some of the trimming details, but unequivocal in his praise for the chassis:

> There is no question but that the MG Rover's Sport and Racing division has done its work on the SV's chassis.

RIGHT: *Autocar*'s Richard Bremner put the SV-R through its paces for the magazine in June 2004. (*Autocar*)

BELOW: Dave Stokes is keen to see an MG XPower SV on the race tracks – and this is his concept of how one could look with Motorsport sponsorship. (Dave Stokes)

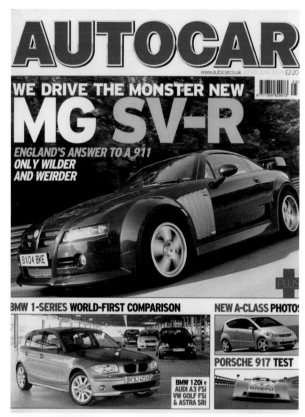

Celebrity Status

The promotional efforts of 2003, when XP3 was sent to provide a touch of glamour at the Cannes film festival, finally appeared to have paid dividends when, in May 2004, it was announced at the 2004 event by 'Box Office Films' that an SV would star in a new $10m action adventure film entitled *Run*, the filming of which began two months later. The SV – car number 113 – was specially finished with chromed side gills, a substantial chrome rear wing and chromed wheels – plenty of 'flash' for the 'fast and furious' set. Playing supporting roles to the SV would be the actor Rick Yune and Simon Webbe, one of the mainstays of popular British boy-band 'Blue'. As the press release explained with breathless enthusiasm: 'Rick Yune heads the cast in the lead role of Harry "Mac" McKenna, an American bounty hunter who hits the streets of modern urban England searching for the truth, only to find a non-stop nitrous-injected world, a beautiful but mysterious woman, and more truth than he ever bargained for...'

RIGHT: Simon Webbe, member of the British boy-band 'Blue', poses with the MG XPower SV-R at the NEC show in May 2004. (MG Rover)

Actors Rick Yune and Steve Hart will also star in the film Run. *(MG Rover)*

Seen outside MG Sport & Racing HQ at Longbridge, this is the custom-finished MG XPower SV built especially for the film, with one-off chromed louvres and 'bling-bling' chrome wheels, specially sourced from the USA. (Author)

At the rear of the Run SV is an equally bold chrome-finished wing. (Author)

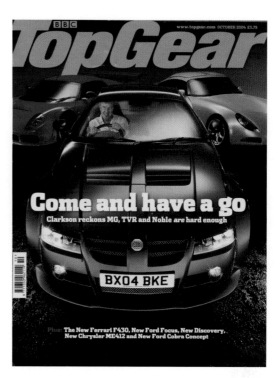

Top Gear magazine revisited the MG XPower SV-R for their October 2004 issue. (Top Gear)

Around Brands Hatch it's grippy, it steers with precision, and its damping not only controls the body with the vigour of an over-zealous traffic cop, but allows the springs to mop up bumps, too. So a chassis that has been optimized towards road use proves more than man enough for a work-out on the track – something the SV has in common with lesser MGs. All of this means that its neutral balance can be indulged to satisfying effect, especially since the brakes shed speed with great efficiency.

Meanwhile, *Auto Express* was clearly very enamoured of the SV; unlike *Autocar*, they had no criticism to make of the fit and finish: on the contrary, they said:

Inside, the car is a revelation. Given the low volume of the project, we were expecting an interior hastily thrown together from bits of old Rovers; but we're pleased to say we were wrong, and the SV-R has a hand-finished bespoke cabin, trimmed in leather and Alcantara, and the quality is much, much better than we had dared to hope for. ...It might not be the last word in refinement – in fact, it's a bit of an animal – but the SV will surprise those who didn't expect cash-strapped MG to turn out such a well engineered supercar.

A CHALLENGING FUTURE

With a planned production life of up to four years, there is obviously a lot more potential for the MG XPower SV family as yet unseen; it is clear that MG's most dramatic

LEFT: Peter Stevens is no less keen to see a Motorsport future for the SV – as evidenced by his own artist's impression of how a GT version might look. (Peter Stevens)

LEFT: Peter Stevens oversaw the creation of this clay representing a competition version of the SV. (Peter Stevens)

BELOW: Indian-born driver Phiroze Bilimoria hopes to be one of the first to take the SV-GTR to the track in the 2006 GT Championships. He is seen here at a special publicity photo-shoot at the Rockingham race circuit in November 2004, with a specially liveried MG XPower SV loaned by MG Sport & Racing. (Terry Lee)

In November 2004, MG Rover unveiled an 'ultimate' iteration of the road-going MG XPower SV-R, aimed at the reasonably well-heeled enthusiast who fancies a car which can be driven to and from the track as well as around it. Massive six-spoke twenty-inch wheels (a factory option from early in 2005) barely conceal uprated Brembo disc brakes. The paint finish is 'Orange Fire', while there are optional 'natural' finish carbon-fibre side air vents. (MG Rover)

Whatever happens to the MG XPower SV itself, there is the strong likelihood that its brave and adventurous styling will pave the way for future MG sports cars, as suggested in this artist's impression by _Autocar_ magazine. (_Autocar_)

supercar could have an exciting lifetime ahead of it. However, there was a dramatic turn of events in April 2005, when – following the collapse of negotiations between MG Rover and their Chinese partners SAIC, MG Rover – and MG Sport & Racing – were precipitated into administration. It seems likely that the SV will emerge from this process – yet another of the many crises it has faced in its short life – and new owners will doubtless pick up the threads of the developments that were already in hand before the collapse. The first of the proposed additions to the family was the automatic transmission variant – an easy enough exercise to achieve and one that was easy to justify even if the idea of an MG XPower SV automatic hardly advances the hard-core message of the range. Beyond that, there can be more-powerful engine options – such as a 765bhp

version, using lessons learned from the crazy Bonneville ZT-T based 'X15'. Even more powerful versions remain entirely feasible, although their eventual existence will probably depend upon the proffering of a suitably expansive wallet. As a taster of what a more extreme version of the SV could look like, Peter Stevens and Ian Moreton conjured up a special one-off show version which the company unveiled in November 2004. A further project under consideration – which might yet appear as the MG XPower SV-S – is a variant fitted with a supercharged version of the Ford V8, specially developed by Rousch Engineering in the USA.

Beyond this there is also a return to Motorsport with the planned MG XPower SV 'Club Sport' GT-class contender, and the possibility that the SV will be sold in small numbers in the United States, breaking almost 25 years of enforced abstinence from what was once MG's biggest market. Stevens reckons that the necessary certification work could be picked up from where the Mangusta left off and completed for around half a million dollars – although of course marketing, distribution and other costs would add to that figure. Some would argue that it would only be worth doing as part of a concerted plan to return MG to the United States on a larger scale; others would say 'what the heck? Let's do it and generate the demand anyway'. With new ownership on the cards as these words were written, and a renewed focus on MG's sports car heritage, the jury is still out on how those dice will roll…

Late in 2004, MG Rover unveiled this 'MG GT' concept, based upon the MG TF but clearly taking styling cues from the MG XPower SV. (MG Rover Group)

As MG XPower SV's future was again thrown into doubt, the _Financial Times_ of 15 April 2005 carried this advertisement for the MG Sport & Racing business, makers of the SV.

Specification

Performance		
Acceleration (SV)	0–60mph: 5.3sec	0–100km/h: 5.4sec
Acceleration (SV-R)	0–60mph: 4.9sec	0–100km/h: 5.1sec
Top speed (SV)	165mph	268km/h
Top speed (SV-R)	175mph	284km/h

Power	SV	SV-R	SV-GTR
Engine	Front-mounted longitudinal 90° V8		
Capacity	4,601cc	4,996cc	4,996cc
Bore x stroke	90.2 x 90.0mm	94.0mm x 90.0mm	94.0mm x 90.0mm
Material	Aluminium alloy block and heads		
Valves	Double overhead camshafts, four valves per cylinder		
Compression ratio	10.0:1	11.4:1	to be confirmed
Power	320hp SAE @ 6,000rpm (230kW @ 6,000rpm)	385hp SAE @ 6,000rpm (294kW @ 6,000rpm)	264hp (restricted) (202kW)
Torque	410Nm @ 4,750rpm (302lb/ft @ 4,750rpm)	510Nm @ 4,750rpm (375lb/ft @ 4,750rpm)	to be confirmed

Transmission type	Rear-wheel drive	
	Electronic traction control	
Gearbox	Five-speed Tremec manual	(Five-speed sequential on SV-GTR)
Ratios 1st:	3.37:1	3.37:1
Ratios 2nd:	1.99:1	1.99:1
Ratios 3rd:	1.33:1	1.33:1
Ratios 4th:	1.00:1	1.00:1
Ratios 5th:	0.73:1	0.73:1
Ratios reverse:	3.22:1	3.28:1
Ratios final drive:	3.46:1	3.46:1
Mph/1,000rpm in top:	30.1	35.5
Km/h/1,000rpm in top:	48.5	57.1

Exterior	Front aerodynamic splitter
	Rear air diffuser
	Black finish side air vents
	Green-tinted glass
	Electrically heated and adjustable power-fold door mirrors
	Roof-mounted aerial
	Projector headlights
	Front and rear fog lights

Interior (SV and SV-R)	
Instrumentation	Green dial speedometer and tachometer
	Green dial fuel and coolant temperature gauges
	Analogue clock
Climate control	Automatic temperature control
	Rotary controls for temperature, distribution and fan over-rides
	Recirculation control
Audio	Single CD player and tuner
	Four Infinity® speakers plus front tweeters
Interior	Reclining leather and Alcantara® seats; Electric seat-height adjustment
	Alloy centre console; Carbon-finish header and cant rails and door posts
	Leather steering wheel with height adjustment
	Leather and alloy finish gear knob; Driver's clutch footrest
	Leather upper door waist rails and rear trim

	Centre console storage bin with armrest; Two cup holders
	Leather and bright stainless steel sill trims
	Leather handbrake, gearshift gaiter and console lid; Colour-keyed cut pile carpet
	Colour-keyed carpeted rear luggage shelf and boot
	Lights-on and driver's door-open warning buzzers
	Courtesy delay lights in roof and rear compartment sides
	Door open/puddle lamps
	Electric front windows with driver's one-touch-down control
	Heated rear window with timed switch-off

Interior (SV-GTR)	Carbon-fibre racing seat
	FIA-approved fire extinguisher by Safety Devices
	Computer-controlled wiring loom

Protection

Safety	Dual-action (inertia and fixed) four-belt, three-point safety harnesses
	Remote control, central door locking
	Alarm system and tracker with remote telemetry and SOS call-out
	Electric internal boot and fuel filler releases
	Lockable wheel nuts
Brakes	Brembo® discs and four-pot calipers
	Bosch 5.7 electronic ABS (no ABS on SV-GTR)
	Electronic brakeforce distribution
	324mm diameter ventilated and cross-drilled front discs (350mm on SV-GTR)
	310mm-diameter ventilated and cross-drilled rear discs (all models)
Tyres (SV and SV-R)	Michelin Pilot Sport
	Front 225/40 ZR18
	Rear 265/40 ZR18
	Spare Instant mobility system
Tyres (SV-GTR)	Dunlop Sport 'slicks' and 'wet' tyres as appropriate

Dimensions

Length	4,480mm
Width	1,900mm excluding mirrors
	2,076mm including mirrors
Wheelbase	2,670mm
Front track	1,678mm
Rear track	1,626mm
Height	1,320mm
Weight	1,495kg (3,296lb)
Cd	0.38
CdA	0.68

Construction

Body	Two-door, two-seater coupé with unique carbon-fibre construction
Chassis	Steel box frame with integrated FIA-specification roll cage
	(FIA-approved by Safety Devices for SV-GTR)
Unladen weight	SV – 1,495kg (3,296lb); SV-GTR – 1,100kg (2,425lb)

Handling

Suspension	Independent coil springs
Front	Double wishbones and 25mm anti-roll bar
	Spring rate 73N/mm, wheel rate 29 N/mm, bump travel 70mm
Rear	Double wishbones and 25mm anti-roll bar
	Spring rate 53N/mm, wheel rate 31 N/mm, bmp travel 60mm
Steering	Power-assisted rack and pinion
	Turns lock-to-lock 3.0
	Overall ratio 17.2:1
Turning circle	10.6m (34.7ft) between kerbs

	SV	SV-R
Wheels	Alloy OZ two-piece, five-spoke	Alloy MG-OZ, five-spoke
Front	8J x 18 x 40	8J x 18 x 40
Rear	10J x 18 x 41	10J x 18 x 41

Chronology of Events

Month /Day	Year	Description of Events
5 March	1996	At the 1996 Geneva Salon, De Tomaso exhibits the 'Bigua' prototype of a smaller car aimed at creating an 'Italian TVR'.
March	1998	The arrangement between De Tomaso and Qvale is announced; 'DAL' (De Tomaso Automobiles Limited) will build the production version of the 'Bigua' – rebadged as 'Mangusta' – and the Qvales will distribute the car worldwide with the exception of the UK and Italy. De Tomaso will continue to produce the Guarà at the rate of about fifty per annum, and there is talk of a further new car, likely to be called 'Pantera' in homage to another successful De Tomaso model name.
10 November	1999	The first production Qvale Mangusta leaves the production line at Qvale Modena.
6 January	2000	At the Los Angeles Motor Show, the Mangusta marks the return to the US market of the De Tomaso marque.
17 March	2000	The Qvale and De Tomaso parties announce that they have dissolved their business arrangement. Qvale is rumoured to have invested some $30 million in the venture. The project will be taken forward as the Qvale Mangusta.
9 May	2000	The 'Phoenix Consortium' bid is successful in agreeing terms to buy Rover and MG from BMW. Phoenix comprises John Towers, Nick Stephenson, David Bowes, Terry Whitmore, John Edwards, Brian Parker and Peter Beale. A joint press release is issued by BMW and the Phoenix Consortium.
9 May	2000	A brief press release on behalf of Alchemy Partners states: 'We note today's announcement. Alchemy Partners wish the Phoenix Consortium and its employees good luck for the future. Alchemy Partners looks forward to fresh transactions.'
May	2000	Kevin Howe is appointed as the chief executive of Rover Group.
June	2000	Other appointments announced to the MG Rover Board during the month: Chris Bowen as operations director, Bob Beddow as human resources director, John Parkinson to sales and marketing, John Millett to finance and strategy, Rob Oldaker to product development.
27 June	2000	Rob Oldaker joins Rover Group as its new product development director.
7 July	2000	Peter Stevens joins Rover Group as design director.
20 July	2000	Nick Stephenson meets with David Sharples (Rover Group export director) and Bruce Qvale for initial discussions about possible collaboration on the UK or European distribution of the latter's Qvale Mangusta sports car. Further discussions during August and September.
25 August	2000	Plans announced for a joint Le Mans venture between MG (owned by Rover Group) and Lola Cars International Ltd. Nick Stephenson, deputy chairman of Rover Group and a Lola car director says: 'We are delighted to have the expertise of the people at Lola, who won at Le Mans this year, working on this exciting project. It demonstrates how serious we are in developing the MG brand, which has been underdeveloped previously. The return to international motor racing is a major part of injecting excitement and performance into the brand.'
9 September	2000	Rover Group formally announces a change of name to MG Rover Group Limited. Kevin Howe, CEO, says: 'Given that we are establishing a new company, the opportunity has been taken to reflect this in a new name which emphasizes that we are totally committed to the design, engineering and manufacture of world-class MG and Rover products.'
30 October	2000	The formal change of name from 'Rover Group Limited' to 'MG Rover Group Limited' is registered at Companies House.
30 January	2001	The new MG saloon range, derived from heavily re-engineered Rover saloons, is unveiled to the press at a special event in the Longbridge Conference Centre. The three MG saloons are based on the Rover 25, 45 and 75, and are referred to by their respective code-names of X30, X20 and X10.
12–13 February	2001	Bruce Qvale meets MG Rover's Nick Stephenson and Peter Beale at Longbridge to discuss the basis of 'Heads of Agreement' for a formal deal to sell Qvale Modena to The Phoenix Consortium.
27 February	2001	Geneva Motor Show: the MG saloons are unveiled to the public, along with the Rover 75 Tourer. The MG saloon names are revealed for the first time: 'X30' becomes MG ZR, 'X20' is MG ZS, while 'X10' is MG ZT. MG Rover also unveils the proposed sports estate version of 'X10' – coded 'X11' and named the MG ZT-T.

27-28 February	2001	The MG Rover management team, including Nick Stephenson, Peter Beale, Kevin Howe, Rob Oldaker and Peter Stevens, meet up at Qvale Modena to discuss with Bruce Qvale and his team the possibility of a deal to acquire the Italian manufacturing assets of Qvale Automotive Group. Peter Stevens and Kevin Howe have come fresh from the launch of the MG saloons and ZT-T estate at Geneva. Nick Stephenson and Peter Beale stay in the Mini Hotel Le Ville in Modena.
5 March	2001	An MGF is placed on show on the Chapman-Arup stand at the SAE Show at Cobo Center, Detroit, Michigan for the duration of the show (5 to 8 March). MG Rover says that this is to allow some market research in a market (the USA) where the MG marque has been dormant for twenty years. A statement also adds the rider, however, that 'the MG Rover five-year business plan assumes no planned sales in the US market.'
21 March	2001	Dick Wallrich, one of the organizers of 'MG 2001' – what is hoped will be the largest ever gathering in the USA of MG cars and enthusiasts – contacts the author and asks if he can assist in encouraging MG Rover to support the event. Wallrich says: 'We have been holding the torch for them for twenty-one years now, and I figure that even if they aren't coming this way anytime soon, the least they could do is help us keep the torch burning a little longer until they do come.'
10 April	2001	The 'MG XPower' trademark is registered at the UK Patent Office (TM No. E2172989).
26 April	2001	MG Rover launches its new 'XPower' Motorsport brand at a special ceremony at the NEC, just prior to the Sportscar Show. The codenames for the Le Mans, TOCA and Rally cars are revealed as EX257, EX259 and EX258 respectively. Also announced is the creation of a new company – MG Sports & Racing Limited – that will oversee the 'XPower' brand and co-ordinate motorsports activities.
10 May	2001	MG Rover announces that it is developing 'extreme' versions of some of its mainstream models, including the MGF-derived 'MGF Extreme' and MG ZT-based 'MG ZT Extreme'.
14 June	2001	The US publication *Autoweek* says that 'rumours are circulating that someone – perhaps Rover – will buy Qvale Automotive Group. 'We've talked to MG Rover for a year,' Bruce Qvale, whose company produces the Mangusta sports car, tells *Autoweek*. 'They've looked at our factory. It's speculation on all this buy/sell stuff. They like our production, but we've had other suitors before.'
15 June	2001	MG reveals the first in a series of Extreme cars – the MGF X Power 500 – on the eve of MG's assault in the Le Mans 24 Hour race. 'MG Extreme vehicles are one-off demonstrators, not intended for series production, and will each be outrageously powerful and road legal. The XPower 500 features a race-bred 500Ps engine and six-speed sequential transmission in a much modified MGF monocoque structure.
16 and 17 June	2001	Two MG Lola EX257 race cars compete in the first Le Mans race for MG since 1965, when Paddy Hopkirk and Andrew Hedges finished 11th in the race – the best an MGB had achieved there, and 2nd in its class. Having qualified 1st and 2nd in the LMP675 class, the MG Lola reached 3rd overall within two hours of the start, and established the fastest wet-weather lap, with a blistering 3rd fastest time overall; but both cars had retired by half-way.
19 June	2001	MG Rover and Qvale Automotive of San Francisco California announce that the former has entered into an agreement to purchase the assets of the latter's Italian subsidiary, builder of the Ford Mustang V8-powered Qvale Mangusta. A concept sketch of the proposed re-engineered car – codename 'X80' – is revealed. Kevin Howe states: 'The MG X80 will be an excellent fit at the top of our family of MG cars. It also provides an opportunity to look at markets where we are not currently represented. In particular, the US markets, the world's largest sports car market, where we can now seriously evaluate the full potential of the MG brand.'
27 June	2001	MG Rover announces that it will send a delegation and vehicle display to the major 'MG2001' gathering in St Paul, Minnesota, USA – the latest event in a series that takes place only every five years and brings together MG enthusiasts from all over North America. 'MG 2001' takes place between 2 and 6 July.
27 June	2001	MG Rover registers the company name 'MG X80 Limited' at Companies' House, the nature of business being described as 'manufacture of motor vehicles'.
July	2001	MG X80 Ltd Italy is set up at Modena, initially using part of the Qvale Modena building, until November 2002.
11 September	2001	MG Rover unveils a full-size plastic foam model at the Frankfurt Motor Show of the proposed new MG sports coupé, based on the Qvale Mangusta and labelled 'MG X80'. Projected production is put as summer of 2002. Also unveiled is a road-going version of the MG ZT XPower 385. On the very same day, terrorists hijack two planes, and fly them into the twin towers of the World Trade Center in New York City.
28 November	2001	MG Rover Parts, a newly formed company of MG Rover Holdings, announces the finalization of its agreements with Caterpillar Logistics to build a world-wide parts operation. 'The new company will open its doors for business in March 2002. The deal creates the infrastructure for MG Rover to fully develop the commercial benefits of its parts operation, which has an expected turnover in the region of £250 million.'
20 December	2001	MG Rover and China Brilliance Holdings Co Ltd (CBH), part of the Brilliance Group, announce that they are in discussions relating to the formation of a wide-ranging strategic alliance and co-operation agreement.

15 January	2002	MG TF is publicly unveiled, for the first time, at the Brussels Motor Show. British pop singer Sophie Ellis-Bextor assists with the unveiling. The MG TF shows the first production version of Peter Stevens' new concept for the MG 'grille' shape, with a horizontal central bar, as previewed on the MG X80 Frankfurt show car.
30 January	2002	At the MG TF press launch in Portugal, Kevin Howe indicates that the MG X80 programme has slipped. 'We also received many positive and a few critical comments at Frankfurt, and we've been busy addressing these in the development programme. Consequently with these two live issues we decided to delay production for a little later than we had originally envisaged.'
12 February	2002	Internal options report to review the best way forward for the MG X80 project, the costs and timescales for which have escalated; this is a critical review of the project.
14 February	2002	MG Rover employees receive what the local press calls a 'shape up or ship out' message, telling them that outside consultants were being brought in to create a 'job shop' to help those who did not want to give 100 per cent to leave. On the same day, the story breaks in *Automotive News* that 'MG Rover is delaying by one year plans to begin production of as many as 1600 MG X80 sports cars at the former Qvale plant in Modena.'
14 February	2002	The story breaks in the Indian media that MG Rover and Telco – parent company of 'Tata' – are talking about the possibility of MG Rover marketing a variant of the Tata Indica, a small Indian-produced hatchback.
17 February	2002	MG Rover's sales and marketing director John Parkinson confirms that the MG 'X80' has been delayed until the summer of 2003 (for the coupé), with an as yet undisclosed date for the roadster.
20 February	2002	MG Rover faces the prospect of strike action due to disaffected elements of the workforce who are particularly unhappy about the company's desire to hang on to some of BMW's working practices. On the same day, the last car rolls out of the famous Ford plant at Dagenham, Essex.
5 March	2002	Geneva Motorshow. MG Rover unveils a concept for a new Rover – the 'TCV' or 'Tourer Concept Vehicle', which is the first demonstration of the design theme being mapped out for the Rover brand by Peter Stevens.
1 May	2002	Ian Moreton joins the reformed MG X80 project team.
4 June	2002	The *Financial Times* claims that the Chinese government is looking into financial irregularities by Yang Rong, chairman of China Brilliance, and other senior executives of the company.
6 June	2002	*Autosport* magazine carries a story that David Price Racing was developing a version of the X80 to become a Le Mans GT contender, as well as an entrant in the N-GT category of the FIA GT Championship.
17 June	2002	MG Rover confirms that it has temporarily suspended production of all models in order to alleviate a parts crisis that has been looming, due to difficulties being experienced in transferring its spare parts handling business from Unipart to Caterpillar.
19 June	2002	MG X80 Prototype 'XP1' sets off in a covered trailer from David Price Racing's premises at Great Bookham, England on a testing trip to Nardó, Italy.
20 June	2002	Brilliance China announces that it has replaced its chairman Yang Rong by Wu Xiaoan, formerly vice chairman.
July	2002	MG X80 Prototype 'XP1' is tested at the Nardó race circuit in Italy, where it achieves a speed of 203mph (327km/h).
3 September	2002	*Autocar*, in the issue dated 4 September 2002 (but on sale the previous day), reveals 'scoop' details of the revised MG X80, including two photographs of a lightly disguised 'mule' (actually 'XP1').
16 September	2002	MG X80 Prototype 'XP3' is despatched from Dove Company to QCR Motors for fit-up and final preparation for display as the 'MG XPower SV' show-car.
2–3 October	2002	Photo shoot of the MG XPower SV at the 'Dimlock Building', a disused warehouse behind a BBC car park in Wood Lane, White City, West London.
7–8 October 7	2002	Video shoot of the MG XPower SV at a disused power station near Dover, Kent.
21 October	2002	Formal presentation of the MG XPower SV to the MG Rover Group board.
22 October	2002	MG XPower SV unveiled at the British Motor Show at the NEC.
24 October	2002	Special supplier and sub-contractor conference held at Studley Castle in Warwickshire, providing an opportunity for different partners in the MG X80 project to meet one another, make presentations about their aspects of the programme and to share any concerns.
4 November	2002	After the British International Motor Show, MG Rover Group reports great interest in its car ranges and in excess of 1,000 orders, representing over £12m at showroom prices. 'Interest in the new MG XPower SV has been especially high. Customers have shown a keenness to be the first to enjoy the thrills of this exciting new car, and the first three months' production has already been sold.'
20 November	2002	At the '*Autocar* 2002 Awards' ceremony held today in Battersea, London, MG Rover Group receives the '*Autocar* award for Outstanding Achievement', and Peter Stevens the '*Autocar* Designer of the Year'.
10 December	2002	MG XPower SV 'XP3' is shown at the Bologna Motor Show – the local show to the factories where much of it is built.
17 January	2003	MG Rover chief executive Kevin Howe signs off approval for initial production run of 835 MG XPower SV. Peter Stevens commits to delivery of the first production car by 1 May 2003.

4 March	2003	Geneva Motor Show: 'XP3' appears on the fairly low-profile MG Rover Swiss distributor's stand, but with the formerly black 'gills' refinished in bright aluminium.
11 March	2003	First MG XPower SV 'off tools' taken from OPAC to MG X80 factory at Modena, where it is to be kept for about a week before travelling via OPAC to UK and into the paintshop at QCR by 24 March 2003.
20 March	2003	MG Rover's production director Rob Oldaker steps aside from his secondary role as managing director of MG Sport & Racing and his place is taken by Kim Johnson.
26 March	2003	Kevin Howe and Nick Stephenson witness the third car being assembled in the jigs at OPAC.
20 April	2003	The Sunspot Yellow display car 'XP4' is completed, using a GRP body on an automatic transmission Qvale Mangusta chassis.
1 May	2003	The first production-specification MG XPower SV, car '101', finished in Starlight Silver, is driven to Longbridge for a viewing by enthusiastic MG Rover management and staff.
25 June	2003	MG Rover board conduct a 'ride and drive' assessment.
27 June	2003	MG X80 UK team relocate from the ARUP offices at Leamington Spa to temporary accommodation at Longbridge.
July	2003	Nigel Gordon-Stewart leaves the MG X80 project; his position would eventually be filled by David Watson as commercial manager, MG Sport & Racing.
12 and 13 July	2003	Car #3 (P103), finished in XPower Grey, appears at the Goodwood Festival of Speed, where Peter Stevens is on hand to show the car to potential customers. Sir Jack Brabham tries the car and professes approval, qualified for a desire for more power.
14 July	2003	Car #3 is shipped via Heathrow to Rousch in Detroit, USA, for EEC emissions compliance testing (Rousch has great experience of the Ford engine).
19 July	2003	In a process of name-swapping, the company known formerly as 'MG X80 Ltd' (manufacturer of motor vehicles) becomes 'MG Sport & Racing Ltd' (manufacturer of motor vehicles), while 'MG Sport & Racing Ltd' (nature of business described as 'other sporting activities') becomes 'MG X80 Ltd'.
27 August	2003	Business planning meeting chaired by Kevin Howe authorizes the extension of production beyond the first fifty cars, allowing forward programming of tooling and order commitments.
18 September	2003	Kevin Howe takes delivery of his personal MG XPower SV, a British Racing Green car (car '106').
10 October	2003	Phoenix Consortium deputy chairman Nick Stephenson takes delivery of his personal MG XPower SV, a Trophy Blue car (car '108').
29 October	2003	MG Sport & Racing announces the official on-sale date of 1 November 2003 for the MG XPower SV, with the SV-R to follow in spring 2004. The company states that 'the MG XPower SV line-up starts from £75,000 and will be available through a network of specialist XPower dealerships, or directly from the MG Sport & Racing factory.'
1 December	2003	John Parkinson, already director of 'XPart', assumes responsibility for MG Sport & Racing. Kim Johnson is operations manager.
8 and 9 December	2003	Still studio photography of Peter Stevens' personal MG XPower SV-R (car '118' in a special finish of Ferrari Titanium [silver]) in association with BBC *Top Gear* magazine and television programme.
10 December	2003	Testing and filming of Peter Stevens's MG SV-R for BBC Top Gear; the result is broadcast on BBC2 TV on Sunday 14 December 2003.
6 January	2004	MG Rover Group announces that it has entered into a sale and long-term leaseback arrangement of 228 acres of land, including 4.25 million sq ft of buildings, on its Longbridge site with St Modwen Properties plc for £42.5 million. MG Rover Group will invest the funds directly in the car company's business activities. MG Rover has been granted a long-term lease of up to thirty-five years over this land and provision is made for the sensible release of surplus land at MG Rover's option.
26 January	2004	Consideration begins of Project Odyssey, a study into the relocation of much of the MG XPower SV assembly from Italy to Longbridge.
6 February	2004	MG Rover board and senior management – headed by Kevin Howe, John Parkinson, Rob Oldaker and Peter Stevens – conduct a further comparative 'ride and drive' assessment, taking four MG XPower SVs in convoy to Wales with representative competitor 'benchmark' vehicles including a Porsche Carrera 4S, TVR Tuscan R, Maserati 4200, Noble 340.
26 February	2004	At the very last minute, after final preparations, the Geneva SV-R show car is despatched on a covered trailer to be taken to Geneva.
2 March	2004	MG Sport & Racing announces the MG XPower SV-R, a higher-powered version of the SV, at the Geneva Show. The extra performance comes from a Sean Hyland-built, 5ltr, XPower version of the all-aluminium, 32-valve, double overhead camshaft V8 engine. 0–60 mph in less than 5sec, and top speed circa 175mph/ 282km/h. Power output is 400hp at 6,000 rpm and torque 510Nm at 4,750 rpm. Prices announced start at £65,750.00 for the 'entry level' SV, and from £82,950.00 for the SV-R. The show car is finished, like Peter Stevens's car, in Ferrari Titanium (silver) and is car '109'.
8 March	2004	MG XPower dealers are invited to spend a day at Oulton Park where they have the chance to see and try the MG XPower SV, SV-R and talk to Peter Stevens, Giordano Casarini and Ian Moreton.
22 March	2004	MG Sport & Racing announces that 'following the revealing of a more powerful "R" version of its high performance MG XPower SV at the recent Geneva Motorshow, the waiting list has now reached six months on certain specifications.' On the same day, Ian Moreton steps aside from direct involvement

		in the MG SV production programme, and MG Rover commercial manager David Sharples is now overseeing the MG XPower SV project.
March	2004	First production car for an external customer (car '112' in Sunspot Yellow) is delivered in a brief ceremony at Longbridge.
April	2004	Second external customer car ('133') is delivered. This car is subsequently taken by its owner on a trip to Le Mans in June 2004, calling in at MG Sport & Racing on the way there, and again on the way back.
19 April	2004	MG Sport & Racing showcases the MG XPower SV sports car as the main attraction at the 'SubCon' Subcontractors show, aimed at promoting local businesses, at the National Exhibition Centre, Birmingham.
21 May	2004	At the Cannes Film Festival, Box Office Films announces that their $10m action adventure movie *Run* would feature the MG XPower SV alongside stars Rick Yune (*The Fast and the Furious*, *Die Another Day*) and Simon Webbe of pop band 'Blue', who would be making his feature film debut. Simon Webbe later makes a photo-call appearance on 25 May at the NEC. Meanwhile the film car, chassis '113', is readied at MG Sport & Racing.
25 May	2004	MG XPower SV-R (car '139' in Dusty Blue) shown at the '*Sunday Times* British Motor Show' at the National Exhibition Centre, near Birmingham.
27 May	2004	De Tomaso business enters receivership.
14 June	2004	MG XPower SV-R (the NEC show car) appears at the London '*Daily Telegraph* Motor Expo'.
16 June	2004	MG Rover Group with parent company Phoenix Venture Holdings (PVH) and Shanghai Automotive Industry Corporation (SAIC) announces that following the signing of an agreement, they have now entered into an exclusivity arrangement in order that the companies can develop a 'far-reaching strategic relationship'.
22 June	2004	*Autocar* magazine publishes a brief 'test' of the MG XPower SV-R based on driving the car as part of a track session at Brands Hatch, Kent.
23 June	2004	*Auto Express* magazine publishes its first road impression of the MG XPower SV-R. The magazine sums up by saying: 'It might not be the last word in refinement – in fact, it's a bit of an animal – but the SV will surprise those who didn't expect cash-strapped MG to turn out such a well engineered supercar.'
2 July	2004	MG XPower SV-R (the NEC show car) appears at the 'Max Power' show at the NEC.
9 July	2004	Phoenix Venture Holdings announces the sale of its 'XPart' business to Caterpillar Logistics for £100 million, thereby freeing up capital for other parts of the business.
16 July	2004	Ian Moreton leaves the MG XPower SV project for the time being. On the same day, the fifty-first SV (an SV-R) is completed – car 151, destined for Phoenix chairman John Towers.
September	2004	Steve Hudson leaves MG Rover Group. At around the same time, Ian Moreton returns to oversee the creation of a special show version of the MG XPower SV-R alongside one-off MG TF and Rover 75 coupés.
11 November	2004	The 'Project X' race team reveal plans to enter an MG XPower SV-GTR in the 2005 British GT Championship (later deferred until 2006). The bold plan is the beginning of a proposed three-year campaign which it is hoped will see the SV-GTR compete in the British GT Championship Cup Class (GT3), climbing to the British GT NGT Class (GT2) the following year and ultimately the FIA World GT Championship.
15 November	2004	MG Rover unveils a trio of concept cars – including a special one-off version of the MG XPower SV-R finished in 'Orange Fire' and intended to demonstrate the feasibility of a road-going track-specification version of the car.
27 February	2005	British Chancellor of the Exchequer, Gordon Brown, visits China and lobbies on behalf of an early conclusion to the MG Rover – Shanghai Automotive Industry Corporation (SAIC) deal.
20 March	2005	The first MG XPower SV-R to compete in a race takes to the track at Jarama, Spain. Raced privately by Peter Lloyd Racing, the car finishes in 33rd position overall (out of 43 starters) and 7th in class.
31 March	2005	A spokesman for SAIC says that its planned strategic alliance with MG Rover remains on track despite press coverage claiming that the Longbridge manufacturer could run out of cash before the agreement is signed. The spokesman says: "Things are unchanged and the negotiations are ongoing – any transaction of this nature takes time to complete." No firm dates have been given for when the deal will be finalised, although there is speculation that it could be timed to coincide with the Shanghai Motor Show from 19-21 April.
2 April	2005	Following an offer by the British Government to provide a £100m 'bridging loan' to help the MG Rover/SAIC deal reach conclusion, Whitehall officials fly to China over the weekend for talks with executives from SAIC to try to resolve all the outstanding issues.
7 April	2005	The Board of directors of Phoenix Venture Holdings meets with PriceWaterhouseCoopers in the morning, and announce later the same day that they will be taking the necessary steps to appoint administrators from PWC for MG Rover Group and Powertrain.
8 April	2005	MG Rover Group and Powertrain enter administration.
12 April	2005	MG Sport & Racing enters administration.
Summer	2005	The future of the MG brand – and the MG XPower SV – enters another crisis period. There seems little doubt that MG will survive – and that the SV has moved on the evolution of one of Britain's greatest brands.

Build Details of Early Cars

Chassis number	Destination	Type	Drive	Engine	Transmission Type	Gears	Body colour	Trim	Notes
101	Internal	SV	RHD	4.6	Manual	5	Starlight Silver	Royal Black	First Production Specification car
102	Internal	SV	RHD	4.6	Manual	5	Starlight Silver	Royal Black	
103	Internal	SV	RHD	4.6	Manual	5	XPower Grey	Bloomberry	Car shown at Goodwood, then sent to Rousch
104	Internal	SV	RHD	4.6	Manual	5	Red Hot	Oyster	
105	Internal	SV	RHD	4.6	Manual	5	XPower Grey	Bloomberry	
106	Internal	SV	RHD	4.6	Manual	5	British Racing Green	Royal Black	Kevin Howe
107	Internal	SV	RHD	4.6	Manual	5	Pearl Black	Gunsmoke	Phoenix board member
108	Internal	SV	RHD	4.6	Manual	5	Trophy Blue	Gunsmoke	Nick Stephenson
109	Internal	SV	LHD	4.6	Manual	5	Ferrari Titanium	Azurite	Geneva Motor Show 2004
110	Dealer	SV	RHD	4.6	Manual	5	Red Hot	Oyster	
111	Internal	SV-R	RHD	5.0	Manual	6	XPower Grey	Bloomberry	
112	Customer	SV	RHD	4.6	Manual	5	Sunspot (yellow)	Royal Black	First external customer
113	Internal	SV	RHD	4.6	Manual	5	VW Reflex Silver	Royal Black special finish	Show/ film car –
114	Customer	SV-R	RHD	5.0	Automatic	-	Satin Silver	Royal Black	Nick Stephenson
115	Dealer	SV	RHD	4.6	Manual	5	XPower Grey	Bloomberry	
116	Customer	SV	RHD	4.6	Automatic	-	Pearl Black	Oyster	Phoenix board member
117	Dealer	SV	RHD	4.6	Manual	5	Trophy Blue	Royal Black	
118	Internal	SV-R	RHD	5.0	Manual	5	Ferrari Titanium	Royal Black	Peter Stevens
119	Dealer	SV	RHD	4.6	Manual	5	British Racing Green	Oyster	
120	Dealer	SV	RHD	4.6	Manual	5	Pearl Black	Oyster	
121	Dealer	SV	RHD	4.6	Manual	5	Solar Red	Royal Black	
122	Dealer	SV	RHD	4.6	Manual	5	Starlight Silver	Royal Black	
123	Dealer	SV	RHD	4.6	Manual	5	Royal Blue	Oyster	
124	Dealer	SV	RHD	4.6	Manual	5	Cobalt	Custom	
125	Dealer	SV	RHD	4.6	Manual	5	Garnet	Royal Black	
126	Press	SV-R	RHD	5.0	Manual	6	Emperor Blue	Custom	Press car
127	Customer	SV-R	RHD	5.0	Manual	6	Fantasy ('Chromactive')	Custom	Kevin Howe
128	Dealer	SV-R	RHD	5.0	Manual	6	Grigio Titanium	Royal Black	
129	Dealer	SV-R	RHD	5.0	Manual	6	Orange Fire	Royal Black	
130	Customer	SV	RHD	4.6	Manual	5	Cobalt	Oyster	
131	Dealer	SV	RHD	4.6	Manual	5	Amazon Orange	Royal Black	
132	Dealer	SV	RHD	4.6	Manual	5	Dusty Blue	Azurite	MG Rover board/ dealer demonstrator

Chassis number	Destination	Type	Drive	Engine	Transmission Type	Gears	Body colour	Trim	Notes
133	Customer	SV	RHD	4.6	Manual	5	Red Hot	Royal Black	External customer car
134	Dealer	SV	RHD	4.6	Manual	5	Royal Blue	Azurite	
135	Dealer	SV	RHD	4.6	Manual	5	Emperor Blue	Oyster	
136	Dealer	SV-R	RHD	5.0	Manual	6	British Racing Green	Saddle	
137	Customer	SV-R	RHD	5.0	Manual	6	XPower Grey	Royal Black	MG Rover board member
138	Tba	SV-R	RHD	5.0	Manual	6	Solar Red	Oyster	Press car
139	Tba	SV-R	RHD	5.0	Manual	6	Dusty Blue	Oyster	Birmingham NEC Motorshow 2004
140	Customer	SV	RHD	4.6	Manual	5	Raven Black	Oyster	MG Rover board member
141	Dealer	SV	RHD	4.6	Manual	5	British Racing Green	Custom	
142	Tba	SV	RHD	4.6	Manual	5	Starlight Silver	Bloomberry	
143	Tba	SV	RHD	4.6	Manual	5	Trophy Blue	Oyster	
144	Press	SV	RHD	4.6	Manual	5	Garnet	Oyster	
145	Tba	SV	RHD	4.6	Manual	5	Sunspot (yellow)	Royal Black	
146	Tba	SV	RHD	4.6	Manual	5	Mirror Silver	Azurite	
147	Tba	SV	RHD	4.6	Manual	5	Tba [customer spec]	Azurite	
148	Tba	SV	RHD	4.6	Manual	5	Fantasy ('Chromactive')	Royal Black	
149	Tba	SV	RHD	4.6	Manual	5	Jewel ('Kinetic')	Royal Black	
150	Tba	SV	RHD	4.6	Manual	5	Cobalt	Tba	
151	Customer	SV-R	RHD	5.0	Automatic	-	Mirror Silver	Tba	John Towers
152	Tba	SV-R	RHD	5.0	Manual	5	Tba [customer spec]	Tba	
153	Customer	SV-R	RHD	5.0	Automatic	-	Fantasy ('Chromactive')	Oyster	Phoenix board member
154	Tba	SV-R	RHD	5.0	Manual	5	Tba	Tba	
155	Tba	SV-R	RHD	5.0	Automatic	-	Tba	Tba	
156	Tba	SV-R	RHD	5.0	Manual	5	Tba	Tba	
157	Tba	SV-R	RHD	5.0	Automatic	-	Tba	Tba	
158	Tba	SV-R	RHD	5.0	Manual	5	Tba	Tba	
159	Tba	SV-R	RHD	5.0	Automatic	-	Tba	Tba	
160	Tba	SV-R	RHD	5.0	Manual	5	Tba	Tba	
161	Tba	SV-R	RHD	5.0	Automatic	-	Tba	Tba	
162	Tba	SV-R	RHD	5.0	Manual	5	Tba	Tba	
163	Tba	SV-R	RHD	5.0	Automatic	-	Tba	Tba	
164	Tba	SV-R	RHD	5.0	Manual	5	Tba	Tba	

Index